SODOMY

A HISTORY OF A CHRISTIAN BIBLICAL MYTH

BibleWorld
Series Editor: Philip R. Davies, University of Sheffield

BibleWorld shares the fruits of modern (and postmodern) biblical scholarship not only among practitioners and students, but also with anyone interested in what academic study of the Bible means in the twenty-first century. It explores our ever-increasing knowledge and understanding of the social world that produced the biblical texts, but also analyses aspects of the bible's role in the history of our civilization and the many perspectives – not just religious and theological, but also cultural, political and aesthetic – which drive modern biblical scholarship.

Forthcoming in the series:

SODOMY

A HISTORY OF A CHRISTIAN BIBLICAL MYTH

MICHAEL CARDEN

LONDON   OAKVILLE

Published by

Equinox Publishing Ltd
Unit 6
The Village
101 Amies St.
London
SW11 2JW

www.equinoxpub.com

First published in the UK 2004

British Library Cataloguing-in-Publication Data
A catalogue record for this book is available from the British Library.

Library of Congress Cataloging-in-Publication Data
Carden, Michael, 1952-
 Sodomy : a history of a Christian biblical myth / Michael Carden.--1st ed.
    p. cm. -- (Bibleworld)
 Includes bibliographical references and index.
 ISBN 1-904768-29-6 (hardcover) -- ISBN 1-904768-30-X (pbk.)
 1. Bible. O.T. Genesis XIX--Criticism, interpretation, etc.--History.
 2. Bible. O.T. Judges XIX-XXI--Criticism, interpretation,
etc.--History. 3. Homosexuality--Religious
aspects--Christianity--History of doctrines. 4.
Homosexuality--Religious aspects--Judaism--History of doctrines. I.
Title. II. Bible world (London, England)
 BS1238.H66C37 2004
 222'.1106--dc22

ISBN 1-9047-6829-6   (hardback)
        1-9047-6830-X   (paperback)

Typeset by CA Typesetting, www.sheffieldtypesetting.com
Printed and bound in Great Britain by Antony Rowe, Chippenham, Wiltshire

Sodomy, fellatio, cunnilingus, pederasty
Father! why do these words sound so nasty?

'Sodomy', from the musical, *Hair*

There are two crimes that would merit death – murder and sodomy. For either of these crimes I would wish to confine the criminal till an opportunity offered to deliver him as a prisoner to the natives of New Zealand, and let them eat him. The dread of this will operate much stronger than the fear of death.

Arthur Phillip, first governor of the convict colony at Sydney Cove 1788–92 [cited Johnston and Johnston, 1988: 87]

CONTENTS

ACKNOWLEDGEMENTS

This book began as a dissertation for my PhD in the Studies in Religion Department at the University of Queensland and I want first to thank my principal supervisor, Professor Edgar Conrad, for his invaluable support, advice and guidance. Thanks must also go to his partner, Dr Linda Conrad, for her own support and hospitality. I also want to acknowledge my associate supervisor, Professor Philip Almond, now head of the School of History, Philosophy, Religion and Classics and the support of the School that enabled me to transform the dissertation to a book. I am also very grateful to Philip Davies for his editorial assistance and to Equinox for bringing the book to publication.

I must also acknowledge the assistance of several faculty colleagues in translation matters. Professor Michael Lattke's translation of a crucial passage in Syriac proved invaluable. David Luckensmeyer confirmed my translation of a fifth-century Christian, Greek-language text. The greater part of untranslated texts with which I worked, however, were medieval Latin texts including the extensive commentaries of Nicholas of Lyra. My work on these texts was dependent on the very generous assistance of Dr Keith Atkinson from the Romance languages department, now retired.

Very special thanks must go to Rabbi Z. Cohen, the former Jewish chaplain at the University of Queensland, for his generosity in introducing me to various aspects of traditional Jewish biblical interpretation. I also want to acknowledge the role of the H-Judaic Jewish Studies email list in helping me clarify various aspects of rabbinic texts, most of which I only access in translation. In particular, thanks must go to Anna Urowitz-Freudenstein, the moderator of the H-Judaic List, together with Ulrich Berzbach, Ben Begleiter, E. Pellow, Yoel Kahn, Admiel Kosman, Israel Sandman and Jonathan Schofer, whose answers to my questions relating to the original Hebrew of texts I worked with in translation and other matters proved most helpful and enlightening. While I have mostly lurked there, I must also acknowledge that the Donmeh West Kabbalah lists of Reb Yakov Leib HaKohain have provided me, a Gentile, with important insights into aspects of Jewish tradition.

The time spent completing a dissertation and bringing it to publication often fluctuates between poverty and, if not plenty, then sufficiency. Towards the end it seems like it is mostly poverty that predominates and so it is important to thank many people who helped me through various critical moments. Both my mother, Betty Carden, and my sister, Mary Carden, together with Sue Kentlyn, Majella Franzmann, Ayana Craven, Roland Boer, Marie Porter and Wai Kin Chan, came to the rescue in some crucial times. I also have to thank Jason Parker, Amanda Tink, Geoff Shang, Ann Burlingham, Shayne Wilde, Joseph Nadler, Mark Bahnisch and Gwendolyn Alden Dean. Thanks must also go to Sarah Harward, Benedikte Palings and John Argus for many sanity-saving tea and coffee sessions. I must also thank my housemates Stephen Brown and Colin Griffiths for putting up with me throughout this time.

ABBREVIATIONS

Except where otherwise indicated all biblical quotations, including the Apocrypha, are from the New Revised Standard Version (NRSV). Hebrew and Greek quotations are from the British and Foreign Bible Society Hebrew Bible, the United Bible Societies Greek New Testament and the Septuagint, the Lancelot Brenton edition (Hendrikson Publishers, 1986). Pseudepigrapha (including Pseudo-Philo) quotes are from Charlesworth's edition (1985) and New Testament Apocrypha quotes from the English translation of Schneemelcher's edition (1974). Quotes from Philo and Josephus are from the Loeb Series editions of their works. Talmudic references are from the Soncino Press English translation of the Babylonian Talmud.

1 Clem.	1 Clement, First Epistle of Clement to the Corinthians
1 Chron.	1 Chronicles
1 Sam.	1 Samuel
2 Pet.	2 Peter
2 Sam.	2 Samuel
3 Macc.	*3 Maccabees*
Asat.	*The Asatir*
Abr.	*De Abrahamo* (*On Abraham*), Philo
ARN(A)	*Abot de Rabbi Nathan, The Fathers According to Rabbi Nathan*, Neusner translation of Text A
ARN(B)	*Abot de Rabbi Nathan, The Fathers According to Rabbi Nathan, Version B*, Saldarini translation of Text B
Ad Fortunatus	*Exhortation to Martyrdom, to Fortunatus*, Cyprian
Adv. Haer.	*Adversus Haereses* (*Against Heresies*), Irenaeus of Lyon
Adv. Iud.	*Adversus Iudaeos* (*Against the Jews*), Tertullian
Adv. Marc.	*Adversus Marcionem* (*Against Marcion*), Tertullian
Adv. Oppugn.	*Adversus oppugnatores vitae monasticae* (*Against the Opponents of the Monastic Life*), John Chrysostom
Ant.	*Antiquitates Judaicae* (*Jewish Antiquities*), Josephus
Apoc. Paul	*Apocalypse of Paul*
Apost. Const.	*Constitutions of the Holy Apostles*
BDB	F. Brown, S.R. Driver and C. A. Briggs, *A Hebrew and English Lexicon of the Old Testament* (Oxford: Clarendon Press, 1907)

Bieler	*The Irish Penitentials*
War	*De bello Judaico* (*The Jewish War*), Josephus
Can. Hib.	*Canones Hibernenses* (*Irish Canons*)
Carn. Chr.	*De Carne Christi* (*On the Flesh of Christ*), Tertullian
Exhort. Cast.	*De Exhortatione Castitatis* (*An Exhortation to Chastity*), Tertullian
CCCM	*Corpus Christianorum Continuatio Mediaevalis*
Cher.	*De Cherubim* (*On the Cherubim*), Philo
Christ Ed.	*Christ the Educator*, Clement of Alexandria
Chron.	*The Chronography*, Bar Hebraeus
Chrys. Hom. 1 Cor.	*Homilies on 1 Corinthians*, John Chrysostom
Chrys. Hom. Gen.	*Homilies on Genesis*, John Chrysostom
Chrys. Hom. Isa.	*Homilies on Isaiah*, John Chrysostom
Chrys. Hom. Mt.	*Homilies on Matthew*, John Chrysostom
Chrys. Hom. Rom.	*Homilies on Romans*, John Chrysostom
Chrys. Hom. Stat.	*Homilies on the Statues*, John Chrysostom
Carm. Nis.	*Carmina Nisibena* (*Hymns on Nisibis*), Ephrem Syrus
Comm. Es.	*Commentary on Isaiah*, Jerome
Comm. Hiez.	*Commentary on Ezekiel*, Jerome
Conf. Ling.	*De Confusione Linguarum* (*On the Confusion of Tongues*), Philo
Deut.	Deuteronomy
D. Try.	*Dialogue with Trypho*, Justin Martyr
Div.	*The Divinity of Christ*, Prudentius
D-R	Douay-Rheims
E. Comm. Gen.	*Commentary on Genesis*, Ephrem Syrus
Ebr.	*De Ebrietate* (*On Drunkenness*), Philo of Alexandria
Epiph.	*Hymns on the Epiphany*, Ephrem Syrus
Ep. Basil	*Letters* (*Epistola*), Basil
Ep. Jerome	*Letters* (*Epistola*), Jerome
ER	Eliyyahu Rabbah, major subdivision of the *Tanna debe Eliyyahu*
ESF	*The Early Syrian Fathers on Genesis*
Exod.	Exodus
Ezek.	Ezekiel
Flight	*Flight from the World*, Ambrose of Milan
Fug.	*De Fuga et Inventione* (*On Flight and Finding*), Philo
Gen.	Genesis
Gen. R.	*Genesis Rabbah*
Gen. R. (Soncino)	*Genesis Rabbah*, Soncino edition *Midrash Rabbah*
GCD	Genesis Commentary Digest, *Bereishis: Genesis / A New Translation with a Commentary Anthologized*, Mesorah Publications
Gk Apoc. Ezra	*Greek Apocalypse of Ezra*
Gomorrah	*Book of Gomorrah: An Eleventh-Century Treatise against Clerical Homosexual Practices*, Peter Damian, Trans Pierre J. Payer
Gub. Dei	*De Gubernatione Dei* (*The Governance of God*), Salvian the Presbyter

Ham.	*Hamartigenia (Origin of Sin),* Prudentius
Heb.	Epistle to the Hebrews (Hebrews)
Hom. Pss.	*Homilies on Psalms (Exegetical Homilies),* Basil
Hos.	Hosea
HSP	*Hellenistic Synagogal Prayer*
Ieun.	*De Ieiunio Adversus Psychicos (On Fasting, against the Psychics),* Tertullian
Inst. Virg.	*De Institutione Virginum et Contemptu Mundi (The Training of Nuns and the Contempt of the World),* Leander of Seville
Isa.	Isaiah
Iso. Comm. Gen.	*Commentary on Genesis,* Iso'dad of Merv
Iso. Comm. Judg.	*Commentary on Judges,* Iso'dad of Merv
Jer.	Jeremiah
Josh.	Joshua
JPS	Jewish Publication Society, *Tanakh: The Holy Scriptures*
JSOT	*Journal for the Study of the Old Testament*
Jub.	*Jubilees*
Judg.	Judges
JCD	Commentary Digest on Judges, *Judges: A New English Translation,* Judaica Press
KJV	King James Version
Lam.	Lamentations
LCL *Jos.*	Loeb Classical Library, *Josephus*
Leg. All.	*Legum Allegoraie (Allegorical Interpretation),* Philo
Lev.	Leviticus
Lk.	Luke
LS(S)	*Liber Scholiorum,* Seert recension, Theodore bar Konai
LS(U)	*Liber Scholiorum,* Urmia recension, Theodore bar Konai
LXX	Septuagint
McNeill/Gamer	*Medieval Handbooks of Penance*
Mt.	Matthew
Mk	Mark
MM	*Memar Marqah*
Monog.	*De Monogamia (On Monogamy),* Tertullian
Mor. Job	*Moralia in Job (Morales sur Job),* Gregory the Great
Nat.	*Hymns on the Nativity,* Ephrem Syrus
NEB	New English Bible
NIV	New International Version
nov.	*novella*
NRSV	New Revised Standard Version
NT	New Testament
NT Apoc.	*New Testament Apocrypha,* Ed. W Schneemelcher (1974)
Num.	Numbers
Origen, *Hom. Gen.*	*Homilies on Genesis,* Origen
Origen, *Hom. Jer.*	*Homilies on Jeremiah,* Origen
Origen, *Hom. Lev.*	*Homilies on Leviticus,* Origen

OT	Old Testament
Pall.	*De Pallio* (*The Ascetic's Mantle*), Tertullian
Pes. R.	*Pesikta Rabbati*
PG	*Patrologiae cursus completus Series Graeca*
PRE	*Pirke de Rabbi Eliezer*
PL	*Patrologiae cursus completus series Latina*
Post. Caini	*De Posteritate Caini* (*The Posterity and Exile of Cain*),
Ad. Prax.	*Adversus Praxeas* (*Against Praxeas*), Tertullian
Prov.	Proverbs
Ps.	Psalms
Ps.-Philo	Pseudo-Philo, *Biblical Antiquities*
Ps.-Titus	Pseudo Titus, *The Pseudo-Titus Epistle*
PSTB	*Postilla Super Totam Bibliam*
QHG	*Hebrew Questions on Genesis*, Jerome
Quaest. in Gen.	*Quaestiones et Solutiones in Genesin* (*Questions and Answers on Genesis*), Philo
Rebus	*De Rebus Suis* (*Concerning His Own Affairs*), Gregory Nazianzus, in *Three Poems* (1987)
Regist. Epist.	*Registrum Epistularum*, Gregory the Great
Reg. Past.	*Regula Pastoralis* (*Pastoral Care*), Gregory the Great
Ren. Saec.	*De renuntiatione saeculi* (*On the Renunciation of the World*), Basil, in *Ascetical Works* (1962)
Ruth R.	*Ruth Rabbah*
Sanh.	*Sanhedrin*
S. 'Ol.	*Seder 'Olam*
Sir.	Sirach (Ecclesiasticus)
Somn.	*De Somniis* (*On Dreams*), Philo of Alexandria
SY	*Sefer ha-Yashar* (*The Book of Yashar*)
T. Abr.	*Testament of Abraham*
T. Isaac	*Testament of Isaac*
Test. XII Patr.	*Testaments of the Twelve Patriarchs*
T. Ash.	*Testament of Asher*
T. Benj.	*Testament of Benjamin*
T. d. Eliyy.	*Tanna debe Eliyyahu*
Targ.	*Targum*
Targ. Jon.	*Targum Jonathan to the Former Prophets*
Targ. Neof.	*Targum Neofiti*
Targ. Onq.	*Targum Onqelos*
Targ. Ps.-Jon.	*Targum Pseudo-Jonathan*
T. Levi	*Testament of Levi*
T. Naph.	*Testament of Naphtali*
T. Reub.	*Testament of Reuben*
Trin.	*The Trinity*, Novatian
TS	*Thesaurus Syriacus*
Uxor.	*Ad Uxorem* (*To his Wife*), Tertullian
Virg.	*Hymns on Virginity*, Ephrem Syrus

Vulg.	Vulgate
War	*The Jewish War* (*De Bello Judaico*), Josephus
Wis.	Wisdom (of Solomon), Book of
Zech.	Zechariah
Zeph.	Zephaniah

Chapter 1

INTRODUCING SODOM/OLOG/Y:
A HOMOSEXUAL READING HETERO-TEXTUALITY

1. *Motivation: Suicide, Biblical Studies and Social Control*

Throughout 2001 I was a member of a Queer Men's Discussion Group that met regularly at Queensland University. At one of our meetings the group decided to talk about suicide. Most of the people in the group were young, in their late teens and twenties. During the course of the discussion I was appalled to hear how many had considered suicide, and actually attempted it, and the ages at which they had made their attempts. On reflection, I should not have been surprised. I could do the mental sums working out what year it was when these attempts were made and recalling how homosexuality might have been handled in public debate at the time. I wondered how many others had been successful in their attempts. I also realized that another reason I was so affected was that this was the only occasion I had sat down in a group of gay and bisexual men to talk about suicide. Yet suicide lurks in the background of day-to-day life, surfacing regularly in the deaths of friends who, having reached adulthood, decide that the struggle to get there wasn't worth it. Nevertheless, it is not only public controversies that might compel a person to commit suicide. We live in a society in which a paramountcy of value is assigned to the heterosexual over the homo/bi/sexual. This heterosexual paramountcy is unchallenged everywhere and underlies the everyday routine of life – a fact behind Geoff Parkes' painful question,

> What happens to those of us who are left behind, swept under the carpet, pushed into our hiding places by a society that appears to believe that one's greatest chance of fulfilment lies in a middle-class suburb on a Sunday afternoon with partner, kids and four-wheel drive in tow?' (http://www.remyforum.net/geoff/gsuicide3.htm).

He then continues:

> I survived a childhood that was filled with neglect, pain, alcoholism and religious intolerance, often unintentional but nevertheless, deeply disturb-

ing; I survived Catholic education, and yet I'm still recovering, still burning with the anger at what the bastards inflicted on me for seven years straight; I even survived Toowoomba. I am alive. But I am not unique, or extraordinary because of this (http://www.remyforum.net/geoff/gsuicide3.htm).

Part of why Geoff does not consider himself unique or extraordinary is that the problem is not just Catholic schools or even Toowoomba. This heterosexual paramountcy is not neutral or passive in its effect. As Eve Kosofsky Sedgwick points out,

> The number of persons or institutions by whom the existence of gay people – never mind the existence of *more gay people* – is treated as a precious desideratum, a needed condition of life, is small, even compared to those who may wish for the dignified treatment of any gay people who happen already to exist…the scope of institutions whose programmatic undertaking is to prevent the development of gay people is unimaginably large. No major institutionalized discourse offers a firm resistance to that undertaking; in the United States…most sites of the state, the military, education, law, penal institutions, the church, medicine, mass culture, and the mental health industries enforce it all but unquestioningly, and with little hesitation at even the recourse to invasive violence (1994: 42).

The heterosexual paramountcy actively strives to enforce uniformity and abhors sexual plurality.

If biblical studies can be considered a major institutionalized discourse then it certainly belongs in Sedgwick's list. Biblical studies has participated fully in sustaining the regimes of compulsory heterosexuality responsible for so much suffering and death. The biblical texts themselves have long been employed as the ideological basis of such regimes. They have been twisted and braided to form the nooses that have choked out many a life. It is my consciousness of that fact that caused me to write this book to help unravel some of those lethal braids and loops. In so doing, I hope that I can help facilitate more queer people to *Take Back the Word* (Goss and West 2000) such that biblical studies might one day become an institutionalized discourse that celebrates the existence of queer people and works to encourage our increased presence and participation.

2. *Reception, Intertextuality, Readers and Politics*

That such a possibility might arise is assisted by the fact that, as Ken Stone notes, the discipline of contemporary biblical studies has been 'undergoing a rapid transformation…with the appearance of a range of new interpretative questions and types of reading' (Stone 2001: 11). While Stone adds that this process happened over 'the last few decades', it has most notably taken place in the last two decades. One of these transformations has been a shift in biblical studies to what Morris calls 'post-critical exegesis' (Morris 1992: 27) This way of reading links current literary strategies with both the critical biblical studies of the last 150 years and the pre-critical studies that preceded it. This new field is also known as the study of biblical reception. Thus, there have been studies such as Jeremy Cohen's on the reception of Gen. 1.28 in early and medieval Rabbinic and Christian thought (1989) and anthologies such as *A Walk in the Garden* (Morris and Sawyer 1992) which sketched a history of images of Eden, Adam and Eve and the Fall. John Sawyer (1996) has written a study on the role of the book of Isaiah in Christianity. Marina Warner (1995) contributed an essay discussing images of the Queen of Sheba in Islamic, Ethiopian and European art and literature to an anthology of women writing on the Bible. Norman Cohn (1996) has also written on Noah's flood in western thought. Most recently, Yvonne Sherwood (2000) has written a study of the reception of the book of Jonah in Christian and Jewish traditions. However, as if to show that there is nothing new under the sun, it is necessary to also cite Jack P. Lewis' 1968 study of the interpretation of Noah and the Flood in early Jewish and Christian literature which anticipated the current interest in biblical reception.

Previously, biblical studies had been dominated by the historical-critical method, which aimed at ascertaining the meaning of biblical texts in the context of their own historical, cultural setting. Its quest was to discover the intentions of the authors of the biblical texts and to reconstruct that historical setting. Historical criticism was a quest for ancient Israel and its religion and so dismissed pre-critical exegesis in both Christian and Jewish traditions, not to mention the broader use of biblical texts in Jewish and Christian cultures. But the results of archaeology in Israel/Palestine have challenged the reconstructions of ancient Israel developed in critical biblical scholarship. Biblical texts are no longer confidently seen as windows into the past, and ancient Israel is now understood to be a shadowy world only glimpsed, 'as through a glass darkly', in the biblical texts. A darkened glass serves better as a mirror than a window, and so the world of ancient Israel, found by historical critics in the texts, turns out to be in large measure the world of the historical critical readers themselves, their assumptions and ideologies, not an objective, historical entity.

This changing understanding has led biblical scholars to adopt new approaches to biblical study, in particular to draw on literary theory to read the biblical texts as literature rather than history. The new interest in biblical reception has been aided by the development in literary theory of the concept of intertextuality as a tool for interpreting texts. The concept of intertextuality recognizes that texts do not exist in isolation but are always in relation with one another:

> ...any text is a mosaic of quotations; any text is the absorption and trans-formation of another. The notion of intertextuality replaces that of inter-subjectivity, and poetic language is read as at least double (Kristeva, cited in Carroll 1993: 57).

Texts echo and allude to each other. Similarities and differences between texts both invite 'conversation' between them and allow 'each text to be affected by the other' (Fewell 1992: 13). Every text has a pre-text, the texts that existed before it came into being, and a post-text, those texts subse-quently generated by the text. A text is both a pre-text and a post-text of another. The post-texts of a text shape the pre-text that a reader brings to that text and employs in reading that text. Consequently, Penchansky gives three broad meanings of text by which an intertextual approach can be applied. First, there is the text itself, which an intertextual approach regards as existing in a relationship of juxtaposed texts. Second, there is the social text, the cultural conditions in which a text is read (Bal describes this as the pre-text, 'the historical, biographical and ideological reality from which the text emerges' [Bal 1989b: 14]). Finally, there is the interpretive text, the interaction of interpreters and audience with texts to create something new (Penchansky 1992: 77-78). The role of the reader is crucial in this process. Beal points out that it is the reader's ideology that determines the legiti-macy of intertextual relationships and how to 'rightly' negotiate those rela-tionships (Beal 1992: 28). The reader alone can set the boundaries of texts and establish textual relationships.

The study of biblical reception illustrates the processes of intertextual-ity, through what Carroll calls 'the discombobulations brought about by time' (Carroll 1992: 68) of the biblical text. Carroll reminds us that:

> Different theoretical perspectives inevitably produce very different read-ings of texts, and texts as traditional and ideological as the Bible are always vulnerable to changing paradigms of interpretation (Carroll 1992: 84).

Or, as Paul Hallam complains, '...the more I read the commentaries, the more they all seem like autobiographies, albeit disguised' (Hallam 1993: 84). The biblical text is actually fraught with 'obscurity' (Handelman 1982: 29). It does not describe motivations or even the physical appearance of its characters. It is a text filled with gaps that create obscurity. Readers nego-tiate these gaps by filling them according to a regnant ideology, making 'the interpretive act...similar to the creative act' (Zornberg 1996: xviii).

Bal points out that, because of this obscurity, a biblical narrative easily becomes an ideo-story, a narrative, taken out of context, 'whose structure lends itself to be the receptacle of different ideologies' (Bal 1988: 11). The study of reception helps to illuminate this process and sheds light on us as readers. Finally, the cumulative process of reading and interpretation, the post-text of the biblical texts, shapes the pre-text, which a reader employs in any interpretation of the biblical text. The biblical texts are also sacred texts to a variety of religions and cultures, so it is inevitable that there have been many different readings. The study of reception rediscovers those readings, either rejected or marginalized, and enables them to challenge the assumptions of the dominant pre-text. Thus, the study of reception can be a political process, which makes it well-suited to a project of anti-homophobic inquiry in a way that the old historical approach could not encourage.

3. *Introducing Sodom and Gibeah*

The story of Sodom is an ideo-story that has served to entrench homophobia and is still used for that purpose in conservative Christianity. However, the story in Genesis 19 is very much full of gaps. We are not told the nature of the evil of the city. There is no description of the Sodomites. The only indication we have of their character is the siege of Lot's house by the men of the city, demanding that Lot's guests be brought out to be 'known' by them. When Lot remonstrates with the mob, he nowhere makes plain how he understands their intentions. The rest of the story tells us no more than the fate of Lot and his family and the destruction of the city. Yet, when John Huston portrayed the story of Sodom in his film, *The Bible...In the Beginning*, Sodom appeared as a city almost taken over by a lesbian and gay Mardi Gras. The men of Sodom are shown as queeny, campy types, definitely not manly. Their speech is sibilant, they wear make-up, they are effeminate and they are predatory. Huston filled in the textual gaps so as to present the city as a hothouse of homosexuality, something not found in the biblical text. The political ramifications of this portrayal are best illustrated by my own experience. I first saw the film as a teenager wrestling with my sexuality, in the days before Stonewall. It was the first representation I had seen of homosexuality and, with its lethal consequences, was very much a text of terror for me. As the film has been subsequently regularly televised, I wonder how many other people, like myself, first saw their sexuality represented in that deadly way. I also wonder how many straight people had their homophobia reinforced by this film. My experience illustrates the political nature of many biblical texts and their subsequent representations.

Huston's film also shows how texts are read, reread, even rewritten, in the development of a post-text, which is 'any rewriting of a previous text, which is always a reading, be it a commentary or a different version' (Bal 1988: 254). The post-text of Sodom and Gomorrah is an ongoing process of commentary, exegesis, midrash and representation, starting within the Hebrew Bible and continuing with apocrypha, pseudepigrapha, Christian scripture and onward with Christian, Jewish and other readings and representations of the story right through to modern times. Huston's film is part of a homophobic post-text of Sodom and Gomorrah that homosexualizes the story and forms the dominant pre-text used today in reading the biblical text (the ante-text).

Turning from film to commentary, it is instructive to examine both the use of the homophobic interpretation in Robert Alter's reading of Sodom and its uncritical acceptance, in my view, by the queer theorist, Jonathan Goldberg. Alter reads the story in the light of the promises of posterity to Abraham. For Alter, Sodom stands as a type of anti-civilization which serves as a warning of the precariousness of national existence and procreation which must depend on 'the creation of a just society' (Alter 1994: 32). Of the attempted rape of the angels, Alter declares:

> ...in regard to this episode's place in the larger story of progeny for Abraham, it is surely important that homosexuality is a necessarily sterile form of sexual intercourse, as though the proclivities of the Sodomites answered biologically to their utter indifference to the moral prerequisites for survival (Alter 1994: 33).

Although Goldberg questions this incompatibility of nationhood and same-sex relations (Goldberg 1994: 6), he nevertheless accepts the validity of Alter's reading of the story and includes it as the first essay in his anthology, *Reclaiming Sodom*, dealing with homosexuality and American culture. However, in part 3 of his *Sodometries: Renaissance Texts and Modern Sexualities* (1992), Goldberg explored the fear of 'sodomy' and its interplay with the precariousness of survival in early American colonial experience, especially that of the Puritan colonists in American New England. One could ask, therefore, whether Alter's reading is a natural reading of the story or whether he replays an ongoing white American (male) anxiety. Hallam's observation on commentaries is appropriate here, '(t)oo much autobiography...(e)veryone so certain they've been there, seen Sodom' (Hallam 1993: 84).

Bailey, McNeill, Horner and Boswell, however, have all challenged the homophobic interpretation of Sodom and Gomorrah. Bailey and McNeill argue that the crime of Sodom should be understood as inhospitality towards strangers (Bailey 1955: 5; McNeill 1977: 45). Horner and Boswell argue that the crime should be understood as one of attempted rape of strangers (Horner 1978: 51; Boswell 1980: 93) something very different to consensual homosexuality. Additionally, Bailey and Boswell point out that the homophobic reading of Sodom and Gomorrah has never been the only way the story has been read. In particular, Rabbinic Judaism has never read the story as divine punishment of homosexuality. These arguments were reprised by Nancy Wilson (1995).

Acceptance of the homophobic interpretation of the story has never been an issue in critical scholarship. While individual authors are too many to enumerate, it was uncritically accepted and only in the last two decades does it appear to have been quietly dropped. With the exception of Simon Parker (1991), I have yet to find evidence that, until the early 1990s, any biblical scholar had ever publicly questioned the homophobic interpretation, which is still promoted by religious conservatives. Parker aside, of the five people mentioned here who have challenged it, McNeill, Horner and Boswell are all self-identified gay men and Nancy Wilson is both a lesbian and a minister in the queer inclusive Metropolitan Community Church. All five are outside the guild of biblical scholarship. In fact, it is only in the second half of the 1990s that visibly queer hermeneutical approaches have emerged within the discipline known as biblical studies. It is sobering to reflect that the landmark *Postmodern Bible* (Bible and Culture Collective 1995) had nothing to say about lesbian and gay hermeneutics, let alone queer, bisexual or transgender hermeneutics. It is also ironic, because any queer person of faith in the biblical religions must, *ipso facto*, be a skilled biblical interpreter if they are to survive in their traditions and at the same time validate their own sexuality/gender identity.

An intertextual approach to reading texts establishes textual relationships through the similarities, echoes and allusions that the reader establishes for one text with an/other/s. It is not difficult to establish an intertextual relationship for Genesis 19 because there is a remarkably similar story to that of Sodom in the Bible, the outrage at Gibeah recounted in Judges 19–21. Here, a Levite and his concubine spend the night in the town of Gibeah. As with the Sodom story, the house in which they stay is besieged by the men of the town, making the same demands as the men of Sodom. In this story, however, there is no divine intervention. Instead the Levite throws his concubine to the mob who rape her to death. The Levite leaves the next day and incites Israel to engage in a punitive war against Gibeah and the tribe of Benjamin. Thus, Gibeah is destroyed. This particular story remains a ghost haunting the cities of the plain. Its political sig—nificance lies in the fact that we have the words 'sodomy' and 'sodomite' to refer especially to male homosexuality, but not 'gibeathy' and 'gibeathite'. The story does not form part of the homophobic pre-text, in which the biblical texts are used against homosexuality today.

It is also striking that this similarity of both stories has been recognized. Bailey, Boswell, Horner, McNeill, Parker and Wilson include the story in their discussions of Sodom and Gomorrah. Many commentaries on both Genesis and Judges link the two stories (e.g. Moore 1895: 419; Ryle 1921: 213; Skinner 1930: 307; Von Rad 1961: 213; Boling 1975: 278-79; Martin 1975: 205; Trible 1984: 75; Soggin 1987: 289; Webb 1987: 189; Wester-mann 1987: 142; Bal 1988: 93;). When the focus has been on their similar-ity, the main issue has been which story has priority. Thus, Boling points out that Wellhausen regarded the Judges story as a 'late imitation of the sory of Lot...and arbitrarily dismissed it as having no positive value'. (Boling 1975: 278). Both Niditch (1982) and Lasine (1984) also compare the two stories to ascertain priority, Niditch arguing a Judges priority and Lasine a Genesis priority. Only recently have the two stories been subject to inter-textual analysis. Penchansky (1992) uses both stories along with Genesis 24 to demonstrate the application of intertextuality to biblical texts. Tapp (1989) reads both stories with that of Jephthah's daughter (Judges 11) to demonstrate an ancient Israelite ideology of virgin daughter expendability. Matthews (1992) gives an anthropological reading of both stories to show hospitality, its rituals, obligations and subsequent violations within both narratives, as the crucial theme that they share. Stone focuses primarily on the outrage at Gibeah, but is critical of Matthews' reading for ignoring 'the interrelations among gender, power, homosexuality and hospitality' (Stone 1995: 103). I agree with Stone that these interrelationships are fundamen-tal and will analyse them in detail in the following chapter.

So there is a recognized relationship and similarity of both stories and discussion of one now commonly includes some reference to the other. However, the career of both stories has been very different in the history of homophobia. The story of Sodom has become a foundational myth of Christian homophobia; the story of Gibeah has not. In fact it is only recently that Christian homophobia has begun to impose a homophobic understanding on the events at Gibeah (cf. Lovelace 1979: 101; Webb 1994: 78), largely in response to queer counter-readings that invoke the outrage at Gibeah to undermine the homophobic reading of Genesis 19.

4. *Assumptions and Objectives*

This book is an exercise in Sodom/olog/y or Sodom-talk, which can often include sodomy-talk.[1] I am a homosexual reading hetero-textuality, the post-text/s of Sodom and Gibeah. Essentially, I am bringing together a variety of now scattered and often obscured texts to expose them to view. In so doing, I bring to light a history of how these stories have been read. Thus, the project is an exercise in intertextuality. Unlike historical critics, who are interested in teasing out an original context (cultural, ideological situation) behind a biblical text, I tease out the subsequent career, the post-text/s, of a biblical text. Unlike historical critics, I am also not attempting to ascertain what, if anything, 'really happened' behind the stories of Sodom and Gibeah. I agree with Paul Hallam when he says, 'Just a rumour. There is no Sodom, there are only Sodom texts' (Hallam 1993: 275). Nevertheless, I have taken as my starting point that the stories of Sodom and Gibeah are accounts of rape, attempted and perpetrated, and are not concerned with same-sex love and desire. Furthermore, my reading of both stories employs literary, anthropological and historical tools and the insights from employing those tools will be applied to the subsequent history of the two stories.

In this exercise, I bring a certain background and assumptions, the most obvious being my political engagement as a gay man. I apply a queer perspective to my reading and an agenda of exposing and countering homophobia. Consequently, my engagement with the texts will not pretend any dispassion. As Clines points out:

> My own set of distinctive beliefs – cultural, ethnic and religious commitments and inheritances – are what make me an individual... I would...call them the components from which I construct my identity... But in... developing a literary interpretation of a text, much more of my self is involved, and I cannot...casually screen out my identity (Clines 1993b: 74).

And, as Ekua Omosupe points out, 'we must distill theory from the "texts" of our lives and proceed to use these theories to expand our visions, challenge our thinking and living, inspire our growth' (Omosupe 1991: 110). I believe that this understanding is fundamental to anti-homophobic inquiry and also to biblical studies.

---

1.   I have taken my cue for this usage from Rosemary Radford Ruether's *Sexism and God-Talk: Toward a Feminist Theology* (1983). If theology is god-talk and Christology is Christ-talk then Sodom/olog/y is Sodom/y-talk.

This history aims at bringing together and exposing the post-text/s of Sodom and Gibeah, which exist scattered through books and libraries. I do so especially to provide a resource for the struggle against religious homophobia. Sodom is still invoked against us and yet, for the most part, we do not know its history. The Christian homophobic reading only developed over time and was not part of the original Christian package. Furthermore, while Sodom has become a foundational homophobic myth in Christianity, it has not in Judaism. This fact cannot be ignored in any account of Sodom's Christian career, not least because the alternative Jewish tradition always existed alongside the Christian one and was originally a standard interpretation from which the homophobic reading deviated. By uncovering this history we can effectively counter the Christian homophobic myth. So much of queer experience involves such quests for information as Sedgwick poignantly observes,

> Nothing – no form of contact with people of any gender or sexuality – makes me feel so, simply, *homosexual* as the evocation of library afternoons of dead-ended searches, 'wild' guesses that, as I got more experienced, turned out to be almost always right. Why, when I ask the *Britannica* about the crime of Oscar Wilde, does it tell me about 'offences under the Criminal Law Amendment Act' nowhere summarised? If information is being withheld (and to recognise even that is a skill that itself requires, and gets, development) must it not be *this* information. I don't know whether there can be said to be for our culture a distinctive practice of 'homosexual reading,' but if so, it must surely bear the fossil marks of the whole array of evasive techniques by which the *Britannica*, the *Readers Guide*, the wooden subject, author, and title catalogs, frustrate and educate the young idea (1993: 207).

Radclyffe Hall, in *The Well of Loneliness*, portrays the young lesbian in the novel, Stephen Gordon, finding her identity searching her dead father's locked bookcase of sexological texts. Ed Madden comments on this portrayal

> (t)his uncanny scene of recognition in the library surely rings true for gay and lesbian readers, who do not grow up in their own cultures, but often find their identities and cultures in the library (1997: 169).

It certainly does for me and is one of the main reasons I took on this project. It was not enough for me to read that, unlike Christian readings, Jewish interpretation of Genesis 19 was not focused on homoeroticism. I wanted to know exactly how Judaism read this story and I wanted to bring as much of it together into the one resource as I could. In other words, this Jewish interpretation fits Sedgwick's classification of information withheld by the Mainstream culture. Furthermore, by bringing together the reception of the two stories in both traditions, I can discover earlier conversations which allowed 'each text to be affected by the other' (Fewell 1992: 13). Most importantly, I wanted to know if anyone had recognized the likeness of both stories and how they had explained the differences and similarities. While such instances have been rare, as will be seen, those explanations do not support a homophobic interpretation of either story.

This book is the first, I believe, to give a history of the reception of both stories. While Bailey and Boswell point out differences in Christian and Jewish interpretation of Genesis 19 they have not presented a comprehensive study of this reception. Ide (1985) studies the development of the homophobic reading of Sodom in the intertestamental period and early Christianity. However, the work is both full of gaps and limited by its narrow Christian focus. This focus is also reflected by the polemical nature of the work. Ide writes as if Christian fundamentalists are looking over his shoulder or as if he is in a constant sniper battle with them. While I do not 'pull any punches', I do not see myself as primarily addressing fundamentalists. The hermeneutical divide between Christian fundamentalists and myself is vast, and furthermore, I refuse to acknowledge their (usurping) claim to be the sole custodians or performers of genuine Christianity. Christianity is a large tapestry of which they are merely a rather unpleasant part. Ide's final shortcoming is that he focuses solely on Sodom and makes no link with the Gibeah story. Similarly, Loader's study (1990) focuses solely on the reception of Sodom and Gomorrah and, like Ide, does not go beyond the sixth century CE. However, he includes a detailed survey of Sodom in early rabbinic texts such as the Talmud. Loader's approach is a historical-critical one in that he posits a rich tradition concerning Sodom and Gomorrah outside the Genesis account, in the subsequent texts of its reception. While I find his work interesting, my main problem with Loader's study is that he completely ignores issues of sexuality and gender. He displays no understanding of the politics invested in this story both in the period under study and beyond. Very influential for me has been Paul Hallam's anthology, *The Book of Sodom* (1993), in which he brings together a variety of texts on Sodom and Gomorrah (some only tangentially). His introductory essay, 'Sodom: A Circuit Walk', I regard as a profound piece of biblical commentary. An indispensable guide for me has been Mark Jordan's study of the development of medieval Christian moral theology categorizing and condemning homoerotic acts and desires, *The Invention of Sodomy* (1997). The title refers to the invention of the word/concept *sodomy* (L. *sodomia*) as a clearly homophobic device by the eleventh century monk, Peter Damian, in his *Book of Gomorrah*. In the history of homo-phobia, this is an event of profound consequences and I will give my own detailed analysis of Peter Damian's work. However, while invaluable, Jordan's is a theological study that includes some exegetical material on Sodom rather than a detailed account of the interpretive history of Sodom. Finally, none of these studies examines the reception of the Gibeah story and no other account of Gibeah's reception exists.

It is important to stress that this is not a study of the acceptance of homosexuality. Nor am I arguing that non-homophobic readings of Sodom demonstrate an acceptance of homosexuality. Certainly, Judaism has tradi-tionally condemned homoeroticism, but has not based that condemnation on Sodom and Gomorrah but has found the Levitical proscriptions suffi-cient in themselves. Furthermore, I am not arguing an essentialist approach to sexuality, whereby lesbian and gay people are any automatic 'given' in any culture or era. Homosexuality takes on many forms and is culturally determined, as is heterosexuality. Nevertheless, I regard same-sex attrac-tion and homoerotic behaviour as cross-cultural phenomena, despite being socially constructed in many forms. Thus, homophobia, the aversion to and fear of homosexuality or the homoerotic, is something that can mani-fest itself cross-culturally, again in different forms. On that basis, I refer to readings that homosexualize a story as giving it a homophobic reading. Finally, Carroll points out that a complete study of biblical reception

> would have to be a multi-lingual enterprise which took into account the many uses made of the Bible in all the various languages of societies, communities and groups for whom the Bible had had any significance (Carroll, 1992: 62).

One book alone could never be a complete and comprehensive survey of the reception of the stories of Sodom and Gibeah. Such a task would be a collaborative exercise, stretching over a long time frame with a result that would run into volumes. However, in embarking on this project I have cast my net widely to see what can be retrieved and acquired quite a collection of Sodom's post-textual materials, as well as those of Gibeah. While most of them are discussed in this book, its mediaeval *terminus ad quem* has meant that many texts remain to be incorporated into further studies.

5. *In Closing*

I argue here that reading the stories of Sodom and Gibeah together reveals them as stories of injustice and abuse. Of particular importance is the use of rape as a metaphor for oppression and victimization. Ironically, one implication of this metaphor is that homophobia is more appropriately a sin of Sodom rather than homoeroticism. But is it that simple to invert a site of homo-cide into a judgement of homophobia? John Linscheid throws down this challenge:

> Do queer theologians, who note the rapacity or inhospitality of the city's inhabitants, unwittingly pitch camp with right-wing theologians who preach Sodom as the homosexual archetype? In both arguments we seek refuge by emphasizing our difference from those who were destroyed. Both theologies arise from our fear of destruction. We must reassure ourselves that the voice is wrong which whispers, 'you too deserve the fire' (Linscheid, www.seas.upenn.edu/~linsch/Sodomtxt.html).

It is my hope that detoxifying Sodom does not merely reinscribe this story as a license for other genocides. Furthermore, Connell O'Donovan declares,

> I want that tiny hamlet of Sodom to be Queer Space. And really, it's ours whether we want it or not. Enough of our blood has been spilled in its name to warrant ownership of that land several million times over (O'Donovan, www.geocities.com/WestHollywood/1942/sodom).

I agree with O'Donovan: Sodom is ours now. In Ezekiel, it is said, 'I will restore their fortunes, the fortunes of Sodom and her daughters… Sodom and her daughters shall return to their former state' (Ezek. 16.53, 55). By their former state, the text means that Sodom will be restored to life with all of its people and all of its wealth in the garden that was its land. The fires of homophobia keep that land a wasteland. It is my hope that detoxification of this story will help end that homophobic project and promote the full acceptance of the homoerotic. Then, on the once blasted plains of Sodom, we will see 'a sowing of peace…the vine…yield its fruit, the ground …give its produce, and the skies…give their dew' (Zech. 8.12). Loosened from the sustaining salt, Lot's wife will lift up her eyes and laugh.

Chapter 2

READING SODOM AND GIBEAH

1. *Disaster, Civil War and Rape*

Before embarking on a history of the interpretation of Sodom and Gibeah, I will present my own interpretation of these two stories in an intertextual reading that explores the parallels and inversions of rape imagery in both stories. My reading of the stories will be in two parts. The first part is a literary reading of the intertextual relationship of the stories that recognizes Sodom as the paradigmatic disaster story, and I will draw on the insights of Susan Sontag and Maurice Yacowar into the disaster story genre in film and literature. The second part, using anthropological and historical analysis of Mediterranean cultures, examines the ways homophobia, rape and compulsory heterosexuality are integral to the events of both stories. In particular, I will draw on the anthropological work of Carol Delaney and the concept of monogenesis she identified in the gender structures of Mediterranean cultures. Richie McMullen's analysis of male rape and Eve Kosofsky Sedgwick's insights into the role homosexual panic plays in structures of masculinity will also be important.

   In comparing the two stories, I will argue that the story of Sodom is an account of YHWH's mighty deed in overthrowing injustice and oppression and not punishment for homoeroticism and same-sex love and desire. The story of Gibeah is one of a society in which injustice and oppression lead to social breakdown and civil war, but finally the oppressive system remains in place. Nevertheless, while countering and denaturalizing the dominant homophobic reading of Genesis 19 to detoxify both stories of homophobic accretions, the broader issue remains of the genocide at the heart of YHWH's mighty deed. Elie Wiesel reminds us that in Jewish thought it is permissible to 'oppose God as long as it is in defence of God's creation' (cited in Sherwood 2000: 122). There can be no detoxification of Sodom's story without condemnation of the genocide wrought by the deity. In Gibeah's case, while the Israelites repent of the genocide they have carried out, the underlying injustice that led to it remains in place and uncondemned. That injustice is the system of patriarchal heterosexuality that subordinates women to men and employs homophobia to sustain itself. It was that system that invented the homophobic interpretation of Sodom in the first place.

2. A Tale of Two Cities

In their survey of Hebrew mythology, Graves and Patai point out that cities 'divinely destroyed in punishment of ungenerous behaviour towards strangers are a commonplace of myth' (Graves and Patai 1964: 169). They continue by listing a number of eastern Mediterranean sites that local legend tells were cities supernaturally destroyed for inhospitality. Sodom and Gomorrah, however, remain the prime examples of such cities whose story impacts even on our contemporary world, not least by inscribing the words *sodomy* and *sodomite* on language. But cities do not have to be divinely destroyed to incur moral justification and rereadings of their fate. The fate of the ancient southern Italian city of Sybaris has left us with the word *sybarite* and its disapproving connotations of luxurious living. Nevertheless, the story in Judges, of the outrage at Gibeah and its destruction in the ensuing war between the tribe of Benjamin and the rest of Israel, has remained largely ignored. Mieke Bal points out that, up until the 1980s, the story remained largely unknown even within the world of biblical scholarship (Bal 1988: 16). Yet the crucial events tipping the balance for the destruction of both the cities of the Plain, Sodom and Gomorrah, and the Benjaminite town of Gibeah are remarkably similar. I will use this similarity of the two stories to let each shed light on the other. By focusing on women, who are the powerless ones in both stories, I will present Genesis 19 as an account of one of YHWH's liberative, mighty deeds rather than a story about divine punishment for homosexuality.

a. *The Cities of the Plain*
The destruction of Sodom and its fellow cities is a gripping disaster story. Disaster stories have long proved a popular genre[1] but this story contains the added thrill of divine retribution for unspeakable evil. Therefore, in addition to its necrophiliac appeal, it also appeals to the moralist inside us. Such moralist appeal is enhanced by the 'extreme moral simplification' of the disaster genre, which 'can give outlet to cruel or at least amoral feelings' (Sontag 1966: 215). And like a good horror story, Sodom's story

1. Susan Sontag notes that disaster 'is one of the oldest subjects of art' (1966: 213).

enables us to vicariously enact our own fears of a greater vengeance – god, karma, hubris – in the comfort of our own living room.

While the story of Sodom's destruction is related in Genesis 18–19, there are also earlier references to Sodom and the cities of the Plain in Genesis that foreshadow the catastrophe. The first, Gen. 10.19, names four of the cities – Sodom, Gomorrah, Admah and Zeboiim – as part of the patrimony of Canaan, son of Ham. Since Canaan is specifically cursed in the preceding chapter (9.25), the reader's bias is already encouraged against the cities. The next is in Genesis 13 when Abram and Lot separate to keep the peace between their respective households. Abram and Lot survey the land and Lot notes that the Jordan valley is rich and well-watered particularly around the cities of the Plain. Lot opts to settle there moving 'as far as Sodom' (13.12). The narrator informs the reader that this event takes place in the time before 'the LORD had destroyed Sodom and Gomorrah' (13.10) and that the people of Sodom 'were wicked, great sinners against the LORD' (13.13). Thus, a sense of anticipation is created for the reader that, following the catastrophes of the Deluge and the Tower of Babel, another one is about to unfold. Lot's move to Sodom will narra-tively enable an inside view of Sodom's destruction, further adding a quality of suspense. As Yacowar says of the disaster genre:

> The basic imagery of the disaster film would be disaster, a general, spec-tacular destruction, but usually this imagery occurs only at the end, though often with brief and promising samples along the way. More than by its imagery, then, the genre is characterized by its mood of threat and dread (1995: 268).

Lot's opting for Sodom, has introduced a sense of ominous dread to the narrative.

The account in Genesis 14 of the war between the cities of the Plain and the Elamite king, Chedorlaomer, and his allies is the next element prior to the final catastrophe. Indeed, Genesis 14 could be regarded as an example of one of Yacowar's 'brief and promising samples' (1995: 268) of disaster before the final conflagration. This account reports that there are five cities of the Plain – Sodom, Gomorrah, Admah, Zeboiim and Bela/Zoar – and that they have been vassals to the king of Elam for twelve years. In the thirteenth year they rebel and Elam, in alliance with Shinar, Ellasar and Goiim, goes to war with them. The rebel armies are defeated, and the vic-tors plunder the cities and deport their populations. This plunder and depopulation foreshadows Sodom's final fate of devastation and mass death. Amongst the deportees is Lot. This fact heightens the ominous tension: Lot has not escaped but shares the fate of his fellow citizens. What will happen to Lot in the final catastrophe? While Lot is taken captive, one of his fellow citizens escapes and comes to Abram telling what has become of his nephew. This news prompts Abram to intervene. He goes to war, defeating Elam, rescuing Lot, winning the plunder and releasing all the other captives. The king of Sodom then offers Abram his pick of the spoils in reward but Abram, not wishing to be known as being enriched by the king of Sodom, refuses (14.22-23). No reason is given why he declines the offer but, as Abram is the hero in the narrative, his decision reflects negatively on the king of Sodom, especially since the incident follows Abram's blessing by Melchizedek, a priest of the Most High.

In chs. 15–17, the focus is on Abram/Abraham, Hagar and Sarai/Sarah and the narrative returns to the story of Sodom in Genesis 18. Abraham is settled at the oaks of Mamre. Here he has a vision of YHWH during which Abraham is visited by three men, to whom he is lavish in his hospitality. The exchange between Abraham and his guests is ambiguous. While one of the men predicts Isaac's birth, it is YHWH who responds to Sarah's laughing response (18.9-15). When, in Gen. 18.16, the men set off to Sodom, the rest of the chapter sets the scene for the catastrophe to come. YHWH addresses Abraham to reveal that the outcry of Sodom's sin has become so great that YHWH has decided to investigate it. If matters are as bad as they appear, YHWH has determined to destroy Sodom and its fellow cities (18.17-21). Abraham bargains with YHWH to spare the cities even if only ten just men are found there (18.23-33). This episode heightens the sense of ominous dread, announcing the destruction of the cities, foreshadowed in 13.13, and setting the process in motion. The tension is further heightened in that Abraham, who in Genesis 14 goes to war to rescue Lot, makes no mention of his nephew when pleading with YHWH. There is, thus, no assurance that Lot will escape the coming catastrophe.

The final tragedy unfolds quite rapidly in Genesis 19. It opens with two angels arriving at Sodom in the evening where they meet Lot sitting at the city gates. The angels had planned to spend the night in the city square but Lot urges his hospitality on them, which they accept only after initially refusing him (19.1-3). When they are in Lot's house, all the men of Sodom gather outside and demand that Lot bring out the angels so that the men may 'know them' (19.4-5). Lot goes out to the mob and pleads with the men, eventually offering them his two virgin daughters to do with as they please (19.6-8). The mob rejects this offer, prompting the angels to intervene by striking the mob blind (19.9-11). The angels then reveal to Lot that they have been sent to destroy the city for its wickedness and order him to leave with his entire household. Lot warns his sons-in-law, but they reject him mockingly, illustrating another frequent theme of disaster stories. Survival prospects are strengthened when people unite to help each other – interpersonal conflicts only aid the forces of destruction (Yacowar 1995: 271).

From the events of the night, the text shifts abruptly to the early morning. Amazingly, Lot's Cassandraesque[2] experience with his sons-in-law appears to have undermined his own resolve. The angels anxiously wake Lot first thing the next morning urging him to flee. They then rush Lot, his wife and two daughters out of the city, actually taking them by their hands. Outside Sodom, Lot and his family are urged to flee to the hills lest they be caught in the general destruction of the cities. However, Lot pleads with the angels that he and his family take refuge in the nearby town of Zoar. His request is granted and the family takes refuge there (19.12-23). The destruction and overthrow of the other cities of the Plain with fire and brimstone from the heavens immediately follows. Despite the angels warning them not to look back, Lot's wife turns to look back on the conflagration, as they arrive at Zoar, and is turned into a pillar of salt (19.24-26). The narrative then shifts briefly to Abraham who, rising early, looks out over the Plain from the high country and witnesses the smoke of the burning cities billowing up from the land below. The reader is told nothing about Abraham's reaction, not even if he is anxious for Lot's safety. However, the narrative immediately makes the point that Lot has been spared because 'God remembered Abraham' (19.29).

The story then shifts from the unfolding of catastrophe to the theme of survival. Indeed, the flight of the Lot family is a brief example of a particular disaster story type, 'survival after a disastrous journey' (Yacowar 1995: 265). Lot's wife looked back to be turned to salt as the family arrived at Zoar. The narrative then relates that Lot is afraid to stay in Zoar and he flees to the hills with his daughters where they take shelter in a cave (19.30). The theme of survival and human continuity now becomes paramount. The daughters of Lot, believing that no others are left in the world, decide they must become pregnant by their father to have children and assure human continuity. To this end, the elder daughter proposes that they get their father drunk, to have sex with him without his knowledge. The younger daughter agrees to this plan, which they implement over successive nights. On the first night the older daughter has sex with her father

---

2.   Sontag identifies the Cassandra phenomenon as a frequent convention of the disaster genre and one of the standard hallmarks of the heroes in sci-fi disaster films of the 1950s and 1960s – 'the hero tries to warn the local authorities without effect; nobody believes anything is amiss' (1966: 211).

and the following night the younger daughter likewise. Genesis states that on both occasions Lot 'did not know when she lay down and when she rose' (19.33, 35). From these unions are born Moab, from the elder daughter, and Ben Ammi, from the younger. These are the ancestors of the Moabites and Ammonites respectively (19.30-38).

What has Genesis told us about Sodom and its fellow cities? They are wealthy and are located in rich and well-watered country. Each city has its own king but there is a community of interest in that the cities have formed a league or alliance. The people of these cities are wicked and sinful but, prior to Genesis 19, the nature of their iniquity remains unspecified. In Genesis 14, Abr(ah)am refuses any share in Sodom's wealth. Yet he is willing, in ch. 18, to bargain with YHWH to save the cities from their impending doom.

The account in Genesis also raises a number of questions that have been asked repeatedly by interpreters over the centuries, as will be seen later in this book. Who are the three men who visit Abraham and why, when they set off towards Sodom, is it YHWH who speaks with Abraham as he sees them on their way? What is the relationship of YHWH to these men? Although three men leave Abraham, why do two angels arrive at Sodom? Why does Lot sit at the city gates and why does he press his hospitality on the angels? Does he recognize their angelic identity? Is he simply generous in his hospitality like his uncle or is he anxious for the welfare of the strangers who intend to stay in the city square?

More questions surround the siege of Lot's house, which marks a turning point in the story. They hinge on an important convention in the disaster genre: poetic justice, 'the assumption that there is some relationship between a person's due and his or her doom' (Yacowar 1995: 276). What is the connection between this siege involving all the men of Sodom and the ultimate catastrophe that claims the lives of all the Sodomites? A major issue in most commentaries is whether to understand this incident as illustrative, in that it now gives a picture of the evil prevalent in Sodom and Gomorrah, or determinative, in that the Sodomites achieve a new depth of infamy that tips the balance against them. Both positions have been adopted in homophobic and non-homophobic readings of the story.

Regardless of whether this incident is illustrative or determinative, there is a crucial question for the use of this narrative as a homophobic ideo-story. What do the men of Sodom want when they besiege Lot's house? They demand Lot bring out his guests so that they may 'know' them. The Hebrew word in the text, *wĕnadʿah*, from the Hebrew word, ידע (*ydʿ*), 'to know'. The word can mean, 'to have sex with', but Bailey points out that

> in the Old Testament, excluding the present text and its undoubted deriva-
> tive Judg. xix. 22, it is only used ten times (without qualification) to denote
> coition. In combination with *mishkabh* (*sic*), which signifies in this context
> the act of lying, yadha` (*sic*) occurs in five further places (Bailey 1955: 2-3).

Critically, homophobic readings of the story are based on these sexual connotations of *yd'*.

Lot's reaction to the mob makes it apparent that the men of Sodom did not merely want to get acquainted with his guests. He offers his virgin daughters to the mob telling the men to do with the women as they please, but the mob rejects his offer. Lot's daughters have no say here – they are his property. For the wellbeing of his guests he is prepared to hand them over to be raped by all the men of Sodom. No doubt, it is this action of Lot that has encouraged a sexual reading of the Sodomites' demand. However, Boswell points out that

> (t)his action, almost unthinkable in modern Western society, was conso-
> nant with the very low status of female children at the time and was not
> without its parallels even in the more 'civilised' Roman world: Ammianus
> Marcellinus recounts…a similar instance where the Roman consul Tertul-
> lus offers his children to an angry crowd to save himself. There is no
> sexual interest of any sort in the incident (Boswell 1980: 95).

The sexual interest of the mob hinges on how the word 'know' is read. It re-appears three verses later when Lot offers his daughters to the mob. He describes them as having 'not known (*yāḏ'û*) a man' (19.8). It would seem here that the word has a sexual connotation, and for this reason I am prepared to accept that the Sodomites use the word in the same way. It could be argued that Lot is attempting to connect with the mob by mirroring their own speech mannerisms.

However, I don't accept a sexual connotation to the Sodomites' demand in an unnuanced manner. Instead, I agree with Mieke Bal's argument that the Hebrew word, *yd'*, should not be understood as a simple euphemism for sexual intercourse. She points out that the word has a particular significance in relation to women:

> What the expression conveys…is that the threat of sexual intercourse with
> someone other than the exclusive possessor, is the knowledge that turns
> the woman who experiences it into an *other*, an autonomous subject…that
> subjectivity…threatens the exclusivity of the possession (Bal 1989a: 225).

Her insight suggests that, in the case of males demanding to 'know' males, such meaning might work in reverse. A man that is 'known' by other men loses autonomous subjectivity and becomes a possession of the man that has 'known' him. This understanding of the word would be most consistent with a reading that stressed attempted rape as the intent of the Sodomites and not the expression of, or surrendering to, same-sex desire itself. The Sodomites have not come to Lot's house to invite the angels to an orgy. Furthermore, such an understanding accords with the fact that the scene outside Lot's house is one of potential violence, however one might read the Sodomites' demand. I would argue that if we are to read the story sexually there is only one way to read it and that is as a case of threatened rape. Rape would have been the fate of Lot's daughters if the mob had accepted his offer. The consent of the daughters was not an issue for Lot, and the consent of the angels does not appear to have been a consideration of the Sodomites.

What the story doesn't do is specify same-sex desire *per se* as the wickedness of Sodom. However, reading the incident as attempted rape provides clues on how to understand Sodom's evil. The siege of Lot's house clearly contributes a sense of tension and crisis in the story. Nevertheless, that the angels subsequently reveal to Lot their purpose is to destroy the city, not investigate it, suggests that this incident is not necessarily determinative of the fate of Sodom. Instead, the incident clearly indicates that strangers may not be welcome, or have no rights, in Sodom. Attempted rape here is illustrative of the evils of inhospitality and abuse of outsiders that are typical of Sodom – an argument I will return to later in this chapter.

Questions also gather around the character of Lot. How are we meant to understand his apparent willingness to hand over his daughters to the mob? Why is Lot so apparently reluctant to leave a city he knows is to be destroyed? Indeed, it appears, ironically, to be Lot's prevarication the next day, not Abraham's bargaining with YHWH, that preserves, at least, some of the people of the Plain. He refuses to flee to the hills, because he believes that he will still be overtaken by the disaster, and wins a reprieve for the town of Zoar so that he can take shelter there. Meanwhile his sons-in-law, who do not believe his warnings and were apparently not in the mob the night before, perish with the rest of Sodom. Furthermore, Genesis suggests that Lot is rescued on the basis of his kinship with Abraham and not for any intrinsic merit on his part (and with him the people of Zoar).

It can be strongly argued that Lot is not a positive character in the story, and hence I don't believe we are meant to approve the offer of his daughters. Eventually he and his daughters will take to the hills, because Lot is afraid that Zoar will be destroyed. There, his daughters get him drunk in order to have sex with him without his knowledge or consent. Thus, the image of rape returns when last we see Lot, but this time it is reversed in a strange twist of poetic justice. The daughters, who were offered up for rape by their father, are now in control of events. They speak and act; their wishes, not Lot's, determine events. The story ends with Lot, drunk and unconscious, the progenitor of two of Israel's enemies, but not only of Israel's enemies. There are messianic implications in the daughters' agency that have long been recognized by both Jewish and Christian commentators, as will be seen later in this book.

b. *Gibeah: Strangers Not Welcome*

The story of Gibeah in Judges 19–21 is remarkably similar to that of Sodom and sheds light on many of these questions. The one major difference between the two stories is that in Gibeah there is no denouement involving catastrophic unleashing of elemental forces. Instead the disaster is that of civil war and resulting genocide. These characteristics make the story of Gibeah a disaster story and not a war story, because in this narrative 'the image of carnage and destruction predominates over the elements of human conflict' (Yacowar 1995: 266).

Unlike the story of Sodom, the story of Gibeah is not foreshadowed earlier in Judges (although an anonymous Levite does figure in Judges 17 and 18, the stories of Micah's sanctuary and the Danite migration). The events unfold from Judges 19, which opens, disarmingly, as a story of marital break up. A Levite in the area of Ephraim takes a concubine, but she commits adultery[3] and abandons the Levite, returning to her father's house in Bethlehem. The Levite decides to go after her and bring her back, taking with him two donkeys and a servant or boy (*na'ar*). On arriving at Bethlehem he is welcomed fulsomely by his father-in-law who pressures him to stay. The Levite accepts and the two men spend three days eating and drinking (19.1-4). Over the following two days the Levite plans to depart, but is talked out of it by his father-in-law who continues to ply him with food and drink. It is only late on the fifth day that the Levite begins his journey home with the concubine. Since they have set off so late, they need to stop somewhere to stay the night. The servant suggests Jebus (Jerusalem) but, as that is not an Israelite town, the Levite refuses – 'We will not turn aside into a city of foreigners, who do not belong to the people of Israel; but we will go on to Gibeah' (19.11). This declaration of distrust is ironic because the Levite's decision will have horrific results.

---

3.   Bal (1988: 81-89) disputes this reading of the Hebrew text preferring to see here echoes of a struggle between patrilocal and virilocal forms of marriage. In the ancient LXX and Vulgate versions, the text is changed to say that the concubine leaves because of a quarrel.

When they eventually arrive at Gibeah, a Benjaminite city, they sit in the square waiting for someone to offer hospitality. But the townspeople ignore them until an old man, also originally from Ephraim, comes in from the fields. On questioning them the old man finds they have food and fodder for the donkeys, but need somewhere to stay the night. The Levite's replies to the old man appear to me to be somewhat ambiguous in the Hebrew. In particular, he appears to refer to his concubine as 'your female slave' (*wĕla'āmateka*) (19.19). The ambiguity is erased in the NRSV translation but is present in the King James version which renders the verse as: 'Yet there is both straw and provender for our asses; and there is bread and wine also for me and *thy* (my emphasis) handmaid (*wĕla'āmateka*)' (19.19).[4] This ambiguity suggested to Trible (1984: 72) that the Levite is offering the concubine to the old man in return for his hospitality. Trible's suggestion fits the subsequent behaviour of both the Levite and the old man towards the concubine.

Whether or not the Levite offers the concubine in exchange for hospitality, the old man invites the Levite and his party to spend the night in his house. On repairing to the old man's house, the Levite and his host commence eating and drinking. This convivial atmosphere is abruptly interrupted when 'the men of the town, a perverse lot, surrounded the house, and started pounding on the door' (19.22). They demand that the Levite be brought out to them so that they may 'know' (*wēnēda'ennû*) him (19.22). Like Lot, the old man pleads with them and offers both his own daughter, a virgin, and the Levite's concubine to them to do with as they please (19.23-24). This offer does not appease the men so the Levite forces his concubine out to them. She is seized by the men who proceed to rape her 'all through the night' (19.25-26). When they have finished raping her, 'the woman came and fell at the door of the man's house' (19.26). The next morning the Levite comes out and tells her to get up as they are leaving. Getting no response, he puts her on his donkey and returns to his home in Ephraim (19.27-28). On his return 'he cut her into twelve pieces, limb by limb, and sent her throughout all the territory of Israel' (19.29). This is a summons to the tribes of Israel to gather to hear his case and to seek retribution.

The narrative in Judges 20–21 describes the aftermath. Israel assembles and hears the Levite's case, which is markedly different from the events that took place in Gibeah.

4.   The NRSV renders this passage as 'We your servants have straw and fodder for our donkeys, with bread and wine for me and the woman...'

> I came to Gibeah that belongs to Benjamin, I and my concubine, to spend
> the night. The lords of Gibeah rose up against me, and surrounded the
> house at night. They intended to kill me, and they raped my concubine
> until she died (Judg. 20.4-5).

The Levite has stated that the mob sought his death and omitted his
responsibility in handing the concubine over to them. He also removes any
ambiguity about how she died saying that she died at the hands of the
rapists. The assembly decides in favour of the Levite, but the Benjaminites
support Gibeah resulting in a civil war between Benjamin and the rest of
Israel. The Benjaminites win the first two battles (even though YHWH
seems to have promised victory to Israel) but are defeated in the third
(thus vindicating YHWH's promise). Most of the Benjaminites are wiped
out save for 600 men. Chapter 21 describes how the Israelites, aghast that
the tribe of Benjamin might die out, seek to redress the attempted genocide. The problem is that, because of the outrage at Gibeah, the Israelites
have sworn not to give their daughters to Benjaminites. However, for the
tribe of Benjamin to continue, the 600 male survivors must have female
partners to bear children. Conveniently, it is determined that one town,
Jabesh Gilead, had stayed out of the war. The town is attacked and all the
citizens put to the sword save for 400 virgins who are then given to the
surviving Benjaminites. That is still not enough and the remaining 200
Benjaminite men are allowed to abduct the requisite number of women
from amongst the daughters of Israel when they dance during the annual
festival at Shiloh. Thus, through abduction and rape, the tribe of Benjamin
is preserved

    The story of Gibeah can truly be said to be a horror story set in a night-
mare men's world. Except at the beginning, when the concubine leaves
the Levite, women remain subject to men throughout the narrative. Before
the outrage the main male characters, the Levite and his father-in-law
and the Levite and the old man, seem to spend most of the time eating
and drinking together. The Levite regards the concubine more as property and may even offer to hand her over to his host in return for his hospitality (hence the old man's readiness to offer her along with his own
daughter to the men of Gibeah?)[5]. It is the Levite who hands her over to
the mob to secure his own safety and his attitude to her the next morning
is callous to say the least. Until he tells his story to the Israelite assembly,

---

    5.   Bal is not apparently aware of Trible's insight and suggests that the old man
offers the concubine to the mob because he does not recognise virilocal marriage (Bal
1988: 92).

we do not know whether the concubine died at the hands of the mob or when he cut up her body.[6] The text itself, apart from his statement to the assembly of Israel, does not give conclusive evidence either way. Given his behaviour, the Levite is not a character whose veracity would inspire the reader's confidence. The old man is just as disreputable as the Levite whether or not his offer of hospitality is genuine or dependent on the concubine being made available to him. When he offers the concubine and his daughter to the mob he specifically tells the men to '(r)avish them and do whatever you want to them' (19.24). This is much stronger and explicit than Lot's offer of his daughters to the men of Sodom ('do to them as you please' [Gen. 19.8]). It would appear then that, as far as the old man is concerned, women are mere chattels who can be used and abused.

The other question arising from the story concerns the mob's intent with the Levite. The text says that 'they surrounded the house and started pounding on the door' (19.22). It is quite clearly hostile and the Levite himself says that they wanted to kill him. In the NRSV, the mob calls out to the old man 'Bring out the man who came into your house so that we might have intercourse with him' (19.22). As I said earlier, the Hebrew here is 'that we may know him – *wenēda'ennû.*' Once again we come back to the word *know*, יָדַע, *yd'*. I argued that any sexual connotations of this word are best understood in a context of violence and rape. I further concluded that attempted rape in Sodom demonstrates its hostility to strangers and that its people make a habit of abusing them. I would argue that the same conclusion necessarily applies here. Even more so than the story of Sodom, the scene described here is one of mob violence; the men of Gibeah are pounding on the house. Gibeah itself is also clearly not a very welcoming town – only a resident alien even considers offering hospitality to the Levite (albeit under dubious circumstances). Like the Sodomites, the men of Gibeah are also clearly not interested in getting to know the Levite. Boswell says, 'Jews and Christians have overwhelmingly failed to interpret this story as one of homosexuality, correctly assessing it as a moral about inhospitality' (Boswell 1980: 95-6). That the story does not figure in the history of religious homophobia is partly because attention has focused on the fate of the concubine. Her fate shows that the men of Gibeah were not animated by overwhelming homosexual desire (even though they did not accept the old man's offer). How these events are to be understood hinges on the word 'know'. As in Genesis 19, if this word only occurred once in the text it could be said that a sexual meaning may be

6. Both the LXX and the Vulgate make clear that she was dead when the Levite found her the next morning, unlike the Hebrew version.

discounted. However, it is used again in a sexual sense in the text to describe the fate of the concubine. Verse 25 says that the men of Gibeah knew (*wayyēḏ'û*) her and abused (*wayyiṯ'allēlû*) her all the night.[7] Clearly, *yḏ'* in this context has a sexual meaning, but in the context of a scene of extraordinary and explicit violence. The men of Gibeah did not turn up to invite the Levite to an orgy and the concubine had no power over what befell her. There can be no doubt that this story is one about attempted pack rape of a man, which is diverted to the successful pack rape of a woman.

As in Genesis 19, rape also figures at the close of this story. Rather than the image of two daughters raping their father to secure the continuance of the race, the story of Gibeah closes in Judges 21 with the image of the abduction of 600 women (the majority through the slaughter of their people) to secure the continuance of the tribe of Benjamin. As with the concubine, they have no control over events and their own wishes are not a consideration to the male protagonists. I have one more observation to make about the story. The Levite's servant/boy disappears in Gibeah. According to the text he goes in, but he does not come out. This disappearance causes me to wonder if he has been left behind with the old man to replace the concubine (who is clearly no longer a suitable reward for his hospitality). His disappearance has gone unremarked in all the commentaries.

c. *Patterns in Sodom and Gibeah*

When reading the two stories together certain patterns emerge with each shedding light on the obscurities of the other. We are told that Sodom and its fellow cities are wicked, but we are not told the nature of this wickedness. With Gibeah, the Levite's plight in the town square tells us that the people of Gibeah are at least indifferent to strangers if not hostile. The Levite is only given hospitality by a townsperson who comes, originally, from the Levite's own region. On the other hand, the angels are immediately welcomed by Lot and so we are given no immediate impression of how Sodom practices hospitality. The Gibeah story makes the inhospitality of the locals explicit.

---

7.   This question of the meaning of 'know' is crucial even in translation. The LXX renders the word as 'be with' (*sungenometha*) in Genesis and 'know' (*gnomen*) in Judges, the former having a sexual meaning, the latter not. The Vulgate, on the other hand, uses 'know' (*cognoscamus*) and 'abuse' (*abutamur*), respectively. The Jerusalem Bible renders both as 'abuse' while the NIV renders both as 'have sex with'. The NEB renders both as 'have intercourse with'. I believe Moffat most accurately captures the significance by rendering both as 'rape' (Moffat 1953: 17, 291).

What do the mobs in both cities want of the strangers they are demand-ing? It is not immediately clear in either story. The angelic intervention means we never find out in Sodom's case. Both Lot and the old man offer women to the mob to appease them, but this action could merely serve as the easiest means to bribe them. However, the use of the word 'know', suggests a sexual intent. That this intent is pack rape is shown by the fate of the concubine herself. The Levite's own testimony in Judges 20, that the men of Gibeah wanted to kill him, does not rule out his being threatened with pack rape. If the concubine does die at the hands of the mob (and not by being dismembered by the Levite) that fact would support the Levite's claim. Pack rape at the hands of a mob would be a particularly brutal death. Pack rape of a defenceless stranger is a particularly apt symbol of injustice and abuse of the helpless, which I would argue are the real sins of Sodom and Gibeah and not same-sex desire and its mutually consenting expression.

If the angels had not intervened in Genesis 19, Lot would probably have handed his daughters over to the mob. This probability is made explicit in Gibeah through the Levite's behaviour. Not only does he seem willing to use the concubine to purchase hospitality, but he finally casts her out to the mob to secure his own safety. Her brutal death shows what would have happened to Lot's' daughters if the angels had not intervened. Their intervention actually makes Lot look rather ridiculous and is perhaps a judgement on his own confidence in his authority as a male and father.

The male protagonists in both stories are not presented favourably. Both Lot and the old man offer their daughters to the mob; the old man also offers the concubine. Furthermore, Lot appears weak, prevaricating and distrustful of the angels' guarantees. It is almost as if he doesn't want to leave Sodom. Perhaps the mockery of Lot by his sons-in-law (fellow men) has made him distrust these upstart strangers who have already undercut his authority in front of the mob. The Levite emerges as particu-larly callous and brutal. He is not averse to altering the truth when telling his story to the Israelites. In both stories the cities are destroyed, Sodom and its fellow cities by direct divine means, Gibeah and the tribe of Benja-min by war. Furthermore, in Judges YHWH only plays a minor role, that of an oracle giving battle advice. In both stories, there are survivors. Zoar is preserved for Lot to take shelter in. 600 Benjaminite men survive the civil war. At the end of Genesis 19, Lot's daughters believe they and their father are the only ones to survive the catastrophe and, thus, the only humans left in the world.

Both stories conclude with rape as a means to ensure continuance of a community. In Judges, 600 women are abducted to ensure the survival of the tribe of Benjamin. The horror of the concubine's fate is, thus, in no way redressed by the conclusion of the Judges story. In the Genesis story, if read with the understanding that the main victims are Lot's daughters, there is a striking reversal of the rape image. It is only angelic intervention that has saved them from the fate of the concubine. Reading both stories from the vantagepoint of the daughters and the concubine it is clear that women are the ultimate victims, subject to the power of the men. However, Genesis 19 reverses this pattern, closing with Lot being raped by his daughters to secure the continuance of the human race. By doing so the women establish their own agency and speak as characters (the concubine never speaks: her only agency is at the beginning of her story). As a result, Lot, the patriarch, is rendered powerless and silent; drunk and subject to his daughters, his authority is stripped from him. As powerless women, subject to abuse, they rise up and assert their own power. They can do this because YHWH's intervention has destroyed the interlocking systems of power and privilege to which they were subject. Though their action is still rape, it is significantly different from the parallel conclusion in Judges. In Judges 21, the rape is violent and is accompanied by the murder of many thousands in its accomplishment. In Judges, the system of oppressor and oppressed, although adjusted, remains essentially intact. In Genesis, normal power structures are turned upside down. Powerless women take initiative and control.

In both stories rape is the dominant motif and is used to signify the gross injustice that pervades both the cities of the Plain and early Israel. As if to highlight this injustice, Judges 19–21 opens with, 'In those days there was no king in Israel' (19.1), and closes with, 'In those days there was no king in Israel; all the people did what was right in their own eyes' (21.25). It is not the gender of the victims that is crucial, but their status, that of defenceless aliens. Their alien status is reinforced by the fact that they only win hospitality from resident aliens in each of the particular towns. In both cases, too, the ultimate victims, the alien women, are of even lower status.[8] Lot's daughters are saved but there is no such salvation for the concubine. As the lowest, a female alien, she is raped (probably to death) throughout the night by the mob. That this must be her fate is because, in the end, the system is unchanged. The stories of mass rape and murder in Judges 21 confirm this fact. However, in Genesis, YHWH is determined to overthrow the system and so Lot's daughters are saved. Ironically their rape of their father demonstrates that the system has been overthrown. At least for a

8.   Thus, male honour is preserved – I don't believe that gender is irrelevant in these stories.

little while, the victims are victims no longer. In Genesis the victims are freed to find their voice; in Judges the victims remain chained in silence.

3. *Further Exploring Rape, Homophobia and the Sin of Sodom*

Having identified rape as the dominant motif of both stories, it is necessary now to examine the sexual politics of rape and issues of same-sex desire, homophobia and compulsory heterosexuality. My analysis will demonstrate exactly how rape functions to signify inhospitality and abuse of outsiders and the nature of the underlying evil that causes it. Male rape, specifically, will be examined in the context of historical and anthropological studies of Mediterranean/Middle Eastern culture and male sexuality. To detoxify Genesis 19 and Judges 19–21 as texts of terror for queer people, I will address the following questions raised by these stories:

> What is the threat of rape meant to communicate to the angels and the Levite, and how do Lot and the old man of Ephraim interpret the actions of the mobs?
>
> Why are the women considered preferable objects of rape?
>
> Why, in Gibeah, is the offer of two women refused, and the offer of one woman accepted?
>
> And what evil in Sodom and Gibeah is being expressed by way of rape that leads to genocidal divine intervention in the former case and genocidal civil war in the latter. 'Exactly what is the offence that the Levite feels ought to be avenged?' (Stone 1995: 93).

Given the compulsory heterosexuality that underlies mainstream discourse, I would argue that answering these questions requires a reading perspective that foregrounds same-sex love and desire in the reader's experience and not as an issue in these stories. With this queering approach, I consider the interplay of issues of hospitality, honour, shame, gender and sexuality in Mediterranean/Middle Eastern cultures and history. I will argue that the only homosexual issue illustrated by these stories is homophobia as a buttress for compulsory heterosexuality. Inhospitality and abuse of outsiders is signified by male rape as an act of *homophobic and xenophobic* violence.

a. *Gender and Sexuality*
The world of the Bible is one in which women are very much subordinated to men – a pattern consistent with Mediterranean cultures. In these cultures, the literature indicates that female subordination is crucial for male

honour. As Stone points out, 'a man's honour...rests in part on his ability to control the women associated with his household' (Stone 1995: 95). Blok, in his study of adultery, cuckoldry and honour, argues that, in Mediterranean cultures, successful 'claims on a woman entail domination of other men, both from the point of view of the husband...and of the adulterer' (Blok 1981: 431). A man's honour is determined not only by the subordination of his wife, but also by the control of her body and his success in maintaining exclusive sexual use of her body. The pursuit of adultery with another man's wife can therefore be a strategy to diminish his honour and status.

Carol Delaney's work provides very important insights for understanding Mediterranean gender dynamics. Crucial for her argument is the concept of monogenesis, the understanding that 'it is men who give life, women merely give birth' (Delaney 1987: 39). Procreation is understood in terms of seed and soil; the 'male role is to plant the seed; the female role is to transform and bring it forth' (Delaney 1987: 38). Women are, thus, fields that must be fenced in and possessed by men. This male control means that

> (i)f the boundary of what is his has been penetrated or broken by someone else, he is put in the position of a woman and is therefore shamed... Since the seed carries the essential identity of a man, it leaves an indelible imprint which no amount of washing can erase. A woman who has sexual relations with any man other than her husband becomes physically polluted, and, through her, her husband's honour is stained (Delaney 1987: 40, 42).

While Delaney's arguments are based on her observations of twentieth century Anatolian village life, she points out that images of monogenesis run through the sacred texts of all three monotheistic religions. It forms the basis of Aristotelian biology and even in Galen's alternative biological theories, while holding 'that male as well as the female contributed substance...male substance was still held to be generative and formative' (Delaney 1987: 46).[9]

Under this system, it is not difficult to see that the defining mechanism of gender is phallocentrism, the privileging of male paternal over female maternal power. Likewise, phallocentrism is the central structuring mechanism of male sexuality. Under this phallocentric mechanism, normative maleness, masculinity, is defined by penetrating others not by whom one penetrates. The male, penetrated by other men, is stigmatized or, to use our parlance, is 'the queer', while the male, who penetrates, is not so stig-

---

9. It is also through Aristotle and the Bible that monogenesis remains as a subtext for Western cultures.

matized; he is not 'the queer'. Thus, Dover points out that, in ancient Athens, 'the male who breaks the rules of legitimate eros' – in other words, allows himself to be penetrated – 'detaches himself from the ranks of male citizenry and classifies himself with women and foreigners' (Dover 1978: 103).

In Greenberg's survey of male same-sex eroticism in the ancient Middle East the power dynamics of the penetration of males becomes readily apparent. In ancient Babylonian sex-divination texts, anal sex is regarded as a power relationship by which the penetrator is either advanced or diminished according to the status of the men he penetrates. 'To penetrate someone of high social status...anally is favourable; to be involved with one's slave, unfavourable' (1988: 127). Similarly all the ancient Egyptian texts

> ...show the active role in anal sex between men to be one of aggression against an enemy, in which a man can take pride. The passive role, considered feminine, was regarded as shameful (1988: 132).

Throughout his survey it becomes clear that, in the ancient Mediterranean world, the act of penetrating other males did not stigmatize the penetrator and that male-male anal sex was considered an act of aggression by which the penetrated male is feminized by the penetrator. Greenberg concludes his survey by pointing out that, outside 'of a cult context, adult male, effeminate homosexuality was generally scorned as incompatible with the comportment expected of male citizens' (Greenberg 1988: 183). Significantly for my argument, he also notes that male rape was employed as a form of punishment (Greenberg 1988: 181; see also Dover 1978: 105-106).

This pattern continues in much of the (Moslem) Middle East. Schmitt states

> ...the most normal thing is fucking boys. For the man, the buggerer, it is perfectly normal, if he is married and a father. For the boy it is best to do it for extra-sexual benefits... But he must stop at about the age of 16. The longer he continues...the worse for his reputation. A man should not allow others to bugger him. Otherwise he loses his name, his honour... (Schmitt 1992: 7).

There is no shame for a male to bugger other men; his sexuality is not suspect. But for the man who is buggered it is different. Sofer quotes an Arab informant from East Jerusalem:

> I was never fucked, and I will never let anyone fuck me... Men who let themselves get fucked are not men. They have lost their respect... I know

of another man, whose father was fucked before getting married. When the son first heard of it, he immediately cut off contact with his…60-year-old father… We naturally never talked about the subject in his presence, but in conversations he was sometimes referred to as Ibn al manyak i.e., son of the fucked one (Sofer 1992: 119).

In some Middle Eastern societies, men who are fucked become a third gender associated with women (Wikan 1977), or become transgendered such that they are almost equivalent to women (Janssen 1992).[10]

From my perspective, I find it hard to regard men who fuck men in this structure as in anyway equivalent to the Western term, homosexual. Schmitt argues 'that it is not possible to take homosexuality as a starting point' (1992: 2) in understanding these dynamics.[11] However, as a queer identified gay male in a Western culture, I find the most equivalence in these other cultures with the men who are buggered. We are both the sexual deviants in our respective cultures even though the definitions of sexual deviance differ. I would also argue that the men who penetrate in that culture are equivalent to heterosexual men in my culture in terms of normativity and status. In fact, it strikes me that, using our parlance, in this structure of phallocentric male sexuality, there is one sure way for a man to make another man queer (and thus identify who is the queer) and that is by fucking him. In other words, the heterosexuality (honour) of a man is not challenged by his fucking other men. It is, paradoxically, confirmed because male heterosexuality is defined by being the penetrator. Male homosexuality (shame) is confirmed by being fucked. I believe that to call such men homosexual or bisexual distorts what is happening. In terms of best understanding the gender and sexual politics, they are most accurately understood as heterosexual. I would add too that, although Western society has constructed sexuality on grounds of orientation, this phallocentric construction of sexuality still persists in Western culture, most notably in male prison environments. In other words, in some contexts, Western society still allows sexual activity with other males to be a part of male heterosexuality.

b. *Rape and Homosexual Panic*
Rather than representing sexual desire and erotic expression, rape is best understood as sexual violence intended to assert power or express anger

10. For a similar pattern of sexuality outside the Mediterranean, but Mediterranean influenced, see Lancaster (1988) on the *cochones* of Nicaragua.

11. That is not to say that there are not people in such structures who are primarily oriented towards their own sex, but in that structure orientation is not an issue or the focus of homophobia.

(Groth *et al.* 1977: 1242). As an assertion of power, rape is a weapon in the power dynamics of male sexuality and patriarchal gender relations. Put bluntly, rape of women by men is a means to enforce 'the subjugation of women' (Higgins and Silver 1991: 1) to male needs and male privilege (Reeves 1989: 98). But rape of women is also a means by which men struggle for power over each other. Women can be fields where men plant their seed, but women can also be bloodied fields of male contest. This has been illustrated by the use of rape during the ethnic wars in the former Yugoslavia.

However, women do not need to be the surrogates in these male struggles. Men also rape other men. This fact is already implicit in what Delaney and Blok have highlighted about perceptions of adultery in Mediterranean cultures – that, by being cuckolded, the husband is sexually contaminated and bested by the other man through the wife's adulterous body. Studies of male rape have been conducted mainly in Western societies, but these studies show that male rapists are primarily heterosexual men (McMullen 1990: 118). In many cases the perception that a man is gay/queer makes him a target for rape (McMullen 1990: 49). Because many male rapists set out to bring about ejaculation on the part of their victim, the effect of rape on heterosexual men leads them to doubt their sexuality (Goyer and Eddleman 1984: 578; Groth and Burgess 1980: 808-809; Kaufman *et al.* 1980: 223). Both anecdotally and in my own experience, much anti-queer violence also contains an element of sexual aggression. In Western society, then, male rape reinforces the heterosexuality of the rapist while casting that of the victim in doubt. It echoes that earlier phallocentric construction of sexuality rather than the current, Western construction based on orientation. It could be argued that male rape is another context where Western society allows male heterosexuality to include (violent, terrorizing) sexual expression with other males.

At this point, it will be useful to introduce the concept of homosexual panic. The term is originally a legal one, referring to a type of defence mounted by murderers of gay and bisexual men. There, it is taken to mean that the defendant was thrown into a panic by a sexual advance from someone of the same gender, resulting in the defendant losing all control and murdering that other person. Thus blame was shifted onto the target of homophobic hatred. Eve Kosofsky Sedgwick has taken the term, with its connotations of violence and fear on the part of the perpetrators, and used it to identify the psychosocial processes of homophobic enforcement that underlie compulsory heterosexuality. She defines homosexual panic as a process whereby

> Not only must homosexual men be unable to ascertain whether they are to
> be the objects of 'random' homophobic violence, but no man must be able
> to ascertain that he is not (that his bonds are not) homosexual. In this way
> a relatively small exertion of physical or legal compulsion potentially rules
> great reaches of behaviour and filiation... So-called 'homosexual panic' is
> the most private, psychologized form in which many...western men experi-
> ence their vulnerability to the social pressure of homophobic blackmail
> (Sedgwick 1985: 88-9).

Elsewhere she highlights two results of this double bind

> ...first, the acute *manipulability*, through the fear of one's own 'homo-
> sexuality', of acculturated men; and second, a reservoir of potential for *vio-
> lence* caused by the self-ignorance that this regime constitutively enforces
> (Sedgwick 1994: 186).

While Sedgwick is speaking of Western society and its construction of
sexuality based on orientation, I believe this dynamic also exists in a phallocentric construction of sexuality. Sofer reports the following experience
of an Egyptian Israeli Jew with a Palestinian Arab man he picked up in Tel-
Aviv

> ...he was going to fuck me...but he could not keep a hard-on... He could
> not come while fucking me. He directed me to suck him off, but still he did
> not come. I then decided to put a finger in his ass hole, and he came almost
> immediately. He was very insulted and angry... Then I apologised. I said I
> didn't intend to do that, that it was a stupid thing to do, also telling him
> how masculine and manly he was. Telling him how much I enjoyed being
> fucked by such a real man. That I prefer to go with Arab men, like him,
> because they were good fuckers and real men. His anger then tempered
> (Sofer 1992: 110-11).

I read this report as an incidence of homosexual panic with a very real
potential for homophobic violence. As it involves a situation of male-to-
male sex, the Western construction of homosexuality might obscure this
fact for many readers.

Sedgwick points out that homosexual panic works in Western society
because all men must form relationships with each other, which can then
be subject to suspicion (Sedgwick 1994: 186). But in a society where heterosexual men are allowed certain sexual relationships with other men those
relationships are just as fraught with homosexual panic. In these situations
it revolves around guarding the anus (and the mouth) of the man who
fucks, who is the penetrator. I would argue that much homophobic violence arises out of a social regime of homosexual panic because of the
desperate need to identify someone else as the queer. I made the point

earlier that in a world where only the man who gets fucked is queer then the queer is identified by fucking him. But if that man doesn't want to be fucked then the final resort is to rape him. The action alone is sufficient to define the queer. Consent on the part of the man being fucked would actually detract from this dynamic because in rape the rapist is clearly in control of the whole process. Such male control is a defining element of patriarchal heterosexual masculinity.

c. *Hospitality, Rape and Homosexual Panic in Sodom and Gibeah*
Schmitt remarks of Middle Eastern society that '(i)t is the right of men to penetrate and their duty to lie on top' and that '(s)odomisation of one's slaves or of a Christian is not only sanctioned by public opinion, but by some jurists as well' (Schmitt 1992: 3). It is also clear in reading Sofer's accounts of inter-ethnic male-male sex in modern Israel, that it is the Jewish men who are penetrated by Arab men in these accounts and not the reverse. We have seen above how in ancient Athens a man who is penetrated by other men is associated with foreigners. Male prostitutes were normally foreigners in ancient Athens and male rape was employed to signify the victory over foreign enemies in war (Dover 1978: 105). There would appear, therefore, to be a Mediterranean tradition of associating receptive anal intercourse with male foreigners.

In Genesis 19 the reader is forewarned that Sodom and Gomorrah are evil, but not about the nature of the evil. It is not until the men of Sodom besiege Lot's house that we have an inkling of this evil. The evil is not homosexuality but abuse of strangers. Dover points out that in ancient Athens

> anal penetration is treated neither as an expression of nor as a response to…beauty, but as an aggressive act demonstrating the superiority of the active to the passive partner (Dover 1978: 104).

I would argue that the same attitude appears here. Thus, even if the angels had been consenting, it is wrong to read the Sodomites' demand as anything else but an attempted act of abuse of outsiders. The threatened rape of the angels is an attempt to inscribe outsiders as queer and therefore not real men. It is not surprising that misogyny then surfaces through Lot's offer of his daughters in place of his guests. The laws of hospitality demand that Lot protect the male honour (heterosexuality) of his guests. In this world it is better that women be raped than men because rape of men takes away their heterosexuality. In so offering his daughters, Lot is revealed as subscribing to the same ideology as the men of Sodom. Interestingly, in rejecting his offer they confirm Lot's citizenship of Sodom. It could even be argued that Lot offers his daughters because he is uncertain of his own status. Thus, he plays the insider in addressing the mob as brothers but, to cover all options, he plays the outsider in offering them his own daughters in lieu of his guests. Ironically, by so doing he arouses the Sodomites' ire and they determine to treat him worse than his guests, because he has identified himself with outsiders and not insiders.

But in attempting to inscribe the outsider as queer the Sodomites are also attempting to inscribe the queer as outsider. Thus, the tensions of homosexual panic amongst the men of Sodom are relieved in a way that confirms their own heterosexuality (honour). In the words of Sofer's Egyptian Israeli Jewish informant, through rape of outsiders the Sodomites are making a statement that they are 'masculine and manly...good fuckers and real men' (1992: 110-11). Lot is a fellow resident of Sodom and his daughters belong to him not the angels/outsiders hence the Sodomites reject Lot's offer. If Lot's guests had women of their own then those women, as female outsiders, would have been suitable substitutes. Rather than reading the attempted rape of the angels as an instance of homosexual violence, therefore, I believe it should be more accurately read as an instance of homophobic and xenophobic violence. It is a symptom not of a homosexual or bisexual regime in Sodom, but rather one of patriarchal and compulsory heterosexuality.

In Judges 19, the process is similar but with some interesting differences. While the reader is not forewarned about any evil in Gibeah, once the Levite arrives there it becomes clear that this is not a hospitable town. The Levite only receives hospitality from a resident hailing from the Levite's own country. It is because of this, I believe, that the narrative only requires some men to besiege the old man's house. The reader has already discovered that Gibeah is an unfriendly town. The other changes serve to highlight, for me, the complicity of the old man and the Levite in the injustice. Thus, the old man is like Lot in that he offers women in place of his guest. However, in this case it is his daughter and the Levite's concubine who are offered to the mob. The offer of the concubine is a strong confirmation for me of Trible's suspicion that the Levite has offered her in return for the old man's hospitality (Trible 1984: 72). However, his behaviour could also be understood as arising from his own status as outsider and householder. As head of a household of both resident and transient outsiders in Gibeah then all the outsider women could be seen as his to dispose of. Indeed, the old man resembles Lot in that not only does he offer his women as an outsider but he also addresses the mob as brothers, asserting an insider status, just in case. As with Lot, in offering the women the old man is confirmed as no better than his fellow townsfolk and, as with Lot, the rejection of the old man's offer confirms his insider status in Gibeah. Consequently, the Levite throws the concubine to the mob who pack rape her (to death?). To the mob, the Levite is clearly outsider, and the concubine is his woman and shares his outsider status. She is therefore a suitable substitute while the old man's daughter is not.

The rape of the concubine serves to show, more clearly, that the intent of the mob is not homosexual. I will cite Delaney again to underscore this point,

> (i)f the boundary of what is his has been penetrated or broken by someone else, he is put in the position of a woman and is therefore shamed... A woman who has sexual relations with any man other than her husband becomes physically polluted, and, through her, her husband's honour is stained (Delaney 1987: 40, 42).

Consequently, the concubine serves the mob's intentions just as well as the Levite (also demonstrating the blurred boundaries between homophobia and misogyny). As far as the mob is concerned, the concubine belongs to the Levite and so, putting it bluntly, the Levite is made queer by the rape of his woman. It is for that reason that the old man's offer is initially rejected by the mob. His daughter belongs to him and not to the Levite, and so cannot serve as a substitute. It is the same reason why Lot's offer is rejected by the Sodomites (however in the mob's subsequent threat to Lot, I believe, that Lot's daughters were put in peril of the concubine's fate).

Hubris caught up with the Sodomites in that Lot's guests were angels. Hubris catches up with Gibeah in that their intended victim is a fellow *Israelite*. I believe it is this fact that inspires the angry reaction of the assembly of Israel. If a Jebusite or other non-Israelite had reported the same events, I doubt that there would have been the same outrage. In other words, the men of Gibeah are treating fellow Israelites like foreigners. Rape here signifies a breach of ethnic solidarity. It is only fitting, therefore, that as the men of Gibeah rush into rape, Israel, itself, rushes into civil war.

d. *The Sin of Sodom*
In my reading, therefore, inhospitality is signified by male rape as an act of *homophobic and xenophobic* violence. Male rape establishes an equation of outsider and queer, which maintains a system of patriarchal, compulsory heterosexuality. This system is phallocentric, using sexual violence to affirm the penetrating male body as normative and the penetrated male body as queer and other. It is misogynist, because the penetrated male body is, thus, feminized and the feminine is here clearly marked as subject to

male penetrative power. The penetrating male is fully human; the penetrated feminine (female, male or other) is not. Racism and xenophobia
come easily into play because the feminized male is always an outsider. By
being marked as queer, feminized, outsider, males are marked as not fully
human and, appropriately, subordinate to the insider males. But the language of racism and xenophobia is thoroughly grounded in a structure of
patriarchal and compulsory heterosexuality. If there is a sexual sin or evil
to Sodom and to Gibeah, then I would argue that it is precisely this system
itself. My position might surprise many people so used to Sodom being
invoked as a sign of divine abhorrence of same-sex desire.[12]

An interesting critique of my position was offered by bisexual thea/
ologian, Phillip Bernhardt-House (2000), who reads biblical texts through
his 'own bisexual hermeneutical lenses' to determine 'whether an overall
oppressive or liberative reading can be reached' (2000: 18). He argues that
in Sodom and Gibeah what we are presented with is 'plain cultural bisexu-
ality' which appropriates 'homosexual desire to further heterosexual power
relations' such appropriation being 'intrinsically heterosexist in nature'
(2000: 22). He further contends that my own arguments are problematic
on two possible grounds. First, in discouraging the categorization of the
Sodomites as either homosexual or bisexual, I am making a 'noble' attempt
to protect contemporary gay and bisexual men from the sins of our fore-
bears. He argues that 'despite some categorical differences, the behaviour
is often the same (except in terms of rape...)' and so 'the Religious Right...
will still quote these texts against non-heterosexuals' (2000: 23). Secondly,
and more seriously, he argues that I have fallen into a dualistic queer tri-
umphalism, shifting 'all the blame to the heterosexist oppressive majority
– (queer people) have transcended all of that power-politic mess, and it is
only the oppressive majority that perpetuates it' (2000: 23).

My intention is not to prove that heterosexuality is bad, or that gay and
bisexual men can do no wrong, or to set up any sort of dichotomy in which
same-sex desire equals good and opposite-sex desire equals bad. My argument is not about such dualisms. When I state that male rape in Sodom
stems from the basic evil of patriarchal and compulsory heterosexuality, I
am identifying and denouncing a system of power that oppresses heterosexual, bisexual and homosexual alike. While my intent is to detoxify these
narratives for queer people, by rejecting a too rapid equation of gay or
bisexual men with the rapists in Sodom or Gibeah, I am not trying to

12. This invocation only works if the expression of same-sex desire and love is
always and everywhere understood to be rape, because attempted rape is the only
immediately obvious sexual offence in the story.

protect gay/bi men. Instead, I am avoiding the simplistic analogies made by the Religious Right so as to analyse and describe the sexual politics invested in male rape. I can conclude that male rape in these stories serves as a tool of patriarchal and compulsory heterosexuality because this system is very old and not just a modern invention. My analysis also explains why it is that an apparently bisexual culture appropriates 'homosexual desire to further heterosexual power relations' in 'intrinsically heterosexist' ways (2000: 22). The answer is that the culture is not bisexual, but essentially patriarchal and heterosexist. While this sexual system has undergone changes between the time when these ancient stories were written and our own day, the underlying power structures remain fundamentally the same. By analysing how these power structures operate in the biblical narratives I hope to have shed light on how the system operates today, particularly in relation to homophobia and same-sex desire. Not only might these stories be detoxified for queer people, but they might also become resources for social change.

4. *Conclusion*

I will conclude by reviewing several points that have emerged by reading the Sodom and Gibeah stories together. First, I have identified Sodom and Gomorrah as centres of injustice and oppression but not rampant homo/ sexuality. This state of affairs is exemplified by the attempted rape of strangers. The destruction of these cities is an instance of YHWH's mighty deeds aimed at overthrowing injustice and oppression. Second, I have a negative view of Lot's character. He is part of the system of injustice and derives his power from it. Offering his daughters to the mob shows that he shares their ideology. Despite the threat of imminent destruction, he is subsequently reluctant to flee the cities and his flight ends in his ultimate degradation. His fate brings me to my third point, my positive view of Lot's daughters. I have identified their deed, at the end of the story, as the rape of their father, but I have not condemned it. Indeed it can be argued that they are the real victims of the events in Sodom, not the angels. Consequently, the rape of their father is symbolic of YHWH's act of liberation. The victims speak and have agency and are now literally on top. It is important to keep these three points in mind as when reading the history of Sodom's interpretation. The first two are very closely connected. In most cases, the more sexualized the reading of Genesis 19 the more positively Lot is understood. The third point, my positive reading of the daughters, is shared by most readings, even to the chagrin of the individual concerned and could be argued to be encoded in the text. I have not taken a position on Lot's wife but, as will be seen, her fate gives rise to much varying speculation. While the greater number of readings understand it as a form of poetic justice and either condemn her, or, at least, view her negatively, a significant number (primarily Jewish) will regard her as an innocent victim of the catastrophe.

Similar conclusions can be made about Gibeah. It is, like Sodom, a place of injustice and hostility to outsiders – not rampant homo/sexuality. The old man resembles Lot and I have a similarly negative view of his character. Together with the old man, I have also condemned the Levite who, in handing over his concubine, has made explicit the results of Lot's offer. The Levite's action reveals him to be like both Lot and the old man in sharing the ideology that animates the mob. In this story, civil war results in the destruction of Gibeah and of almost the entire tribe of Benjamin. The rush into civil war by the Israelites parallels the rush into rape by the men of Gibeah because rape of fellow Israelites signifies a breach of ethnic solidarity.

Civil war leads to genocide highlighting another feature of both narratives, the mass death, which is the sign of the disaster unleashed. I have stated that the concubine and the daughters are the visible victims in these stories. However, there are also invisible victims – the people of these cities, especially their children and slaves. Not even Abra(ha)m raises his voice for the children of Sodom and Gomorrah. The more spectacular a disaster, the more devastating the destruction thus requiring a greater scale of mass mortality. The disaster genre is one means of playing out the negative utopia of apocalypse. With Sodom, YHWH destroys the system so that the visible victims can speak and act in their own right. But by overthrowing the system, countless others perish as a result. The outrage at Gibeah leads to bloodletting on a massive scale, but here the system was never at risk. Indeed, the mass violence could be argued to be a product of the system itself. However, the Israelites, at least, are portrayed as being appalled at most of what they have wrought.[13] But in Genesis 19, YHWH expresses no regret for the mass death on Jordan's Plain and mass death by fire and brimstone is swift, leaving no rotting corpses to accuse YHWH and ourselves of murder. The story of Gibeah is a reminder that, despite the satisfactions of the negative utopia that the disaster genre provides, the apocalyptic destruction of the cities of the Plain is not an option in the struggle for liberation. Ephrem Syrus portrayed Lot and his daughters as

13. Although they express no regret for the dead of Jabesh Gilead or for the women abducted and raped.

haunted in nightmares by the dying screams of the people of Sodom. The death of Lot's wife can be read as an act of compassionate protest against YHWH's program of genocide. As readers, we continually look back on Sodom and, while in awe of the magnitude of the disaster, as we face no risk of being turned to salt, we, too, should stand beside Lot's wife and condemn YHWH's crime.

Chapter 3

A SHARED HERITAGE: SODOM AND GIBEAH IN TEMPLE TIMES

1. *A Prior World of Temples and Texts*

Both Christianity and Rabbinic Judaism share a textual heritage belonging to a time before either of them came into being, and both claim an uninterrupted continuity with the communities of this earlier period. The defining feature of this common era is the existence of the Temple as the principal point of religious practice and definition, be it through contested or uncritical allegiance. Both Rabbinic Judaism and Christianity are emerging in this period alongside other communities that share a focus on the Temple. This Temple world is also a textual world. All of these communities share Torah and engage with it. Therefore, together with Torah itself, this textual world serves as a background and influence on the literature of Rabbinic Judaism and Christianity.

This chapter will explore that earlier literary world, and is divided into two parts. In the first part, I will discuss what I term scriptural references to Sodom and Gibeah. Included here are not only the Hebrew Canon and the Christian New Testament but also a variety of other texts, some of which were incorporated into later Christian canons or were contenders for canonical status. A number of other texts were important for communities such as the one at Qumran, which did not survive the Temple era or were subsumed into later Christianity and Rabbinic Judaism. In the second part, I will discuss three other ancient writers who were not contenders for scriptural status, but were important both in their own time and subsequently. The turn of the era Jewish philosopher and exegete, Philo of Alexandria, wrote expositions of Torah and drew on it in his philosophical work. Sodom plays an important part in his thought and he not only retells Genesis 19 but also makes frequent reference to it. The second figure is known as Pseudo-Philo because his book, *Biblical Antiquities,* was long included in the Philonic corpus. Pseudo-Philo's work contains a very detailed version of the Gibeah story with important alterations. However, there is no similar account of Genesis 19. The final figure, the first-century

Jewish historian, Josephus, is the only ancient figure to extensively retell the stories of both Sodom and Gibeah.

2. *Scriptural Reflections on Sodom and Gibeah*

a. *Scripture as Commentary*

In this section I will discuss scriptural references to Sodom and Gibeah as commentary on these two narratives, including the Hebrew Bible, Apocrypha and the New Testament, but also Old Testament Pseudepigrapha, Samaritan and Qumran texts.[1] Before Rabbinic Judaism and Christianity become established as separate religions all these texts were held as authoritative at least by some communities in the traditions that preceded them. How the stories are referred to and employed in these ancient texts gives some evidence on how they were understood in the world of Second Temple Judaism. Furthermore, those texts that are eventually accepted as canonical then formed a scriptural foundation on which to base subsequent interpretation. Homophobic associations in these texts provide a basis for subsequent homophobic readings. Texts that do not endorse these associations, however, can provide resources to counter those homophobic readings. The pseudepigraphal texts were also not without influence on some texts that later formed the Christian canon. Many of these texts clearly employ Sodom's story to address sexual agendas and, thus, indirectly influence later Christian homophobic interpretation. However, I will be arguing that the sexual agendas in these pseudepigraphal references are very heterosexual, being focused on inter-marriage with Gentiles and controlling female sexuality, but not concerned at all with homoeroticism.

b. *Gibeah*

Outside of the Hebrew Canon, there are no clear references to Gibeah in any of the literature surveyed here. A possible exception is a passage in the *Testament of Benjamin* (9.1-2), part of the *Testaments of the Twelve Patriarchs*. However, as this passage is also an unmistakable reference to Sodom, I will reserve it for my discussion of scriptural references to Sodom. Apart from the Judges account, most of the references to Gibeah in the Hebrew canon serve a geographic function. Thus, Gibeah's first appearance is in Josh. 15.57 where, oddly, it is included in a list of the towns of the tribe of Judah and not of Benjamin. There is a reference in 1 Chron. 8.6 to a Geba that was the home of the sons of Ehud of the tribe

---

1.   The New Testament Apocrypha I will leave until the discussion of Christian readings and representations in the first millennium CE.

of Benjamin – Geba and Gibeah are etymologically related names. 1 Samuel refers to Gibeah in 10.26, 14.2, 13.2, 13.15 and 14.16 (these last three refer to Gibeah as 'Gibeah of Benjamin'). There are two additional references to Geba in 13.3 (as the site of a Philistine fort) and 13.16 ('Geba of Benjamin'). This latter reference to Geba and most of the Gibeah references in 1 Samuel indicate that the locality seems to be a base for Saul and his army. In 1 Sam. 10.26 Gibeah is specifically referred to as Saul's home. Isaiah 10.28-34 lists a number of Israelite cities and specifically refers to 'Gibeah of Saul' (Isa. 10.29).

There is no odium in any of these geographic references. However, Hosea contains references that clearly associate Gibeah with evil. In Hos. 9.9, Ephraim/Israel is said to be 'deeply corrupted...as in the days of Gibeah'. Then, in the following chapter, the prophet declares: 'Since the days of Gibeah you have sinned, O Israel; there they have continued. Shall not war overtake them in Gibeah' (Hos. 10.9). Despite this clear odium, neither passage gives details of the specific evil associated with Gibeah or refers to the events in Judges 19–21. For readers unfamiliar with those events, these verses in Hosea provide no clues, unlike so many of the references to Sodom, which are frequently specific about both Sodom's fate and the reasons for it.

Most scriptural references to Gibeah, then, are found in 1 Samuel and associated with the story of Saul. A further echo of the story is Saul's first action as king when he delivers the city of Jabesh Gilead from an Ammonite siege (1 Sam. 11). Jabesh Gilead is the city destroyed by the Israelites for their neutrality in the war with Benjamin. Although there are no odious associations with any of these references in 1 Samuel, the character of Saul, his fate and that of his family, could lead the reader to assume that no good can come out of Gibeah and/or Benjamin. This impression is reinforced by the fact that, in the Hebrew Bible, 1 Samuel follows immediately after Judges to make a reader biased against Saul by linking his origins with the events of Judges 19–21. Even in the Christian canon, the two books are separated by the rather brief book of Ruth. As Ruth closes heralding the advent of David, this further reinforces a possible bias against Saul.

c. *Sodom*

In the case of Sodom, references abound in the Hebrew Bible, the deuterocanonical books, the Pseudepigrapha and Christian scriptures. Westermann points out that no 'other incident from Genesis is cited as often in the Old or New Testament' (Westermann 1987: 142). Sodom and its fellow cities are presented both as sites of devastation/destruction and places of great evil. On most occasions the evil is understood as a form of rampant injustice. However, in some texts the sexual theme is prominently linked to Sodom's doom, with one, a late Slavonic version of *2 Enoch*, clearly implicating same-sex desire in Sodom's fate.

I do not intend to discuss every reference to Sodom, as most of them are general, giving no indication of Sodom's evil.[2] In most of these instances Sodom is an example of desolation, the place destroyed by YHWH for sin (*T. Abr.* 6.13; *Gk Apoc. Ezra* 2.19). Often Sodom is invoked as a warning to Israel for not doing right in the eyes of YHWH. For example, in Deut. 29.22-23, Moses prophecies that a future generation of Israel will see the land devastated, 'all its soil burned out by sulfur and salt, nothing planted, nothing sprouting, unable to support any vegetation, like the destruction of Sodom and Gomorrah, Admah and Zeboiim, which the LORD destroyed in his fierce anger'. But the destruction of Sodom can also be used in prophetic texts to illustrate the eventual fate of Israel's enemies such as Edom (Jer. 49.17-18), Moab, Ammon (Zeph. 2.9) and especially Babylon (Isa. 13.19; see also Jer. 50.40). Nevertheless, Sodom is more frequently used in the Latter Prophets as a warning example for Israel's sins and eventual destruction (Isa. 3.9; Jer. 49.18; Lam. 4.6; Amos 4.11; Hos. 11.8 [referring to Admah and Zeboiim not Sodom and Gomorrah]). Similarly, Rev. 11.8 addresses Jerusalem as Sodom because there the 'Lord was crucified' and there the beast kills the two witnesses who prophecy with divine authority at the end time. Sodom here seems to be a place where evil oppresses the good.

Jubilees 13 and *Genesis Apocryphon* 21-22 retell the events of Genesis 13 and 14, but say nothing about the nature of Sodom and Gomorrah and their sins. The added glosses are solely concerned with glorifying Abraham's role in the battle. The Samaritan *Asatir*, a retelling of the Pentateuch, is primarily interested in the events of Genesis 13 and 14 and reduces Genesis 19 to a single sentence: 'On the sixth (day) Sodom was burnt' (*Asat.* VII.28). In the *Testament of Isaac* 5, the seer has a vision of the punishments sinners undergo after death. The seer is shown a river of fire, at the bottom of which sit a group of people, 'screaming, weeping, everyone of them lamenting' (*T. Isaac* 5.26). The angel accompanying the seer says, 'They are the ones who have committed the sin of Sodom; truly, they were due a drastic punishment' (*T. Isaac* 5.27). Nevertheless, while Sodom is clearly associated with serious sin, no clues are provided as to its nature. .

---

2.   These general references include Deut. 29.22-23, 32.32; Isa. 3.9, 13.19; Jer. 49.18, 50.40; Lam. 4.6; Hos. 11.8; Amos 4.11; Zeph. 2.9, *T. Abr.* 6.13; *HSP* 12.61; *Gk Apoc. Ezra* 2.19; Rom. 9.29 (citing Isa. 1.9); Rev. 11.8.

However, a number of texts refer to Sodom and Gomorrah and their sins more specifically, the greater number identifying these sins as injustice and inhospitality. Injustice is the dominant concern of a number of references to Sodom in the Latter Prophets. In Isaiah 1, YHWH addresses Judah condemning its wickedness and comparing it to Sodom and Gomorrah. Verses 2–8 are a general condemnation of the people's rebelliousness and a description of the resulting devastation of Zion. Verse 9, which appears to be a (liturgical?) response of the surviving community, specifically refers to Sodom and Gomorrah in praise of the goodness of YHWH who, unlike the case of those two cities, preserved a remnant of Zion. Verse 10 opens an address to Jerusalem identified as Sodom and Gomorrah: 'Hear the word of the LORD you rulers of Sodom! Listen to the teaching of our God, you people of Gomorrah.' In the following verses YHWH rejects the temple worship because of the evil of the people. Verse 17 contains an appeal to return to the good, in other words to 'seek justice, defend the orphan, plead for the widow'. Verses 21–23 contain a further denunciation of the evil of Zion specifically for murder, theft, bribery and ignoring the plight of the widow and orphan. It would appear, then, that Isaiah understood Sodom and Gomorrah to be places of oppressive power where the rights of the poor and weak are trampled on or, at best, ignored.

In both Jeremiah and Ezekiel, Jerusalem is similarly compared to Sodom for its injustice. However, both books use the sexual metaphor of adultery to underline Israel's unfaithfulness to the deity and Torah. Jeremiah 23.14 condemns the false prophets of Jerusalem saying that they 'commit adultery and walk in lies; they strengthen the hands of evildoers so that no one turns from wickedness'. As a result prophets and people have become like Sodom and Gomorrah. While the reference to adultery could be seen as specifically sexual, it also serves as a strong poetic image for unfaithfulness to YHWH and the Law. The false prophets do not decry but encourage this apostasy. There is a pattern in chs. 21–25, alternating condemnations of Jerusalem's crimes with threats of coming judgement and the promise of restoration. This condemnation of the false prophets follows the judgement of exile and the promise of restoration in 22.24–23.8. Referring back to Jer. 22.11-17 gives a clearer idea of what this evil and wickedness might entail. These verses condemn Shallum, King Josiah's son, for unrighteousness, specifically withholding workers' wages, dishonesty and shedding innocent blood. In vv. 15–16 he is compared to his father who was just, righteous and supported the poor and needy. Injustice and abuse of the poor thus underpin Jeremiah's condemnation of Shallum. The remaining verses of ch. 22 condemn Josiah's other son and successor Jehoiachin, before foreshadowing the fall of Jerusalem and exile to Babylon. Chapter

23 then opens with the promise of return from exile. The condemnation of the false prophets returns to the crimes of Jerusalem in ch. 22, denouncing these prophets as active collaborators in the injustices perpetrated by Shallun and other members of the ruling classes. These injustices have transformed Jerusalem, which should be a beacon of the LORD's justice, into a Sodom.

In Ezek. 16.46-58, Jerusalem is portrayed as a flagrantly adulterous wife and compared unfavourably to both Samaria and Sodom. However, this image of adultery is a metaphor for Jerusalem's abandonment of the LORD because in 16.49-50 the evil of Sodom is clearly specified as social injustice:

> This was the guilt of your sister Sodom: she and her daughters had pride, excess of food and prosperous ease, but did not aid the poor and needy. They were haughty, and did abominable things before me; therefore I removed them when I saw it.

Here again we get an image of a rich and powerful society/class that oppresses the poor. Wealth has made them proud such that they do not try to hide their crimes. Furthermore, Ezekiel declares (v. 51) that Jerusalem has made Sodom and Samaria look righteous. The passage concludes with YHWH's promise to restore both Sodom and Samaria so as to reveal fully Jerusalem's evil to the world.

Pride is the dominant theme in two short references to Sodom made by both Sirach and *3 Maccabees*. These brief references are important because they display a pattern further elaborated in the Pseudepigrapha, the pairing of Sodom's destruction with the destruction of the giants. The giants are the offspring of the unions between the angelic beings, the sons of god, and the daughters of men, as related in Genesis 6. These events set in train the corruption of creation resulting in the Deluge. Sirach 16.1-23 describes the deity's determination to punish wrongdoing. In a list of examples from the past, both Sodom and the giants are paired as explicit examples of disobedience due to pride, incurring divine punishment (Sir. 16.7-8). Similarly, in *3 Maccabees*, the high priest, Simon, calls on the deity's aid against Ptolemy Philopator. He invokes examples of divine intervention in the past, including the destruction of the people of Sodom for their arrogance again pairing Sodom with the destruction of the giants. The linking of Sodom with the giants could imply sexual themes given that the sons of god in Genesis 6 take daughters of men as wives. However there is no sense of sexual offence in Simon's account. The giants trust in their strength and boldness and revolt (*3 Macc.* 2.4). The Sodomites, similarly, act arrogantly (*huperêphanian*) and engage in vice or evil (*kakiais*) (*3 Macc.* 2.5). Both are instances of those who practice injustice (*adikian*) (*3 Macc.* 2.4). The giants are destroyed by a flood of water, the Sodomites by one of fire and sulfur. So while both stories in Genesis contain a sexual element, it plays no part in linking them together in either Sirach or *3 Maccabees*. In the Pseudepigrapha, and with echoes in some Christian scriptures, these sexual elements are made explicit and central in a manner not demonstrated here. However, neither Sirach nor *3 Maccabees* use the stories to exemplify sexual misconduct.

The main point of two references to Sodom in the book of Wisdom (Wisdom of Solomon) is inhospitality, not pride (or sexual sin). The first reference is found in Wisdom 10, an account of Wisdom as Saviour and of her saving acts in history. Wisdom saved Adam, Noah and Abraham and Wisdom rescued 'the righteous man' or Lot from the 'fire that descended on the Five Cities' (Wis. 10.6). The Sodomites are referred to as 'ungodly' or impious (*asebôn*) and v. 7 continues that the smoking wasteland that was Sodom remains as continuing evidence of their wickedness or villainy (*ponêrias*). According to Liddell, Scott and Jones (1940: 1447), this particular word has meanings of knavery, general vice, and cowardice and is used by Thucydides in *The Peloponnesian War* (8.47.2) to portray Athenian democracy as a form of mob rule. Certainly the siege of Lot's house in Genesis 19 is a strong example of such mob rule. But there is nothing specifically sexual conveyed in this passage. Instead the Sodomites are guilty of the folly (*aphrosunês*) of passing Wisdom by (Wis. 10. 8). This particular charge evokes an image of hospitality denied – Wisdom stands ignored and uninvited as the Sodomites pass her by. The passage also refers to Lot's wife, the only female biblical character cited in this entire chapter. While her husband is counted among the righteous, she is a paragon of unbelief, her 'pillar of salt...a monument to an unbelieving soul' (Wis. 10.7). This contrast of husband and wife will also be seen in a gospel reference to Sodom and Gomorrah to be discussed shortly and is the only other scriptural reference to Lot's wife.

Sodom is referred to again in Wis. 19.13-17, an account of the Exodus from Egypt. The Egyptians are compared to Sodom, to highlight their inhospitality and abuse of the Israelites. Sodom's crime is bitter hatred of strangers (Wis. 19.13). They refuse to receive strangers (Wis. 19.14) or, if admitted to Sodom, strangers are received with hostility (Wis. 19.15). But the Egyptians are worse than the Sodomites because they 'made slaves of guests who were their benefactors' (v. 14). Joseph, through his wise stewardship, saw Egypt safely through the exigencies of famine. Consequently, the Israelites settled in Egypt. The Egyptians 'first received them with festal celebrations' but 'afterward afflicted with terrible sufferings those who had already shared the same rights' (Wis. 19.16). By doing so, the Egyptians showed themselves worse than the Sodomites because, while the Sodomites sinned by abusing strangers, they made no pretence about their hatred of strangers. Verse 17 goes so far as to compare the ninth plague of Egypt – darkness – with the blindness inflicted on the men of Sodom by the angels. For the author of Wisdom, Sodom is clearly not associated with sexual sin. Instead, like Egypt of the Exodus, Sodom is a place of injustice and oppression. This oppression is portrayed as a form of inhospitality of which the paragon is Sodom.[3]

This image of Sodom as a paragon or byword of inhospitality appears in ch. 10 of Luke's gospel. Luke's account is almost identical to that in Matthew 10, except Matthew's Sodom is more representative of general iniquity, highlighting Luke's stress on hospitality. Luke 10.1-12 describes Jesus sending 70 disciples off on a campaign of preaching and healing. The disciples are to carry 'no purse, no bag, no sandals' (10.4) but must be completely reliant on the hospitality offered them on their way. Whatever house they enter they must extend peace to all within and if they are

---

3.   This analogy of Sodom and Egypt is also found in the later Samaritan text, the *Memar Marqah*. The focus of this text is the life of Moses not the events of Genesis. However, Moses' call at the burning bush, is compared to earlier angelic visitations including the incident of Abraham and the three at Mamre and the two visitors of Lot in Sodom (*MM* I§1). Later in Book I, a celebratory poem extols Moses and Aaron by comparing them to the angels who went to Sodom

> How excellent to see them enter Egypt like the two angels who entered Sodom!
> The two angels entered Sodom at eventide, sent to open the storehouse of wrath upon all the inhabitants therein.
> Moses and Aaron entered Egypt at eventide, sent to open the storehouse of judgement therein.
> The angels were sent to destroy Sodom. Moses and Aaron were sent to destroy Egypt.
> The angels ate unleavened bread in Sodom. Moses and Aaron celebrated the feast of unleavened bread in Egypt.
> The angels burnt the young in the deep. Moses and Aaron smote Pishon, tributary of Eden.
> The angels drove Lot out in the morning. Moses and Aaron led the Israelites out before morning (*MM* I§3).

This remarkable poem is an even stronger comparison of Sodom and Egypt than the one in Wisdom 19. The events at Sodom, in the *Memar Marqah*, seem to almost foreshadow the events of the first Passover. Some later rabbinic texts will actually date the events at Sodom to the night of Passover.

welcomed they must remain 'in the same house, eating and drinking whatever they provide' (10.7). The image of the hospitable house shifts to that of the hospitable town in v. 8. Jesus charges the disciples that if they are welcomed by a town they are to 'eat what is set before you; cure the sick who are there, and say to them, "The kingdom of God has come near to you"' (10.9). But if they are not welcomed they are to

> go out into its streets and say, 'Even the dust of your town that clings to our feet, we wipe off in protest against you. Yet know this: the kingdom of God has come near.' I tell you, on that day it will be more tolerable for Sodom than for that town (10.10-12).

The healing and the preaching of the kingdom are only offered in return for hospitality. Those towns that do not offer hospitality are not only ineligible to receive the gifts of the kingdom but have shown themselves to be like Sodom. Indeed these towns fare worse. Sodom did not welcome strangers, but these towns denied the emissaries of the coming kingdom of god. It could even be argued here that, without hospitality, the kingdom cannot come to be. This Lucan passage relies on Sodom as the archetype of inhospitality for its force.

The parallel pericope in Mt. 10.5-15 is more ambiguous and concerns a similar mission of the Twelve.[4] Whereas in Luke the disciples have no restrictions on their mission, Matthew's Jesus tells the Twelve to avoid Gentiles and Samaritans and go 'only to the lost sheep of Israel' (10.6). The Twelve are also charged, 'As you go, proclaim the good news, "The kingdom of heaven has come near". Cure the sick, raise the dead, cleanse the lepers, cast out demons' (10.7-8). As in Luke 10, the Twelve are reliant on hospitality. They are to '(t)ake no gold or silver or copper in your belts, no bag for your journey, or two tunics, or sandals or a staff, for labourers deserve their food' (10.9). In other words, the Twelve's mission must rely on the hospitality and support of others in the endeavour. In Luke, on the other hand, the disciples only preach and heal in return for hospitality. Matthew then concludes the pericope,

> If anyone will not welcome you or listen to your words, shake off the dust from your feet as you leave that house or town. Truly I tell you, it will be more tolerable for the land of Sodom and Gomorrah on the day of judgement for that town (Mt. 10.14-15).

Matthew could be highlighting the issue of hospitality *per se* as in Luke or the issue could be the rejection of the proclaimed kingdom and its emis-

---

4.   Luke has a parallel mission of the Twelve in 9.1-6, but with no reference to Sodom.

saries. This latter reading is supported by the nature of the Twelve's commission to come preaching and healing. Sodom and Gomorrah could well represent the epitome of general evildoers who still fare better in the final reckoning than those who reject the message of the kingdom. Nevertheless, Sodom's associations with inhospitality would enhance the reference to the cities in this context in a way that sexual associations do not. While Luke's Kingdom seems grounded in hospitable practice, in Matthew the emissaries of the kingdom rely on the hospitality of others to carry out their mission of preaching and healing.

That Matthew employs Sodom and Gomorrah to epitomize evildoers and wicked cities *per se* is reinforced in Mt. 11.20-24. Here, Jesus condemns the towns of Galilee for rejecting his message despite his 'deeds of power' (11.20). Capernaum is condemned in language virtually identical to that in Mt. 10.15, 'But I tell you on that day of judgement it will be more tolerable for the land of Sodom than for you' (11.23). While Sodom is held up as an example of sinners whose iniquity is not as bad as rejection of Jesus and his message, it is not identified with any particular sin. The parallel account in Lk. 10.13-16, while without reference to Sodom, nevertheless suggests that Sodom's importance for Matthew lies in its fate not so much in its sin. In both Matthew and Luke, Jesus warns Capernaum that 'you will be brought down to Hades' (Mt. 11.23; Lk. 10.15). In many later Jewish texts, such as *Pirke de Rabbi Eliezer*, Sodom and Gomorrah are not just consumed by fire and brimstone from above, but are literally overthrown and cast down into the underworld. So Sodom in Matthew serves to warn that Capernaum will be cast down into Hades just as Sodom was. For Matthew, then, Sodom is a general symbol of unspecified evil, whereas Luke's Sodom is associated with inhospitality, with not welcoming strangers.

There is one more reference to Sodom in Lk. 17.20-27, a short pericope in which the suddenness of Sodom's doom is used to illustrate the suddenness of the coming of the Son of Man. While giving no indication of the evil of Sodom and Gomorrah, this pericope contrasts Lot's wife and her husband as models of doubt and belief in a manner reminiscent of Wisdom 10. No parallel to this pericope appears in Matthew and it is the only other scriptural reference to Lot's wife.

> Just as it was in the days of Noah, so too it will be in the days of the Son of Man... Likewise, just as it was in the days of Lot: they were eating and drinking, buying and selling, planting and building, but on the day that Lot left Sodom, it rained fire and sulfur from heaven and destroyed all of them – it will be like that on the day that the Son of Man is revealed. On that day, anyone on the housetop who has belongings in the house must not

come down to take them away; and likewise anyone in the field must not
turn back. Remember Lot's wife (Lk. 17.26-32).

Lot represents appropriate preparedness being ready to let go of worldly
things when he fled Sodom (Lk. 17.28-29). Lot's wife is used as a warning
not to hold on to the ways of the world, 'Remember Lot's wife' (Lk. 17.32).
This contrasting use of the pair will become a feature of much subsequent
Christian polemic. Interestingly, while Wisdom associates the destruction
of the cities of the Plain with the exodus, this pericope associates the same
incident with the Deluge, specifically naming Noah. There could be an echo
here of the link to Genesis 6 already noted in Sirach and *3 Maccabees*.
However, these two texts link Sodom with the giants, stressing their
punishment, and make no mention of Noah. In contrast, Luke uses Sodom
and the Deluge to illustrate the suddenness of the coming of the Son of
Man in the end times. Luke's combination highlights the story of Sodom
not only as a disaster or judgement story but also as a small-scale end of
the world story. Catastrophic disaster stories rehearse the end of the world,
after all. Lot's daughters justify their raping their father by the belief that
the world had been destroyed leaving them the only survivors.

Two pseudepigraphal texts explicitly connect sex to the evil of Sodom
and Gomorrah, *Jubilees* and *Testaments of the Twelve Patriarchs*, a connection subsequently adopted in 2 Peter and Jude. However, nothing in
these texts links Sodom with same-sex desire, the greatest sexual panic
being caused, in the *Testaments of the Twelve Patriarchs*, by intermarriage
with Gentiles and Israel's abandonment of the Torah.

Sodom is associated with sexual sin on two occasions in *Jubilees*. *Jubilees* 16 recounts the events of Genesis 19, while *Jubilees* 20 is a parting
testament from Abraham to Ishmael and Isaac. *Jubilees* summarizes Gen.
19.1-29 thus:

> During this month the Lord executed the judgement of Sodom and Gomor-
> rah, Zeboiim and all the environs of the Jordan. He burned them with fire
> and brimstone and annihilated them until the present in accord with what I
> have told you (about) all their actions – that they were savage and very
> sinful, (that) they would defile themselves, commit sexual sins in their flesh,
> and do what was impure on the earth. The Lord will execute judgement in
> the places where people commit the same sort of impure actions as Sodom
> – just like the judgement on Sodom (*Jub*. 16.5-6).

From this passage it would appear that the Sodomites are guilty of cruelty
or savagery and unspecified sexual impurity. Sodom is also established as a
warning of what will happen to communities that engage in similar evil.
Omitting Lot's wife, the chapter continues with the escape of Lot and his
rape.

> But we went about rescuing Lot because the Lord remembered Abraham.
> So he brought him out from (the overthrow) of Sodom. He and his
> daughters committed a sin on the earth which had not occurred on the
> earth from the time of Adam until his time because the man lay with his
> daughter (*Jub.* 16.7-8).

Lot is portrayed as committing incest with his daughters and is the one
with agency not the women – 'the man lay with his daughter'. He is then
fiercely condemned through his descendants who will be uprooted and
judged 'like the judgement of Sodom...not to leave him any human descendants on the earth' (*Jub.* 16 9). This verse could serve as a condemnation of
and validating threat against the Moabites and Ammonites. As this father/
daughter incest is said to have never happened before from the time of
Adam, it contributes to Sodom's representation as a place of sexual chaos
and immorality. This sexual immorality is all encompassing, however, and
not associated with any particular type of sexual sin.

The spectre of Sodom and Gomorrah is again invoked, associated with
the giants, in *Jub.* 20.5-6, Abraham's final testament to Ishmael and Isaac.
The sexual nature of the sin of Sodom is paramount, but again only in a
general sense, although Abraham's main anxieties are aroused by idolatry
and exogamy. Abraham begins urging his sons to stay faithful to the
covenant and warns against sexual immorality. In particular, he stresses
strict control of Israelite women's sexuality. If any woman 'commits a
sexual offence, burn her in fire' (*Jub.* 20.4). He then condemns intermarriage with gentiles ('Canaanite women'), equating it with sexual immorality. He backs up these strictures with this warning:

> He told them about the punishment of the giants and the punishment of
> Sodom – how they were condemned because of their wickedness; because
> of the sexual impurity, uncleanness, and corruption among themselves they
> died in their sexual impurity. Now you keep yourselves from all sexual impu-
> rity and uncleanness, and from all the contamination of sin, so that you do
> not make our name into a curse...you will be accursed like Sodom, and all
> who remain of you like the people of Gomorrah (*Jub.* 20.5-6).

This warning is followed by an exhortation against idolatry (*Jub.* 20.7-9). In
vv. 5-6, the sins denounced are unspecified sexual excess and appear to
apply equally to both Sodom and Gomorrah and the giants. The *Jubilees*
version of the Genesis story of the sons of god mating with the daughters
of men does not detail specific sexual sins, simply stating that the giants
were born from these unions. It goes on to say that '(w)ickedness increased
on the earth' and, in consequence, all living beings 'corrupted their way
and their prescribed course' (*Jub.* 5.2). This corruption then spurs the deity

to send the flood to wipe out humanity. The angels (the sons of god) and the giants are punished separately beforehand, the giants being utterly extirpated. A possible reading of Abraham's admonitions is that Israel's way is adherence to the covenant with the Most High. Idolatry is a corruption of Israel's 'prescribed course' as is also intermarriage with gentiles. Intermarriage with gentiles is a form of sexual immorality and if Israel does not adhere to the sexual rules of the covenant then there is greater likelihood of sexual relations with gentiles, including intermarriage. The sons of god abandoned their prescribed course as angelic beings and took human women as wives resulting in the giants. The attempted rape of the angels in Sodom is likewise a departure from the prescribed course of humans by attempting sex with angelic beings. Similarly, Lot's incest is a departure from the prescribed course of a father by having sex with his offspring, which is why his lineage must be extirpated from the earth. Both the attempted rape and incest occur because of the general climate of sexual immorality in Sodom and Gomorrah. Same-sex desire might thus be implicitly associated here with Sodom but it is neither exclusively nor explicitly so, instead being part of a general climate of sexual immorality that both represents and results in a 'corruption of...the prescribed course'. However in *Jubilees* 20, Sodom and Gomorrah stand primarily as a cautionary metaphor warning against the twin and related evils of idolatry and exogamy, not same-sex desire.

The link between idolatry and exogamy is crucial to understanding the references to Sodom and Gomorrah in the *Testaments of the Twelve Patriarchs*, which with *Jubilees* has been dated to the second century BCE (Kee 1983: 778; Wintermute 1985: 44). In the *Testaments*, Sodom is associated with sexual immorality, and, in one important instance, linked to the Watchers, the angelic beings of Genesis 6. Unlike *Jubilees*, *Testaments of the Twelve Patriarchs* includes a clear condemnation of pederasty but without any association to Sodom and Gomorrah. As in *Jubilees*, Sodom in the *Testaments* warns not against same-sex desire but against exogamy and idolatry. What is at issue here is again the crossing of angelic/human boundaries, the prescribed courses of what is human and angelic, as a metaphor for exogamy.

The *Testaments* portray the sons of Jacob giving their final words to their children. They are a combination of exhortation, warning and predictions of Israel's future. In particular, the children of Israel are exhorted to hold to the Law and remain faithful to the LORD. They are also told that they will eventually fail and the consequences that will result. Kee says of the *Testaments'* understanding of the Law that it is 'a virtual synonym for wisdom...is universal in its application...and is equated with natural law' (Kee 1983: 780). Kee further observes that a passage in *Testament of Naphtali* condemns both homosexuality and idolatry as incompatible with the law of nature. This passage, below, links both Sodom and the Watchers. Similarly, Lewis Eron (1990) argues that this passage and other references to Sodom in the *Testaments* clearly assume the condemnation of homoeroticism. It is my opinion that both Kee and Eron have been misled by the reference to Sodom and that reading such references to Sodom as a negative code for same-sex love and desire, particularly when linked to the Watchers, misses their point.

I will begin with the reference to Sodom in the *Testament of Benjamin*, which associates Sodom with general promiscuity, specifically with 'loose' women.

> I tell you that you will be sexually promiscuous (*porneusete*) like the promiscuity of the Sodomites *(porneian Sodomôn)* and will perish, with few exceptions. You shall resume your actions with loose women, and the kingdom of the Lord will not be among you, for he will take it away forthwith (*T. Benj.* 9.1-2).

At issue here is not same-sex desire but sexual promiscuity, which Kee points out is the 'grossest' sin in the *Testaments* (1985: 779). Women are portrayed as 'inherently evil' enticing both men and the Watchers into sin. Such misogyny leads the *Testament of Levi* to equate marriage to gentile women with 'sodomy' and associate such marriages with impiety and abandoning the Law:

> You teach the Lord's commands out of greed for gain; married women you profane; you have intercourse with whores and adulteresses. You take gentile women for your wives (purifying them with an unlawful purification) and your sexual relations will become like Sodom and Gomorrah (in ungodliness) (*T. Levi* 14.6-7).

Association with the gentiles means not only becoming like them but something worse, going against the nature of Israel, the Law.

The importance of Sodom's place in this context becomes clear in the remaining two references. The *Testament of Asher* declares, 'Sodom...did not recognize the Lord's angels and perished' (*T. Ash.* 7.1). What does it mean to not recognize the Lord's angels? The answer is found in *Testament of Naphtali* 3, the passage under question. Here, Sodom and the Watchers are likened for having gone against nature, incurring the curse of the deity.

> Sun, moon and stars do not alter their order (*taxin*); thus you should not alter the Law of God by the disorder (*ataxia*) of your actions. The gentiles,

> because they wandered astray and forsook the Lord, have changed the order (*taxin*), and have devoted themselves to stones and sticks, patterning themselves after wandering spirits. But you, my children, shall not be like that...in all the products of his workmanship discern the Lord who made all things, so that you do not become like Sodom, which departed from the order of nature (*taxin phuseôs*). Likewise the Watchers departed from nature's order (*taxin phuseôs*); the Lord pronounced a curse on them at the Flood...he ordered that the earth be without dweller or produce... I have read in the writing of holy Enoch that you also will stray from the Lord, living in accord with every wickedness of the gentiles and committing every lawlessness of Sodom (*anomian Sodomôn*) (*T. Naph.* 3.1-4.2).

I would argue that the issue here is again that of crossing the boundaries of the human and the angelic or semi/divine. The Watchers married human women and were condemned. The men of Sodom desired Lot's guests but did not realise that they were angels and also perished. The gentiles are like both because they are idolatrous, having gone astray and patterned 'themselves after wandering spirits' (*T. Naph.* 3.3), the Watchers themselves. For Israel, the Law and the associated relationship with the deity are its nature. To abandon the Law, especially through sexual promiscuity, but also through idolatry and intermarriage with the gentiles, is to change the order of Israel's nature in as evil a way as both the Sodomites and the Watchers who transgressed the boundaries of the human and the angelic. This crossing of the boundaries becomes the metaphor by which to condemn abandonment of the Law, idolatry and intermarriage with the gentiles. Abandonment of the Law, in fact, results in *porneia*, which gives rise to both intermarriage with gentiles and idolatry, each being facilitated by the other. Such an alteration of Israel's nature will lead to catastrophe being visited upon Israel, such as was sent on the flood generation, the people of Sodom and Gomorrah and upon the Israelites themselves with the Assyrian and Babylonian invasions and deportations (*T. Naph.* 4.1-2).

Eron states that 'the overriding concern of *Testaments of the Twelve Patriarchs* is to admonish its audience to remain faithful to God and loyal to God's ways... Sexual desire, *porneia*, was seen as one of the powerful forces that draw men away from God' (Eron 1990: 37). I would argue that from this concern there is a symmetry between Sodom and the Watchers that makes sense in terms of crossing human and angelic boundaries, in a way that reading Sodom as a site of same-sex desire does not. This symmetry is made clear in the one other reference to the Watchers in the *Testaments*. The account in *Testament of Reuben* 5 portrays women as 'inherently evil' enticing both men and the Watchers into sin.

> For every woman who schemes in these ways is destined for eternal pun-
> ishment. For thus it was they charmed the Watchers, who were before the
> Flood. As they continued looking at the women, they were filled with desire
> for them and perpetrated the act in their minds. Then they were trans-
> formed into human males... (*T. Reub.* 5.4-6)

The *Testaments* are addressed to an audience of men. The story of the
Watchers is one of angelic beings and women, however in Sodom the
reverse occurs – angelic beings and men. The Watchers were tempted by
women and succumbed to *porneia* such that 'these angels who were by
nature sexless took on a sexual identity' (Eron 1990: 36). As a parallel, in
Sodom human males were steeped in lawless *porneia* such that they were
blind to the angelic nature of Lot's visitors. In so doing their fates were
sealed and the cities destroyed. In the gendered and misogynous world of
the *Testaments*, the story of the Watchers serves to warn of the dangers of
not controlling one's wives and daughters and allowing them to surrender
to *porneia* (cf. *Jub.* 20.4). Similarly, the story of Sodom warns of the dangers for men of surrendering to *porneia*. This surrender results from
abandoning the Law.

Thus, unlike Kee, I do not think that homosexuality is necessarily
condemned or employed as a metaphor for abandonment of the Law,
idolatry and intermarriage with the gentiles. Eron is especially arguing
against the contention of Boswell and Scroggs that 'the New Testament
and related writings do not address homosexuality in its modern form'
(Eron 1990: 26). Eron bases his argument on

> (1) ...references to Sodom in the Testaments and contemporaneous
> literature, (2) on the use of the Greek terms *taxis* and *physis* in that
> literature, and (3) on the fact that male-male sexual relations were
> considered to be a form of illicit sexual desire: *porneia* (Eron 1990: 27)

I have no argument with his third point. I have no doubt that male same-
sex relations were considered to be a form of illicit sexual desire in intertestamental Judaism and subsequently in early Christianity. However, I
would not base my argument on references to Sodom and Gomorrah in
the literature unless they are clearly associated with same-sex love and
desire. Eron himself does a brief survey of such literature and comments
that, with the exception of 2 *Enoch* (see below), only 'Josephus and Philo
describe the sins of the Sodomites explicitly as homosexual relations'
(Eron 1990: 32). Later in this chapter I will disagree with Eron's reading
of Josephus. Eron's main argument, however, is based on his reading of
these passages in the *Testaments*, but none of these passages clearly indicate an association with same-sex sexual relations. His assumption of such

an association, I would further argue, is undermined by the obvious association of Sodom with the Watchers – something not found in Philo or
2 Enoch (or even Josephus). It is the crossing of the human/angelic
boundary due to *porneia* that provides the basis for the parallels between
the Watchers and Sodom. I think this parallel explains the problems Eron
identifies in his own argument, that 'to the authors of the *Testaments of the
Twelve Patriarchs* homosexual relations did not attract much attention'
and that the 'major discussion...is relegated to a Testament whose major
concern is not sins of a sexual nature' (Eron 1990: 37). Indeed, it is
instructive to turn to this passage, *T. Levi* 17.11, because here there is a
clear condemnation of same-sex desire in the form of pederasty. Not a
'discussion' but a list of evil priests, it says, 'In the seventh week there will
come idolaters, adulterers, money lovers, arrogant, lawless, voluptuaries,
pederasts (*paidophthoroi*), those who practice bestiality'. There is no reference to Sodom here or anywhere else in this chapter and neither is there
any reference to the Watchers.

Before I leave the *Testaments* I should comment on another feature of
T. Benj. 9.1. It is also significant because some have read here a reference
to the events at Gibeah, if so the first instance where Gibeah and Sodom
are linked. Charles points out that the reference to the kingdom being
taken away in this passage seems to refer to the rise of David replacing
Saul and his line (1908: 210).[5] Bailey then reads the whole verse as a
prediction of the outrage at Gibeah making it responsible for the loss of
the monarchy to Benjamin (Saul) in favour of Judah (David) (Bailey 1955:
19). If Bailey's reading is accepted, then it can be argued that, in its reference to loose women, the *Testament of Benjamin* holds the concubine
responsible for the outrage at Gibeah. Kee reminds us that the *Testaments*
regard women as 'inherently evil,' enticing 'men...to commit sin' (Kee
1983: 779) and such an attitude to the concubine would, thus, be consistent with misogynistic philosophy of the *Testaments*. The responsibility
of the concubine for her fate is something that will be found in some subsequent texts that do refer explicitly to Gibeah. However, I see nothing in
the text that would justify a 'homosexual' understanding of the iniquity of
Sodom let alone of Gibeah. Nevertheless, Eron, who likewise agrees with
Charles, argues that because 'the men of Gibeah rape and kill the Levite's
concubine while the daughters of Lot are not harmed by the men of
Sodom, the *porneia* both groups of men committed cannot be seen as

---

5.   Hollander and De Jonge disagree with Charles and see here a reference to the
exile and the end of the Davidic kingdom 'which will be renewed not before the
coming of Jesus Christ' (1985: 435).

heterosexual rape' (1990: 33). *Porneia* is certainly the issue in this context but I suspect the warning is about the lawlessness and strife to which it leads. Several verses earlier in ch. 7, the patriarch warns his children to 'flee from the evil of Beliar, because he offers a sword to those who obey him' (*T. Benj.* 7.1). Then the patriarch makes this warning, '(b)ut you, my children, run from evil, corruption, and hatred of brothers, cling to goodness and love. For a person with a mind that is pure with love does not look on a woman for the purpose of having sexual relations' (8.1-2). The imagery here of the sword and hatred of brothers fits a context of Judges 19–21 and the genocidal *civil* war arising from the events at Gibeah. The events of Judges 19 and Genesis 19 share the quality of lawlessness[6] both giving rise to and resulting from unrestrained *porneia*. It is this lack of restraint and lawlessness in the (attempted) rape in Sodom and Gibeah that is the connection, not the heterosexuality or otherwise of the events.

The association of Sodom with unbridled sexuality found in *Jubilees* and the *Testaments* recur in the references to Sodom found in the Catholic Epistles, Jude and 2 Peter. Both epistles are inter-related, although the debate about their relationship is outside the purview of this book. Both also appear to be a warning against libertine ecstatics who are disrupting the Christian communities. However, there is nothing in either Jude or 2 Peter to indicate homoeroticism *per se* as an issue. Jude 7 uses Sodom's destruction to warn the community against following the libertine ecstatics. Jude accuses the Sodomites of sexual immorality and pursuing 'other flesh', *heteras sarkos*, (which the NRSV has translated as 'unnatural lust'). The preceding v. 6 also refers to the angels of Genesis 6 who 'did not keep their own position but left their proper dwelling' and were punished. The Sodomites are compared to them, and it would appear that both are used as examples of any who 'defile the flesh, reject authority, and slander the glorious ones' (Jude 8). Certainly both the Sodomites and the angels rejected authority and defiled their flesh by pursuing sexual unions across the angelic/human barrier. But, as in the *Testaments* and *Jubilees*, the important referent for Jude is the disruptive lawlessness of *porneia* arising from following the libertines. Authority and community cohesion are the main issues here. The libertines are dividing the community and they preach nothing but surrender to *porneia*. *Porneia* breaks down communities and leads to disastrous consequences as exemplified by the sons of god in Genesis 6 and Sodom and Gomorrah in Genesis 19. However, there is nothing in this reading that requires a predominantly homosexual understanding of Sodom and its sin.

6. It is also this 'lawlessness of Sodom' that is identified in *T. Naph.* 4.1.

In 2 Pet. 2.4-10, Sodom is likewise mentioned in company with the angels of Genesis 6 (and the Flood generation). Rather than expand on Sodom's fate, the text is more concerned to hold up Lot as an example of a righteous person who patiently endured the crimes of his neighbours until delivered by the deity. The Sodomites are said to be 'lawless' (*athesmôn*) and engaging in 'licentiousness' (*aselgeia*) (2.7). Thus, 2 Peter repeats themes found in the Pseudepigrapha associating lawlessness and sexual excess as well as echoing Luke in holding up Lot as a model for the godly. The text also stresses that the fate of Sodom and of the angels is an example of what awaits all of the ungodly, especially those who despise authority and give themselves over to 'depraved lust' (*epithumia miasmou*) (2.9-10). But nowhere does 2 Peter identify any specific sexual offence associated with the Sodomites. How a person would understand both 2 Pet. 2.4-10 and Jude 7 depends on what that person understands the evil of the Sodomites to be. I would suggest that, for the authors of these texts, however the sexual evil of the Sodomites is understood, it will accord with the sexual teaching and practices of those libertine ecstatics whom both these letters are determined to condemn.

What is not present in any of these texts is what is found in *2 Enoch*. Andersen points out that both the date and provenance of *2 Enoch* cannot be successfully identified although he favours an early date CE (Andersen 1983: 94-97). The text only survives in Slavonic manuscripts from the fourteenth and fifteenth centuries CE and in both a short and long recension. It is in the long recension only that we find the following:

> This place, Enoch, has been prepared for those who do not glorify God, who practice on the earth the sin which is against nature, which is child corruption in the anus in the manner of Sodom (*2 En.* 10.4).

This explicitness is important because, as already seen, the *Testaments* contain a condemnation of same-sex sexual relations in the form of pederasty in *T. Levi* 17.11. Similar condemnations are found elsewhere in the Pseudepigrapha but Sodom is in no way associated with them. Given that *2 Enoch* only exists in a late medieval Slavonic version, it is just as likely that this passage has been affected by the many centuries of Christian homophobic readings of Genesis 19 as it is that it is responsible for them. This text aside, if there is any specific association of Sodom's sin with homoeroticism in any of this literature then it calls to mind Foucault's much quoted observation on the concept of sodomy in western thought, that it is an 'utterly confused category'.

3. *Philosophy, History and Commentary*

a. *Philo*

Philo is both an exegete of Scripture and a philosopher. The Scripture that he reads is the Torah, the five books of Moses. Thus, Philo does not refer to Gibeah, nor does he enter the world of Judges. Baer says that, for Philo, 'the mystic in pursuit of God...is the true philosopher' and consequently there is an 'underlying identity of purpose of Scriptural exegesis and philosophy' (1970: 6). While regarding the biblical stories to be accounts of historical events, Philo also believed they possessed 'an "undermeaning" (*huponoia*) by which Abraham, Jacob, and other biblical figures were understood to represent...spiritual realities' (Kugel 1997: 597). These spiritual realities were truths applicable to all times and places and, for this reason, Philo pioneered the use of allegory as a tool for teasing out the secret, spiritual messages in scripture in order to develop the spiritual life that is true philosophy. The allegorical approach was subsequently adopted in Christian exegesis, particularly through the work of Origen in the third century CE. Two further crucial points concerning Philo as philosopher and as exegete must also be made before exploring the Philonic corpus.

Firstly, Dorothy Sly emphasizes that Philo, as a philosopher, comes from and is shaped by a world where 'men considered intellectual and spiritual matters to be their domain, and true personhood to belong to them' (1990: 70). In contrast women, 'belonged to a different sphere, out of sight, and for the most part, out of mind' (1990: 70). Philo applies this gendered hierarchy to his understanding of the individual person as a hierarchy of spirit and body, of mind and senses, of reason and desire. The lower and carnal part of a person is female and the higher spiritual part is male. These lower elements are 'dangerous and potentially evil' and must be controlled so that 'the feminine...loses its danger, and enhances the masculine' (Sly 1990: 220-21). It is only by so doing that 'the highest element in the human soul, the mind', can realize its 'essential affinity' with 'the divine spirit itself' (Warne 1988: 117) and enter into communion with the deity.

Secondly, Philo highlights sexual sin, specifically homoeroticism, as the sin for which Sodom was punished. Byrne Fone says that Philo 'may have been the first to give the Hebrew *yadha* (*sic*) a specifically homosexual connotation' (2000: 91). I would go further and consider Philo to be the inventor of the homophobic reading of Genesis 19. In Philo's thought, the homoerotic Sodom represents the consequences of losing control of a person's lower, female, carnal part nature. Consequently, references to

Sodom and the events of Genesis 18–19 occur frequently throughout the Philonic corpus, with the most detailed coverage in *On Abraham, On Dreams, Drunkenness* and an elaborate exegesis of Genesis 18–19 in *Questions on Genesis*.

Philo's portrayal of Sodom in the treatise, *On Abraham*, sets down most concisely the homophobic interpretation of Genesis 19. The story illustrates Philo's arguments concerned with supporting the essential goodness of the deity. The two angels sent to Sodom are proof that the deity leaves 'the execution of the opposite of good entirely in the hands of His potencies acting as His ministers, that so He might appear...not directly the cause of anything evil' (*Abr.* 143). This essential goodness of the deity is further highlighted by Philo's portrait of the cities of the Plain as absolutely evil. Same-sex desire and homoeroticism are crucial elements of this evil. True philosophy is the path of communion with the divine, while the homoerotic is the marker of a false or anti-philosophy.

Thus, Sodom 'was brimful of innumerable iniquities...such as arise from gluttony and lewdness (*lagneias*) and multiplied and enlarged every other possible pleasure' (*Abr.* 133). Sodom's 'never-failing lavishness of...sources of wealth' from being 'deep-soiled and well watered' proves that 'the chief beginning of evils is goods in excess' (*Abr.* 134). As true philosophy is an ascetic path, a superfluity of riches is a peril to be avoided for they only lead to indulgence of the senses. Such abundance caused the Sodomites to throw 'off from their necks the law of nature (*phuseôs nomon*) and [they] applied themselves to deep drinking of strong liquor...and forbidden forms of intercourse (*ocheias ekthesmous*)' (*Abr.* 135). In the Pseudepigrapha, Israel abandons the Law, its covenant with the deity, through sexual license leading to intermarriage with gentiles and adopting their ways. Philo has introduced notions of natural law, constructing homoeroticism as a violation of that law. It is a rebellion against nature that deranges the mind and corrupts the body. The men of Sodom not only,

> in their mad lust for women...they (violated) the marriages of their neighbours...also men mounted males without respect for the sex nature which the active partner shares with the passive; and so when they tried to beget children they were discovered to be incapable of any but a sterile seed. Yet the discovery availed them not so much stronger was the force of the lust (*epithumias*) which mastered them. Then, as little by little they accustomed those who were by nature to submit to play the part of women, they saddled them with the formidable curse of a female disease. For not only did they emasculate their bodies by luxury and voluptuousness but they worked a further degeneration in their souls and, as far as in them lay, were corrupting the whole of mankind (*Abr.* 135-36).

It is this type of explicit homoerotic imagery and homophobic polemic that is missing in references to Sodom in the Pseudepigrapha, and other scriptural texts including those of the Hebrew Bible. Philo argues that male homoeroticism degenerates the male body rendering it feminized and sterile. Philo clearly relies on notions of monogenesis – the male provides the seed, the female is merely the field it grows in. By becoming feminized a male becomes field-like and his seed loses potency. This spurious biology serves to both give 'natural' grounds for homophobia and justify Sodom's fate as the action of a loving deity. Philo continues, 'God, moved by pity for mankind whose Saviour and Lover He was' (*Abr.* 137) made heterosexual unions more fruitful and furthermore

> abominated and extinguished this unnatural and forbidden intercourse, and those who lusted for such He cast forth and chastised with punishments...startling and extraordinary, newly created for this purpose. He bade the air grow suddenly overclouded and pour forth a great rain, but fire not of water... And when the flame had utterly consumed all that was visible and above ground it penetrated right down into the earth itself, destroying its inherent life-power and reducing it to complete sterility (*Abr.* 137-40).

If such an act of destruction and genocide is the work of a loving deity, then Philo has provided a theological grounding for homophobia and a warrant for genocide.

Not content with making Sodom a warning example of the danger of homoeroticism, Philo provides an allegorical interpretation of the story to employ it as a tool for spiritual practice. If Sodom's story portrays the effects of giving free expression to desire and sensuality, it also allegorically contains a set of instructions, the following of which will ensure the control of that desire and sensuality. Allegorically, the five cities stand for the five senses: sight, hearing, taste, smell and touch, 'the instruments of the pleasures which...are brought to their accomplishment by the senses' (*Abr.* 147). Taste, smell and touch are the 'most animal and servile' because they 'cause particular excitation in the cattle and wild beasts most given to gluttony and sexual passion' (*Abr.* 149). Hearing and sight are better, being linked to philosophy, but sight is the 'queen of the other senses' while hearing takes second place being 'more sluggish and womanish than eyes' (*Abr.* 150). Hence four cities of the Plain are destroyed while the smaller fifth city is spared because it represents sight, 'in that it is a little part of all we contain' (*Abr.* 166). Thus, Scripture teaches that the philosopher or godly person must control the lower senses and utilize sight to study and contemplate the works of the deity. In that way the mind will draw close to the divine and enter into communion with it. The destruction of the other four cites/senses teaches that through control of the lower senses the godly person destroys their power and, thus, does not follow the path of the Sodomites. Through allegory, Philo thus turns Sodom into an antidote or vaccine to prevent the contagion of same-sex desire.

Homophobia and genocide colour Philo's use of Sodom in both *On Dreams* and *On Drunkenness*. His argument in both treatises is based on Deut. 32.32, 'the vineyards of Sodom', in a discussion of Joseph interpreting the dreams of two imprisoned courtiers of Pharaoh in Genesis 40 (*Somn.* 2.191-2, *Ebr.* 222). Crucially Philo understands these courtiers to be eunuchs. In both treatises, Philo declares his abhorrence for eunuchs as sterile and barren. They resemble the Sodomites who became so through homoeroticism. In *On Drunkenness*, Philo's abhorrence becomes genocidal invoking Sodom's fate. Sodom 'is indeed by interpretation barrenness and blindness' and the vine of Sodom represents those 'who are under the thrall of wine-bibbing and gluttony and the basest of pleasures' (*Ebr.* 222). In the soul of both Sodomite and eunuch 'all that grows is the lust which is barren of excellence, and blinded to all that is worthy of its contemplation...the bearer of bitterness and wickedness and villainy and wrath and anger and savage moods and tempers' (*Ebr.* 223). Eunuchs, as sterilized males, are interchangeable with the men of Sodom who were rendered sterile through their surrender to homoeroticism. Being sterilized, they have renounced their masculinity and are therefore subject to passions, moods/emotions and lusts. Masculinity hinges on potency and such potency underpins authority and control. Take away that authority and the person and the society become feminized sites of sensual chaos. Sodom and Gomorrah are destroyed because they fall into this state and Philo seeks a similar fate for eunuchs, imploring 'the all-merciful God to destroy this wild vine and decree eternal banishment to the eunuchs and all those who do not beget virtue' (*Ebr.* 224). Banishment for eternity is the most complete form of destruction imaginable.

Elsewhere, in *On Drunkenness*, Philo turns his allegorical attention to Lot and his family. Lot represents the worst type of ignorance that is 'not merely the victim of a want of knowledge, but also, encouraged by a false idea of his own wisdom, thinks he knows what he does not know at all' (*Ebr.* 162). Lot's wife represents Custom, 'hostile to truth', who 'lags behind and gazes round at the old familiar objects and remains among them like a lifeless monument' (*Ebr.* 164). Lot's daughters represent Deliberation and Assent. Thus, the mind of the ignorant man through Deliberation 'examines every point' and Assents 'to every suggestion, however hostile, if what they have to give offers any enticement of pleasure' (*Ebr.* 165). Philo points out that such Assent is a surrender 'as though overcome by wine' and leads to 'complete insensibility' (*Ebr.* 166), which is why one reads that Lot's daughters plied their father with wine. The image of the daughters seducing their father is an allegory for the mind diverted by pride and indulgent self-importance from the pursuit of the good.

Similarly in *The Posterity and Exile of Cain*, Philo names Lot's daughters, Counsel and Consent, and describes Lot as one who, 'having been impelled upwards, wavered and went downwards' (*Post. Caini* 175). Lot is seduced by his daughters who have drenched his senses with wine. The scene is an allegory for the spiritual state of the impious person who refuses 'to acknowledge God as the Maker and Father of the universe', but asserts 'that he himself is the author of everything that concerns the life of man' (*Post. Caini* 175-76). Such a person resembles 'one who is being ruined by drunkenness and sottishness' (*Post. Caini* 176). Likewise, by being barred from the congregation of Israel (Deut. 23.2), the Moabites and Ammonites represent the 'people that suppose sense perception and mind, a male and a female, act as father and mother for the procreation of all things, and take this process to be...the cause of creation' (*Post. Caini* 177). They have allowed their senses to turn them from the divine and forget the true source of all life. Philo's images of intoxication and frenzy echo his portrayal of the Sodomite men frenziedly feminized in their pursuit of homoerotic pleasures. In contrast, Philo's masculine ideal is both potent and in control of that potency. This control is the avenue to knowing the divine, that ultimate potency in Philo's universe.

In *Questions and Answers on Genesis*, Philo gives a more positive picture of Lot and Lot's daughters. Lot is portrayed as a type of a person on a spiritual ascent and Lot's flight from Sodom is a type of progress of the soul. However, Abraham is Philo's chief hero, the model of a perfect, god-aware man. This perspective gives rise to a surprising interpretation of the three men who visit Abraham at Mamre as a trinitarian manifestation of the deity (see also *Abr.* 119-32). Philo says:

> it is reasonable for one to be three and for three to be one, for they were one by a higher principle. But when counted with the chief powers, the creative and the kingly, He makes the appearance of three to the human mind... For so soon as one sets eyes upon God, there also appear, together with His being, the ministering powers, so that in place of one He makes the appearance of a triad (*Quaest. in Gen.* 4.2).

This triadic manifestation demonstrates Abraham's worthiness as a model and brings him into contrast with Lot who is only visited by two. Thus,

Abraham is the perfect man, who 'perceives the Father between His min-isters, the two chief powers', while Lot is a progressive man who can only perceive 'the servant-powers without the Father, for he is unequal to seeing and understanding Him' (*Quaest. in Gen.* 4.30). Although Philo never states it, this understanding of the angels would mean that the men of Sodom were demanding sexual access to hypostases of the deity.

Abraham is Philo's model of all that is worthy, and there is nothing he can do that incurs Philo's reproach. Sarah's character also partakes in this quality. Regarding Sarah's standing behind Abraham in the tent at Mamre (Gen. 18.11), Philo says 'Virtue stands behind the one who is virtuous by nature, not like a slave boy but like a perfect administrator...who...directs the entire soul' (*Quaest. in Gen.* 4.13). Sarah as the dutiful wife represents virtue in contrast to the pederastic image of the slave boy. Being a young male slave is a particularly feminized situation, for slaves were subject to the desires of their masters, who had the right to penetrate their slaves. Ironically, as befits her representing virtue, Sarah has ceased the ways of women (Gen. 18.11) and is consequently no longer part of the economy of penetration. Indeed, she has, thus, become male, allegorically 'absorbed into Abraham as a quality of his character' (Sly 1990: 152). Philo under-stands Sarah's menopause as representing the control of those 'female' aspects of the soul – 'irrational...akin to bestial passions, fear, sorrow, pleasure and desire' – which 'clearly belongs to minds full of Law' (*Quaest. in Gen.* 4.15). Such minds 'resemble the male sex and overcome passions and rise above sense-pleasure and desire' (*Quaest. in Gen.* 4.15). Similarly, in *On Drunkenness*, Philo describes Sarah as representing the virtuous loving mind that has fled the customs of women (*Ebr.* 59) and, in *The Posterity and Exile of Cain*, specifically states that Sarah has been changed into a virgin (*Post. Caini* 134). Such restored virginity is necessary because the deity will only converse with the soul when it has transcended its ef/feminate appetites and become like Sarah, 'ranked once more as a pure virgin' (*Cher.* 50). Sarah's laughter signifies an implicit virginal conception, revealing 'a new act...sown by God in the whole soul for the birth of joy and great gladness, which...is called "laughter"..."Isaac"' (*Quaest. in Gen.* 4.17; see also *Abr.* 206).

There are two ironies in Philo's construction of Sarah being virgin and male. Recall that eunuchs are abhorrent because in their sterilization they are, thus, feminized and subject to the senses. It is only male potency that can enable male (self-) control and to remove that potency is to remove that control. However, women only achieve some measure of (masculine) control in themselves by renouncing their fertility. It is not merely a renunciation of being a penetratee that is the key here. Philo's praise of Sarah's menopause as a restoration of virginity indicates that, for him, women can only achieve the equivalence of male status by renunciation of their very fertility. A sterile woman becomes virgin and thus male. Herein lies the second irony in that, by becoming male, Sarah's relationship with Abraham becomes implicitly homoerotic, a love story of two men. As Abraham's authority is grounded in his potency and his ability to penetrate, this contradiction cannot be sustained. Either Abraham must renounce his penetration stakes and thus become a feminized eunuch or Sarah must be penetrated herself thus becoming slave boy or wife. There can be no true virgin birth of Isaac while Sarah and Abraham are husband and (male) wife.

The twinning of feminization and male sterility together with social and sensual disorder is central to Philo's allegorical understanding of Sodom and Gomorrah. Sodom represents blindness and sterility while Gomorrah represents arrogant human attempts to determine their own worth in opposition to the true measure determined by the Logos (*Quaest. in Gen.* 4.23). The Sodomites represent 'the traits of soul that are blind and unproductive of wisdom' (*Quaest. in Gen.* 4.36). Elsewhere Philo reads the Sodomites who surround Lot's house as those 'barren of wisdom and blind in the understanding' who allow the passions to run 'round and round the house of the soul to bring dishonour and ruin on those sacred and holy thoughts which were its guests' (*Conf. Ling.* 27). The Sodomites' demand for Lot's guests has a twofold meaning. The literal meaning is 'servile, lawless and unseemly pederasty' (*Quaest. in Gen.* 4.37), but it shows, too, that 'lascivious and unrestrainedly impure men…threaten with death those who are self-controlled and desirous of continence' (*Quaest. in Gen.* 4. 37). Philo approves of Lot offering his daughters, seeing in it an allegory for the soul of a progressive man. The progressive soul has both masculine and feminine elements and, while both can be retained in the struggle for perfection, it is often better to discard the feminine 'lesser' elements because they are 'under service to bodily needs and…the dominion of the passions' (*Quaest. in Gen.* 4.38).

Philo reads Genesis 19 allegorically as an ascent of the soul towards perfection, a type of spiritual manual. Thus, the angels' urging of Lot to flee to high ground represents the mind beginning to take the higher road, 'leaving behind earth-bound and low things' (*Quaest. in Gen.* 4.46). Lot's sons-in-law represent false happiness that comes through wealth. They become complacent and resistant to change. Lot's flight shows that the wise pursue peaceful contemplation while the wicked are desirous of the

clamour, wealth and honours of the city. Lot, himself a progressive man, is
in between, which is why he flees firstly to the town of Zoar because 'he is
not...able to get entirely beyond civilisation though he no longer...admires
the city as a great good' (*Quaest. in Gen.* 4.48). However, Philo has it both
ways and translates Zoar as 'mountain' (*Quaest. in Gen.* 4.49) so that Lot is
actually fleeing from town to mountain.

Concerning Lot's wife, Philo initially suggests several reasons for the
ban on looking back at the destruction of Sodom to explain the mortal
consequences of ignoring it. To watch the destruction of the cities could
lead a person to rejoice at the misfortune of others. Alternatively, he
suggests a more serious possibility might be that witnessing the destruction could lead one to grieve greatly over the suffering of all the people that
perish there. An even worse possibility is that looking back might be an
attempt to rationally investigate the workings of the deity, which Philo
condemns as 'an act of impudence and shamelessness and not of reverence' (*Quaest. in Gen.* 4.52). But, allegorically, Lot's wife also represents
sense perception, 'the wife of the mind', which turns back to externalities
such as possessions and pleasures. Thus, 'it changes into an inanimate
thing by separating itself from the mind, for the sake of which it was
animated' (*Quaest. in Gen.* 4.52). As Dorothy Sly points out, unlike Sarah,
Philo does not treat Lot's wife 'as a component part of her husband' (Sly
1990: 119). Like the male characters in Genesis she represents a type of
person in her own right. Lot, on his spiritual ascent, is unlike the person
whose sense perception, the wife of their mind, turns back to possessions
and pleasure. In *Allegorical Interpretation* (*Leg. All.* 3.212-3), she illustrates
the fate of those who do not eradicate their love of pleasure and allow it to
draw them backward. Similarly, in *On Flight and Finding,* she represents
the man who through 'habitual laziness' ignores his teacher and turns his
face backwards...'his thoughts...all for the dark' and so 'turns into a pillar
...a deaf and lifeless stone' (*Fug.* 122).

Lot's wife might not be a component part of himself, but his daughters
are and I am puzzled by the fact that of all the female biblical figures in
Philo's work, Sly overlooked Lot's daughters. In his other works, Lot's
daughters are treated as negatively as their mother, but not so in *Questions
and Answers on Genesis*. On a literal level, Philo excuses the actions of
Lot's daughters because they acted so 'that the human race might not be
destroyed' (*Quaest. in Gen.* 4.56). Allegorically, if Lot represents the one
who 'becomes still purer' and 'separates from the guilty and unlivable way
of life' (*Quaest. in Gen.* 4.55), it does not suit Philo's purpose to condemn
the daughters. Consequently, they represent the daughters of the mind,
Counsel and Consent, with counsel taking priority over consent because

> (i)t is impossible for anyone to consent before taking counsel. And these are necessarily and naturally born to their father, (namely) the mind. For through counsel the mind sows worthy, fitting and persuasive things in those who are not discordant in aiming at the truth. But consent is that which in respect of appearances makes way for the several senses (*Quaest. in Gen.* 4.56).

What is striking, too, is that Philo valorizes the older daughter over the younger, a pattern that will be seen in rabbinic commentary where she is often regarded as being rewarded for initiating these events by becoming the foremother of David through Ruth.

This valorizing of the elder daughter results in the following extraordinary passage on the naming of Moab:

> The literal meaning is (an occasion of) exultation and glorification for those who think rightly. For she did not cease (talking) and remain quiet as if (it were) a reproach but prided herself in thought as if on a great achievement, and with delight said 'I have a deserved honour, which the father, who is the mind in me, has sowed. And having been sown, he did not disintegrate and pass away, but having been born perfect, he was found worthy of birth and nurture' (*Quaest. in Gen.* 4.57).

While he starts with the literal meaning, it is clear from the reference to the father as 'the mind' that Philo has shifted to an allegorical reading. The elder daughter gives birth to a son because to be 'irreprehensible and irreproachable progeny of the mind' (*Quaest. in Gen.* 4.57) the child must be born male. For Philo, there can be no greater commendation than this and so he finds himself utilizing father–daughter incest as an image depicting spiritual growth. Lot's daughters are fields of virtue in which the father-mind sows seed. After all,

> what can counsel do by itself without the mind, and what (can) consent (do). For by themselves they are ineffective and unproductive, unless they are moved by the mind to their proper business and activities (*Quaest. in Gen.* 4.56).

I wonder whether Philo has been seduced by the narrative to unwittingly reveal the unconscious dynamics of the patriarchal rule of the father over the daughter. Unlike Sarah, Lot's daughters do not virginally conceive but act dutifully within the penetration economy respecting due status and authority of the husband/father. Unlike Sarah, the virginal male wife, Lot's daughters, as daughters, are worthy female wives, fertile fields in which to sow male seed for the harvest of worthy fruit. They represent the submission of those worthy but feminine aspects of the psyche to the mind, which is itself masculine and the father of virtue. Consequently father–daughter incest becomes the model of patriarchal marriage. Ironically, in the biblical narrative the reverse is the case – Lot, the father, is forced to submit to his daughters.

b. *Pseudo-Philo*

Pseudo-Philo's *Biblical Antiquities* is a retelling of biblical history from Adam to David and, as Harrington observes, 'transmits legends and motifs not found elsewhere' (1985: 300). He is selective in his account of this history and omits the story of Sodom and Gomorrah. However, Pseudo-Philo provides the first detailed version of the outrage at Gibeah. As in the *Testaments* and *Jubilees*, Pseudo-Philo regards idolatry as the root of all evil and is 'vigorously opposed to marriage with gentiles' (Harrington 1985: 301). In his version of the Gibeah story he does not hesitate to change the biblical narrative to highlight these themes.

The very location of these events is changed. Pseudo-Philo opens the account with the Levite being refused entrance to Gibeah and then journeying to the nearby city of Nob. On arriving there, he sits in the square of the city awaiting an offer of hospitality and is found by the old man, as in the biblical narrative. Jacobson can see no obvious reason for this change of location (Jacobson 1996: 1027), but Murphy suggests that it is meant to stress Benjaminite perfidy in that not one but two of their cities are in the wrong (Murphy 1993: 177). Pseudo-Philo's account names the two male protagonists – the Levite, Beel, and the old man, Bethac. Bethac is another Levite, resident in Nob, and recognizes Beel when happening upon him in the square. Alarmed, Bethac insists Beel take shelter in his house on account of

> the wickedness (*maliciam*) of those who dwell in this city… Get out of here in a hurry and enter my house where I dwell, and stay there today; and the Lord will shut up their heart before us as he shut up the Sodomites before Lot (*Ps.-Philo* 45.2).

This explicit reference to Sodom and Gomorrah likens the men of Nob to the Sodomites, and, with the possible exception of *T. Benj.* 9.1, is the first occasion the two stories are linked. Given this association, the account of Nob's wickedness will indicate how Pseudo-Philo understands the iniquity of Sodom.

When Beel and his party take shelter at Bethac's house all the men of Nob gather outside demanding Bethac bring them his guests. The crowd demands all the party not just the Levite. There is no implication of sexual desire, but rather a mood of threatening violence – 'Bring out those who have come to you today. If not, we will burn in the fire both you and them'

(*Ps.-Philo* 45.3). As in the biblical text, Bethac goes out to intercede with them, 'Are not these our brothers? Let us not do evil with them lest our sins be multiplied against us' (*Ps.-Philo* 45.3). Bethac has not offered the women for rape but instead appeals to ethnic solidarity. The men of Nob reject his pleas and stress his own alien status – 'It has never happened that strangers gave orders to the natives' (*Ps.-Philo* 45.3). The mob makes no such response to the old man in Judges. Instead, Pseudo-Philo has used the Sodomites' retort to Lot.

The assailants then break into the house, seize both the Levite and the concubine and drag them outside. Unlike his biblical counterpart and Lot, Bethac is innocent of what transpires, instead resolutely defending his guests. Pseudo-Philo's Levite is likewise innocent and has not been threatened with rape. The rape happens almost as an afterthought. After the mob releases Beel:

> they abused his concubine until she died, because she had transgressed against her man once when she committed sin with the Amalekites, and on account of this the LORD God delivered her into the hands of sinners (*Ps.-Philo* 45.3).

Up to this point in Pseudo-Philo's version, there has been no indication of any sexual intent by the mob. Rather they are belligerent and threaten unspecified violence. In fact, it is only with her assault that the reader becomes aware of the concubine's very existence in the story. Furthermore, her fate is presented as a punishment for her own actions. She has not only committed adultery but has done so with gentiles. Nevertheless, what befalls her here is quite explicitly rape.

Pseudo-Philo presents Nob's main crime as one of violent hostility towards strangers and, given the explicit association with Sodom, it is how he perceives that city, too. Such hostility is lethal because Beel finds the concubine dead in the morning. He cuts up her body, as in Judges, to summon the twelve tribes. Murder is the basis of his charge against Nob, not rape or sexual perfidy:

> These things have been done to me in the city of Nob, and those dwelling there rose up against me to kill me, and they took my concubine while I was locked up and they killed her. And if being silent pleases you, nevertheless the LORD judges. But if you wish to take revenge, the LORD will help you (*Ps.-Philo* 45.4).

Beel's account enrages the assembly of Israel – 'If such wickedness is done in Israel, Israel will cease to be' (*Ps.-Philo* 45.5). Their concern here is that Nob's violence will rupture the ethnic solidarity on which the survival of the Israelites depends. Nowhere, though, is there any indication that the men of Nob had any sexual interest in Beel and nowhere is there any hint of the homoerotic in the story.

Pseudo-Philo then develops the story as an attack on idolatry. Idolatry threatens Israelite identity and ethnic solidarity. The preceding stories of Micah and the Levite and the migration of Dan (Judges 17–18) have already been presented as accounts of Israel falling into idolatry (*Ps.-Philo* 44). Now the deity, outraged that the Israelites act to avenge the concubine while ignoring the idolatry in their midst, resolves, 'because they were not provoked to anger then, therefore let their plan be in vain; and their heart will be so disturbed that the sinners as well as those allowing the evil deed will be destroyed' (*Ps.-Philo* 46.6). As a result, then, for Pseudo-Philo, the first two defeats of Israel at the hands of Benjamin are the deity's punishment of Israel's acquiescence in idolatry. It is only after the intervention of Phinehas, who explains the reason for the divine anger, that Israel can make amends and defeat Benjamin.

When initially reading Pseudo-Philo's version of Judges 19, I was horrified that the concubine was held responsible for her fate while both the Levite and the old man were exonerated. I originally thought that Pseudo-Philo was disguising the story so that it would bear little resemblance to Genesis 19. However, although I am still disturbed by how the Levite and old man are rendered innocent and all blame put on the concubine, I no longer think that Pseudo-Philo is deflecting attention from the resemblances to Genesis 19. The whole incident is introduced with an explicit likening of Nob to Sodom and Pseudo-Philo draws on Genesis 19 in recounting the outrage. Thus, Sodom functions here as the archetype of violent hostility towards outsiders. The concubine is raped because she is a female stranger stranded and defenceless in a town violently hostile to strangers. As a stranger she is subject to mob violence and being a woman the violence takes the form of pack rape. As a woman who consorted with Gentiles her fate also represents the fate Israel will suffer for similarly consorting with Gentiles and their gods.

d. *Josephus*

Josephus is the only ancient writer to retell extensively both the stories of Sodom and Gibeah, as part of his history of the Jews in *Jewish Antiquities* (*Aniquitates Judaicae*). He makes a further reference to Sodom in *The Jewish War* (*De Bello Judaico*) as a place, once 'blest in its produce and... wealth' (*War* 4.483), that was destroyed 'owing to the impiety of its inhabitants (*asebeian oikêtorôn*)' (*War* 4.484). In *Jewish Antiquities*, Josephus clearly declares that Sodom's crime was hatred of strangers and largely follows the biblical account. His version of Gibeah's story, meanwhile, is so dramatically altered that it bears little resemblance to Judges 19, let alone Genesis 19. Josephus apparently does not recognize any similarity between the stories.

While Josephus claims to be drawing solely on scripture, Thackeray notes that he has expanded this material by incorporating 'a miscellaneous mass of traditional lore, forming a collection of first century Midrash of considerable value' (LCL*Jos*. 4. xii-xiii) together with material from Philo and a number of gentile authors. Significantly, Thackeray believes he is familiar with Philo's *Abraham* (LCL*Jos*. 4. xii-xiii). If so, Josephus has clearly not been convinced by Philo's homophobic interpretation because he does not highlight the evils of homoeroticism but rather violence to outsiders and abuse of hospitality.

This difference in the two writers' understanding is made clear from the outset of Josephus' account, where he explicitly describes the crimes of the Sodomites.

> Now about this time the Sodomites, overweeningly proud of their numbers and the extent of their wealth, showed themselves insolent to men and impious to the Divinity, inasmuch that they no more remembered the benefits that they had received from him, hated foreigners (*misoxenoi*) and declined all intercourse with others (*kai tas pros allous homilias ektrepesthai*) (*Ant*. 1.194).[7]

The Sodomites are proud, avaricious and xenophobic in strong contrast to Philo's description of them as addicts 'of strong liquor...and forbidden forms of intercourse' (*Abr*. 135).

After describing the sins of Sodom, Josephus recounts the events of Genesis 18. The three men that visit Abraham are angels, one of whom is to announce Sarah's imminent pregnancy, while the other two are to destroy Sodom and Gomorrah (*Ant*. 1.198). While Philo had presented the angels as hypostases of the divine nature in a way that anticipates trinitarian ideas, Josephus makes a clear distinction between the angels and the deity. When Abraham learns of the Sodomite's pending fate he 'was grieved for' them and 'made supplication to God' (*Ant*. 1.199). The deity replies to the effect that the angels have been sent because there are not even ten good men in the city. Thus, the doom of Sodom and Gomorrah is already

---

7.   William Whiston's eighteenth-century translation of Josephus rendered this line as 'they hated strangers and abused themselves with Sodomitical practices' (Whiston, undated: 37; see also 1987: 40). Both Bailey (1955: 23) and McNeill (1977: 73) were misled by Whiston's translation into thinking that Josephus understood homosexuality to be Sodom's primary crime.

determined and is not a result of what might happen when the angels arrive there.

On entering Sodom, the two angels encounter Lot whom Josephus praises as being 'very kindly to strangers', having 'learnt the lesson of Abraham's liberality' (*Ant.* 1.200). However, the men of Sodom also see the angels and, 'on seeing these young men of remarkable fair appearance whom Lot had taken under his roof, were bent only on violence and outrage to their youthful beauty' (*Ant.* 1.200). Unlike Philo for whom the main horror is male-to-male sex, perhaps especially anal sex, Josephus emphasizes the violence of the Sodomites' intentions. What I find particularly noteworthy is that Josephus is not troubled by the notion of people being moved by male beauty; instead it is the violent intent of the Sodomites that causes concern. Lot, too, is more concerned about upholding the laws of hospitality rather than homosexuality when he appeals to the mob.

> Lot adjured them to restrain their passions and not to proceed to dishonour his guests, but to respect their having lodged with him, offering in their stead, if his neighbours were so licentious (*akratôs*), his own daughters to gratify their lust (*epithumiais*). But not even this would content them (*Ant.* 1.201).

Josephus has not commented on the morality of offering the daughters, but they are offered to guarantee the inviolability of Lot's hospitality. The crisis is only resolved by divine intervention: 'God...blinded the criminals so that they could not find the entrance to the house' (*Ant.* 1.202). This divine intervention marks the beginning of the destruction of the cities and the disappearance of the angels from the story. Forewarned of the impending doom Lot and his family quit the city in an orderly manner, Lot having failed to convince the daughters' suitors of what will befall. When the city is destroyed by a thunderbolt, Lot neither argues nor prevaricates with the angels about where to take shelter as in Genesis (*Ant.* 1.203). Lot's wife is turned into a pillar of salt because she was continually looking back in curiosity about Sodom's fate in breach of 'God's prohibition' (*Ant.* 1.203).[8] Finally, Lot and his daughters find 'refuge in a tiny spot forming an oasis in the flames: it is still called Zoor (*sic*)...being the Hebrew word for little' (*Ant.* 1.204).

All these changes have built up Lot as a noble or heroic ancestor figure, a pattern Josephus sustains in his account of Lot and his daughters. The three found refuge in an oasis from the flames, but there they are 'isolated from mankind and in lack of food' and passing 'a miserable existence' (*Ant.*

---

8. Josephus himself claims to have seen this pillar which he says 'remains to this day' (*Ant.* 1.203).

1.204). Consequently, he supports the daughters who act 'in the belief that the whole of humanity had perished...to prevent the extinction of the race' (*Ant.* 1.205). But Josephus makes no mention of them getting their father drunk. Instead Lot's daughters 'had intercourse with their father, taking care to elude detection' (*Ant.* 1.205). He does not specify, however, what means were employed to so elude detection.

As for the events at Gibeah, since only minor changes are made to the rest of the Judges account, I will focus on the changes Josephus makes to the events of Judges 19 and the way they dramatically highlight issues of hospitality and rape in the story and obscure any resemblance to the events at Sodom. Another important change anticipates later rabbinic notions that the events at Gibeah took place immediately after the occupation of the land. The biblical narrative places the outrage at Gibeah in the final chapters of Judges. Josephus, however, places it just after the invasion of Canaan at the beginning of Judges.[9] Marcus is puzzled by this transposition suggesting that perhaps it allows time for the tribe of Benjamin to recover sufficiently for the time of Saul (LCL*Jos.* 5.63). Josephus seems unaware of anything unusual about his chronology vis-à-vis the biblical version, but in rabbinic interpretation much will be made of this chronological question.

As his version continues, Josephus puts the spotlight on the concubine, here the much-loved wife of the Levite. The Levite is portrayed sympathetically, being very much in love with his wife, however his feelings are not reciprocated.

> And, whereas she held herself aloof and he thereby only became the more ardent in his passion, quarrels were continually arising between them, and at last the woman, utterly weary of them, left her husband and in the fourth month rejoined her parents (*Ant.* 5.137).

Not adultery but unrequited love compels the concubine to leave the Levite whose love sends him after her. When he comes to her parents' house, he 'redressed her grievances and was reconciled to her' (*Ant.* 5.138). Josephus' version continues as in Judges until they arrive at Gibeah, here Gaba. They wait in the town square for someone to offer hospitality, but it is only the old man from Ephraim who takes them in. The old man offers hospitality because, like the Levite, he too is from Ephraim and there is no hint of menace at this stage.

When they repair to the old man's house, Josephus introduces this striking change:

---

9.   He follows it with the migration of the Danites from Judges 18, but omits the story of Micah and the Levite.

> But some of the young men of Gaba, who had seen the woman in the market-place and admired her comeliness, when they learnt that she lodged with the old man, scorning the feebleness of these few, came to the doors; and when the old man bade them to begone and not resort to violence and outrage, they required him to hand over his woman guest if he wished to avoid trouble (*Ant.* 5.143).

The woman is the object of the mob's attention from the start and there is no sexual or other threat to the Levite. The old man pleads with the young men, as a kinsman and a Levite, not to commit the 'dreadful crime' by violating 'the laws' (of hospitality?) 'at the beck of pleasure (*hêdonês*)' (*Ant.* 5.144). As the concubine, not the Levite, is the focus of attention the old man cannot offer her to the mob, as in the original story, but he offers his daughter. This act is represented as his being driven to extremes to fulfil the demands of hospitality: 'unwilling to suffer his guests to be abused... declaring it...more legitimate...thus to gratify their lust than by doing violence to his guests' (*Ant.* 5.145).

   The mob ignores the old man and breaks into the house. Seizing the concubine, they take her and rape her throughout the night. Unlike Judges, Josephus' version does not implicate the Levite in the concubine's fate. She was always the object of their criminal intentions not the Levite, and she dies melodramatically, 'outworn with all her woes...out of grief at what she had endured and not daring for shame to face her husband – since he above all, she deemed, would be inconsolable at her fate' (*Ant.* 5.147). Shame and notions of infidelity figure more prominently in Josephus' account than the actual violence of the event. These notions are reinforced when the Levite finds her next morning and, not realizing she is dead, tries to wake her 'with intent to console her by recalling how she had not voluntarily surrendered herself to her abusers but that they had come to the lodging house and carried her off' (*Ant.* 5.148). The implication is that by being raped she is somehow at fault or in some way adulterous. Indeed the only mitigating circumstance is that she was taken by force. If she had voluntarily surrendered in an effort to lessen the physical danger to herself, then she would be guilty of collaborating with her abusers and betraying her husband. The cruel irony is that in the biblical account it is the Levite who betrays the concubine and voluntarily hands her over to the mob.

4. *Conclusion*

In the Hebrew Bible and the Apocrypha, Sodom is a place of injustice and oppression. However, in the Pseudepigrapha, Sodom becomes associated with sexual iniquity and lawlessness. These themes are also reflected in the

New Testament Catholic Epistles in polemics against allegedly antinomian rivals who are portrayed as threatening to disintegrate these early Christian communities. This sexual iniquity is always associated with the angels of Genesis 6 and is best understood as transgressing the boundaries of the angelic and the human. It represents the danger of surrendering to *porneia* and, in the Pseudepigrapha, is used to warn against intermarriage with gentiles. With the exception of one text, of very uncertain date, only the works of Philo focus centrally on same-sex desire such that homoeroticism is the defining sin of Sodom and Gomorrah, warranting divine intervention. He employs sexualized negative/positive dichotomies, at the heart of which are homosexual/heterosexual and feminine/masculine, to make Sodom an allegory for both sterility and passion run amok. Outside of Philo, the dominant pattern focuses on Sodom's injustice, lawlessness and hostility to outsiders as the primary evils leading to divine intervention. Hatred of strangers figures along with pride and impiety as the crimes that make the deity decide to destroy Sodom in Josephus' account. While these themes remain dominant in Rabbinic interpretation, ideas of sexual excess will enable Christians to connect with and employ Philo's homophobic interpretation of the story, thus establishing Sodom as paradigmatic of the evil of homoeroticism.

The character of Lot can be evaluated both positively and negatively, more often negatively, especially in comparison to Abraham. In *Jubilees*, Lot is even held responsible for initiating incest with his daughters, while, on the other hand, Wisdom and Christian scriptures present Lot as a positive model for the godly. Philo turns Lot into an imperfect hero who represents the imperfect man's ascent to spiritual perfection, even finding virtue in his offering the daughters. Josephus does not condemn Lot's behaviour, but neither does he turn him into a positive model. Most important for these evaluations is the way his role is perceived in relation to the rape that closes Genesis 19. If Lot is understood as complicit or even the main agent in initiating the events, then he is viewed very negatively if not condemned, along with his daughters. However, if the daughters are understood as the main agents then not only is their father viewed more positively, but the women themselves are almost considered praiseworthy. Philo incorporates both perspectives in his writings even though it leads him into using incest as an image for spiritual growth. Subsequent Christian readings will take up this more positive evaluation, with Jewish readings treading a middle path of regarding Lot negatively but valorizing his daughters. Indeed, Philo seems to anticipate a subsequent Jewish reading that praises the older daughter for initiating these events. The other member of the family, Lot's wife, is viewed negatively over all. This negative understanding will carry over into Christianity as well as Judaism. However, Rabbinic texts will evince an alternative and more positive interpretation of her fate not found in these texts.

Gibeah's story does not receive anywhere near the amount of attention in these texts as Sodom, a pattern repeated in later Christian interpretation of Judges. Josephus' version, which changes the story to remove the similarities to Sodom, will become almost the preferred version for Christians, thus preventing them from turning Judges 19–21 into another homophobic ideo-story. Like Josephus, Pseudo-Philo changes the biblical account and his changes also highlight violence, rape and abuse of hospitality to prevent any possible homophobic interpretation of Judges 19. Josephus' version of events disappears from the Jewish tradition, which, like Christianity, will not show much interest in Gibeah. However, aspects of Pseudo-Philo's version will be found in later Rabbinic texts, one being the tendency to regard the concubine's fate as almost deserved because of her earlier adultery. Pseudo-Philo is the only ancient writer clearly to compare or connect Gibeah to Sodom, employing the latter for its archetypally violent, hostile inhospitality. Similarly, some later Jewish commentators will use the events at Gibeah to show that sex was not the intent of the men of Sodom but, instead, the abuse of outsiders. If it were only sex motivating the Sodomites, the deity would not have intervened.

Chapter 4

BUT THE MEN OF SODOM WERE WORSE THAN THE MEN
OF GIBEAH FOR THE MEN OF GIBEAH ONLY WANTED SEX:
SODOM THE CRUEL, GIBEAH AND RABBINIC JUDAISM

1. *Of Deltas and Backwaters*

To introduce the reader to the world of Jewish interpretation, I want to draw on and re-arrange the river image Yvonne Sherwood used to illustrate the place of Jewish interpretation in a broader pattern of biblical exegesis. She describes Jewish interpretation as one of a number of 'Backwaters...that do not flow as tributaries into the Mainstream' (2000: 91). She is highlighting the fact that biblical studies has been constructed as a form of implicit Christian Studies, 'where to study the Bible without studying Christian theology is regarded by many as strange in the extreme, but where Jewish Studies is regarded as a separate specialist area (an extra string to one's academic bow?)' (2000: 92). Her image works well both to parody the assumptions of the Mainstream, and to dispel any supersessionist notions of the world of Judaism in the Christian Mainstream. Jewish interpretation is not dependent on and nor is it fulfilled in the understandings of Christianity.

However, while recognizing that Jewish interpretation is not a tributary to any Christian river, I confess to being uncomfortable with this image. It tends to reinscribe the assumptions of the Mainstream, making Jewish (and other) interpretation 'a collection of curios, gathered from places foreign to the biblical critic' (Sherwood 2000: 93). Terming Jewish interpretative traditions a Backwater does not adequately represent the relationship of the two traditions, which do not work as two lines, one broad and dark the other thin and faint, running parallel without ever meeting. In fact, I would argue that the Jewish interpretative world to be explored here actually represented a Mainstream in which early Christians shared. Ancient Christian texts are better understood if seen as part of this broader Jewish context, from which the Christian homophobic reading of Sodom later diverged. Consequently, the riverine image I would suggest is that of the delta. Jewish, Christian and other reading traditions (such as Islamic ones) represent the channels of a delta. These channels, at times, run parallel and at other times they criss-cross each other. Sometimes they generate billabongs, backwaters cut off from the lattice of channels. But even these apparently isolated billabongs might potentially be opened up to sub-sequently create new channels. Furthermore, these billabongs are gener-ated by all the traditions, no single tradition having a monopoly on this tendency.

Two types of Jewish texts will be discussed in this chapter. The first consists of a wide variety of legal, narrative, homiletic and exegetical mate-rials, which I will term midrashic. These texts derive primarily from the first millennium CE but some were written in the early centuries of the second millennium. I include in this category the ancient Aramaic versions of the Hebrew scriptures, the Targumim, as they are not just simple trans-lations but creatively amplify and paraphrase the biblical text. The second type comprises the commentaries of individual rabbis from the medieval and Renaissance periods. Despite their variety, midrashic texts share a range of features that distinguish them from the later commentaries. One such feature is their anonymity. Although some of them are attributed to certain individuals their authorship is by and large unknown. Much more important is the literary style and interpretative approach of the bulk of these texts. Midrash is a form of exegesis that attempts to 'fill in the gaps, to tell us the details that the Bible teasingly leaves out' (Holtz 1984: 180). Midrash is creative in its use of wordplay, and, because there is an understanding of the interrelatedness of all Scripture, midrash regularly employs the juxtaposition of secondary scriptural references to elucidate a primary scriptural text. As Neusner comments, through this intertextual play, midrash rewrites 'Torah by means of scripture: writing with scripture the way we write with words' (1991: 13). Consequently, these texts are often highly creative and playful in augmenting the biblical narrative. To enter the world of these texts is to enter a conversation, in part, because many of them are reminiscent of the minutes of an ongoing symposium. Consequently, these texts include a variety of positions and do not strive to uphold a singular, unambiguous account of the biblical narratives.

A final quality most of these texts share is an authority within Jewish tradition, virtually equivalent to the Torah itself. Fundamental to this authority is the belief that when Moses received the written Torah, the Pentateuch, on Sinai he also received an Oral Torah. This second Torah included additional laws, interpretative tools and other information by which to read, interpret and apply the Written Torah. In other words the

Pentateuch does not stand alone in Judaism as scripture does for some fundamentalist Christian groups but is already read in a broader context. Following the Jewish wars with Rome and the destruction of the Temple, these oral traditions begin to be written down. The major compilations are the *Talmuds* and the *Midrash Rabbah* (on the Pentateuch and the five Scrolls). The *Targumim*, too, are understood to be employing Mosaic oral tradition given to elucidate the biblical text. The *Zohar*, in form a commentary on the Pentateuch, comes from much later in the thirteenth century CE, but presents itself as contemporaneous with these other rabbinic texts. Regardless of its age, it is a fundamental text of the Jewish esoteric tradition of Kabbalah and consequently shares the authority of the other works. When reading these texts, therefore, one is not reading mere commentary but scripture itself.

The exegetical writings of the individual medieval rabbis manifest a shift from midrash to a form of exegesis known as *peshat*, which seeks the plain or literal interpretation of the text. Greenstein calls it 'contextual' in that it is more 'rational' than midrash and recognizes the constraints 'of the historical, literary and linguistic conditions in which the text first came to us' (Greenstein 1984: 220). *Peshat* concerns itself more with a scientific approach to language, and the medieval period is also the time that 'the genre of the running, direct commentary on the biblical text comes into its own' (Greenstein 1984: 213). While these commentaries are not on the same level of authority as the earlier midrashim, commentary in Judaism is understood to be a form of continuing revelation, exposing that which is hidden in the text. Nevertheless a particular authority is accorded to the great medieval French rabbi, Solomon bar Isaac or Rashi, who wrote commentaries on both the Hebrew Bible and the *Talmud*.

2. *In Those Days When There Was No King in Israel*

References to Gibeah in early rabbinic texts are sparse and Judges attracted the attention of only a few later medieval exegetes, including the great Rashi. His commentary is typical, being mainly focused on points of geography, law, cult and custom and the military details of the civil war in Judges 20. The Aramaic translation of Judges, in Targum Jonathan to the Former Prophets, keeps close to the Hebrew text with few glosses or changes. However, the Targum gives a different reason for the separation of the Levite and the concubine. Instead of adultery, she is represented as simply 'despising' him (*Targ. Jon.* Judg. 19.2). The Targum appears to follow the tradition found in both the LXX and the Vulgate that the concu-

bine *quarrelled* with the Levite and left him. The Targum of the Minor
Prophets, glosses Hos. 10.9, 'Since the days of Gibeah you have sinned, O
Israel', to explicitly link Gibeah with Saul and Israel's desire to appoint a
king for themselves as the dreadful outrage here. In so doing it erases
entirely the memory of the rape of the concubine.

Other references to Gibeah in early rabbinic literature are few and
brief. The *Pesikta Rabbati* contains a brief reference to the decimation of
Benjamin 'on account of the concubine in Gibeah' (*Pes. R.* 11.3). In the
Babylonian *Talmud*, Gibeah is mentioned as the seat of Saul in *Ta'anith* 5b
and there are general references to Gibeah as the shame of Benjamin
(*Megillah* 25b), to the war with Benjamin (*Yoma* 73b) and the use of the
Urim and Thurrim in the war (*Shebu'oth* 35b). The reference found in
Sanhedrin 103b echoes Pseudo-Philo in that it links Judges 17-18 (the
story of Micah, the Levite and the graven images) with the twofold defeat
of Israel at the hands of Benjamin. Israel is condemned for putting a mere
woman's honour ahead of that of the deity.

A brief discussion of Judg. 19.2 in *Gittin* 6b attempts an explanation of
the concubine's 'playing the harlot' against the Levite in the Hebrew version and the rendering of it as quarrels and disputes in the various translations of the verse.

> He replied: 'Both (answers) are the word of the living God. He (the Levite)
> found a fly and excused it, he found a hair and did not excuse it.' Rab Judah
> explained: He found a fly in his food and a hair *in loco concubitus*; the fly
> was merely disgusting, but the hair was dangerous. Some say, he found
> both in his food; the fly was not her fault; the hair was (*Gittin* 6b, italics in
> Soncino text).

It is not clear why a hair would be dangerous unless it could inflict impurity on the Levite. The use of Latin suggests delicacy on the part of the
Soncino translators and implies the finding of a strange hair either in the
concubine's bed or, possibly, a more personal place, her genitals, which
would support an interpretation that she was having sex with someone
else. The finding of both a hair and a fly in his food, on the other hand,
would give support to a reading that put quarrelling as the reason for the
concubine leaving the Levite. Even so, the concubine is still at fault. The
Levite is willing to forgive the fly in his food because that is something
she has no control over, but the finding of a hair in his food implies poor
housekeeping (or worse) on her part in which case he is in the right to
raise objections.

However, the text continues into a long discussion of the evils of men
terrorizing their households and gives a contrary opinion, condemning the

Levite as primarily responsible for the events without completely exonerating the concubine

> R. Hisda said: A man should never terrorise his household. The concubine
> of Gibea was terrorised by her husband and she was the cause of many
> thousands being slaughtered in Israel. Rab Judah said in the name of Rab:
> If a man terrorises his household, he will eventually commit the three sins
> of unchastity, blood-shedding, and desecration of the Sabbath (*Gittin* 6b).

Commenting in a footnote to this, Simon, the translator, points out that
the man who terrorizes his household will commit these sins as a result of
the fear of his wife and family. They will want to run away from him and
can meet with fatal accidents, his wife will be afraid to confide in him so
he will have sex with her when she is menstruating, and she will light the
Sabbath lamp after dark (Simon, p. 21, nn. 1, 2, 3). This passage, therefore,
is the only instance in which the concubine wins any sort of sympathetic
treatment. Out of fear of her husband, she acts in a way that will precipi-
tate the slaughter of many thousands in Israel.

Two more texts, the *Seder 'Olam* and *Tanna debe Eliyyahu*, address the
chronological questions seen in Josephus. In other words, when, in the
biblical narrative, should the events at Gibeah be located? The *Seder 'Olam*,
a Rabbinic chronography of the events of the Hebrew Bible, follows
Josephus in locating both the incident of Micah's idol and the outrage at
Gibeah in the period immediately after Joshua's death (*S. 'Ol.* 12.10-20).
But the *Seder 'Olam* gives no reason why these events have been recorded
at the end of the book of Judges. An answer is provided in *Tanna debe
Eliyyahu*. The Benjamites are identified as exemplifying those who do not
know 'Scripture and right conduct' because they followed 'filthy ways' and
committed 'such indecencies as one cannot give a name to…in Gibeah'
(*T. d. Eliyy.* ER 56). The text declares that the events at Gibeah occurred
immediately after the occupation of Canaan however,

> Lest the peoples of the world should say that Israel had disgraced them-
> selves by sexual immorality as soon as they entered the Land, He had the
> story of the concubine put off to the very end of the judges rule of Israel, (so
> as to make it appear that Israel had learned such immoral practices from
> the Canaanites long after Israel had entered the Land) (*T. d. Eliyy.* ER 57).

The story is such an embarrassment to Israel that the deity has even
changed the record of Scripture to soften its full seriousness.

Rashi supports this position, commenting on Judg. 17.1, saying that
both events really occurred 'during the days of Othniel the son of Kenaz'
(Rashi 1991: 137). As proof he cites Judg. 19.12 and 1.8. In 19.12 it is
reported that the Levite will not stop in Jerusalem because it is not an

Israelite city, however, 1.8 clearly says that the tribe of Judah took Jerusalem. Therefore the events of chs. 17-21 took place when the Israelites 'had not yet captured Jerusalem' (Rashi 1991: 137). He further reinforces his position when commenting on Judg. 18.1, which states that the Danites had not yet got their land in which to dwell. He links that verse with Josh. 19.47, which portrays the Danites starting to expand their land, and deduces that '(f)rom here we can also derive that this occurred at the immediate beginning of the Judges' period' (Rashi 1991: 141). Rashi makes no comment on the connection of the events of Judges 19 with the preceding events of Micah, the Levite and the Danites. Later commentators, such as Radak, view the events of Judges 19–21 as Israel's punishment for allowing the sin of idolatry initiated by Micah and, by implication, still continuing when the concubine leaves the Levite. The concubine's actions and her subsequent fate become merely the instruments of a broader process of divine punishment of the Israelites.

Overall, Rashi views the concubine disapprovingly, in line with his dislike of concubinage. On Judg. 8.3, Rashi (Rashi 1991: 75) states that a concubine or *pilegesh* is a woman with whom there is no marriage contract implying a certain moral uncertainty to the relationship. This position is critiqued by Nahmanides, who in his commentary on Gen. 25.6 argues that a marriage contract is merely a Rabbinic ordinance and therefore a woman 'is called a concubine only when there is no betrothal' (Nahmanides 1971: 308). It is clear, then, that for Nahmanides, the concubine's status is not shameful or morally questionable. Instead, the relationship of a man and a concubine is a private arrangement as opposed to that of husband and wife, which is also a joining of families (hence the need for betrothal).

So what is it that leads to the separation of the concubine and the Levite? Rashi states that the concubine turned from the Levite's house to the outside, which means she committed adultery. He argues that every expression of the word *znh* 'implies going out...departing from her husband to love others' (Rashi 1991: 151). Subsequent commentators such as Radak follow Rashi in explaining the concubine's departure. While there is an ambivalence towards the reasons for the concubine's separation from the Levite in the *Talmud*, it would appear that, as the rabbinic tradition develops, this ambivalence fades and the concubine is held solely responsible for the breakdown of the relationship and the events that follow.

Rashi says little concerning the events leading up to the rape of the concubine. Concerning the demand of the men of Gibeah for the Levite, he offers the following terse comment on their expressed intention to know him, '*mshkb zkwr*' (Rashi 1991: 157). This phrase echoes the language used to describe male-male sex in Lev. 18.22 and 20.13. Rashi uses the phrase here to identify the meaning of 'know' as expressing a sexual intent when the men of Gibeah say they wish to know the Levite. However, both Rashi and other commentators ignore the old man's offer of his daughter and the concubine or the Levite's casting the concubine out to the mob. Rashi also passes over why the mob accept the concubine after first refusing the old man's offer of his daughter and the concubine in place of the Levite. This issue is addressed by Radak and Ralbag, who argue that the mob had initially rejected the old man's offer, but, when they saw the concubine herself, were appeased and accepted her in place of the Levite (JCD: 157). Abravanel argues that they did not prefer sex with a man but refused out of respect for the old man. Accordingly, they refused his daughter but when the concubine 'alone was given over to them, they accepted willingly' (JCD: 158). Rashi's only further comment on the rape is to point out that the concubine lay dead at the door of the old man's house when the Levite ventured out the following morning.

Of the rest of the story, Judges 20-21, both Rashi and later commentators are mostly concerned with the minutiae of geography, cult details, battle tactics and other such matters. I don't intend to discuss those details here. My interest is if/how the various sexual themes associated with the concubine's fate arise in the treatment of these later events. My main concern is whether any discussion of homoeroticism occurs in judging these events, particularly the Levite's address or the decision to punish the offenders. Rashi says little, merely stressing the common agreement of all the Israelites gathered there on the action decided upon. Abravanel points out that the Benjaminites in Gibeah had planned to rape the Levite and that while one is not normally punished for planning to sin, in Gibeah the crime was 'attempted publicly by a group and therefore caused a desecration of God's name' (JCD: 162). Commenting on the initial victories of the Benjaminites, Rashi now points out that the Israelites were punished because they had not dealt with the idolatry of Micah.

The mass rapes of Judges 21 give rise to some bizarre observations by Rashi and Maharsha, a commentator on Rashi. How did the Israelites determine the virginity of the 400 women spared at Jabesh Gilead? Rashi states that their virginity was determined by placing them over the openings of barrels of wine: 'the non-virgin would allow a fragrance to pass whereas the virgin would not allow a fragrance to pass' (Rashi 1991: 174). Elaborating on Rashi, Maharsha adds that wine was used because it causes sexual immorality. Maharsha's explanation evokes the rape of Lot, which also involved wine and, whether or not either of these commentators had that scenario in mind, I find it a curious intertextual link in the closing events of both stories. Furthermore, Rashi states that Saul was one of the 200 Benjaminites who abducted the Israelite women who danced at Shiloh (Rashi 1991: 177). As will be seen shortly, the rape of Lot in Genesis 19 is understood in rabbinic exegesis to anticipate the Davidic lineage of Israel's kings. Here, the mass rapes closing Judges are used by Rashi to anticipate the failed king, David's predecessor, Saul. The overthrow of Sodom has messianic possibilities, but Judges closes with the system in place and no compensating promise of transformation.

3. *The Men of Sodom Have No Portion in the World to Come*

In contrast to the scant references to Gibeah, the references to Sodom and Gomorrah are ubiquitous in rabbinic literature. The cities are constantly associated with oppression, injustice, greed and hostility towards strangers. These crimes are often augmented with the practice of idolatry and sexual sins, especially adultery, but these evils remain secondary to Sodom's greed and oppression of the poor and outsiders. In fact, Sodom will be seen as a byword for selfish, cruel behaviour. Of great importance will be the image of Abraham as a paragon of hospitality in contrast to the abusive inhospitality of Sodom and Gomorrah. Along with Sodom and Gomorrah, Lot is also set in contrast to Abraham, at best being a poor imitation, at worst a paragon of the apostate Jew. While his offering of his daughters to the mob receives little comment, there is a strong view that he was complicit when raped by his daughters. Both the daughters and Lot's wife receive negative treatment themselves: however, in these texts are strong counter views exonerating their behaviour – especially that even the deity is held to aid and abet the daughters in the rape of their father.

a. *Genesis 18: Abraham at Mamre*
My discussion here will focus on Abraham's reception of the angels at Mamre in Gen. 18.1-8. For rabbinic interpretation, these events present Abraham as the paragon of hospitality and model of Jewish praxis. His virtuous hospitality serves to contrast the abusive inhospitality of the Sodomites. A related topic is the question of the distinction between the deity and the three figures who visit Abraham. According to some accounts the three are two angels together with the deity but the preferred position is that the deity appears separately from the three angels. While I will not explore this matter in detail, the question of the relationship of Abraham's guests and the deity will later be seen as important in Christian exegesis

of these events. Another important topic is Abraham's circumcision in Genesis 17, which further serves to illustrate the importance of Abraham as a model of Jewish praxis and underscoring even more the centrality of hospitality.

In the Babylonian *Talmud*, Abraham's hospitality is a major theme in an extensive discussion of Gen. 18.1-8 found in *Baba Mezi'a* 86b-87a. Here Abraham's practice of hospitality is held to surpass even that of Solomon and this hospitality is finally repaid during the Exodus:

> As a reward for, (*and he took*) *butter and milk*, they received the manna, as a reward for, *And he stood by them*, they received the pillar of cloud; as a reward for, *Let a little water, I pray you, be fetched, and wash your feet*, they were granted Miriam's well (*Baba Mezi'a* 86b).

Abraham's hospitality is highlighted by the fact of his recent circumcision to further portray him as a paragon of hospitality. Only three days have elapsed from his circumcision but Abraham will not be prevented from attending to the needs of travellers. Consequently, the deity caused a heat wave to prevent people from travelling and ensure Abraham's uninterrupted convalescence. However, Abraham is not deterred from prioritizing hospitality above his own needs. He sends his servant out searching for any travellers that might be abroad. Eventually the deity relents and not only visits Abraham but also sends the three angels, identified as Michael, Gabriel and Raphael, each of whom have specific tasks: Michael to announce Isaac's conception, Raphael to heal Abraham and Gabriel to overturn Sodom. Michael will accompany Gabriel to rescue Lot (*Baba Mezi'a* 86b).

Genesis Rabbah is concerned to build up Abraham as paragon of hospitality and friend of the deity, by linking Gen. 18.1 with Ps. 18.36, 'your condescension has made me great', to refer to Abraham's recent circumcision (*Gen. R.* 48.1.1). The deity holds Abraham in such regard that he is not required to stand in the divine presence but, on the contrary, may remain seated while the deity itself stands. This favour is not purely out of concern for Abraham but underlines an important point about circumcision which is developed in the following verses. Through circumcision one is made fit to see the deity for it is only after Abraham's circumcision that the deity appears to him (*Gen. R.* 48.5.1).

As in the *Talmud*, the deity creates a heatwave. But it is not so much to deter travellers, thus enabling Abraham's rest and recovery, but to have the world share his discomfort: 'Said the Holy One, blessed be He, "My righteous man is suffering pain and should the world be comfortable?" ' (*Gen. R.* 48.7.4). However, the lack of travellers causes Abraham anxiety about his ability to continue the practice of hospitality. The deity responds 'Before you circumcised yourself, uncircumcised men would come to you. Now I and my retinue will appear to you' (*Gen. R.* 48.9.1). The centrality of circumcision for seeing the deity is, thus, employed to extol Abraham's paradigmatic practice of hospitality.

Circumcision and hospitality are again two themes emerging in the *Zohar*, one of the central texts of Kabbalah. The reason the deity is said to *appear* to Abraham at Mamre is because before he 'was circumcised he was, as it were, covered over, but as soon as he was circumcised he became completely exposed to the influence of the Shekinah' (*Zohar* I.98b). Prior to his circumcision, Abraham is not described as seeing any manifestations of the heavenly realm. It is only in Genesis 18, following his circumcision, that Abraham is able to see and fully interact with this dimension. Indeed, the *Zohar* addresses the relationship of angels and deity at Mamre in a way that highlights the extraordinary spiritual change circumcision has wrought in Abraham.

> AND HE SAID, ADONAI (my Lord) which shows that the Shekinah (one appellative of which is *Adonai*) had come with them (the angels), and that the angels accompanied her as her throne and pillars, because they are the three colours below her, and Abraham, now that he was circumcised, saw what he could not see before (*Zohar* I.101a)

Circumcision has rendered Abraham holy, a fit person to keep company with the Shekinah, the feminine immanent Divine, herself.

Abraham is also the epitome of hospitality in the *Zohar* and this hospitality is a sign of how worthy Abraham is of the love and special consideration of the deity.

> When Abraham was still suffering from the effects of the circumcision, the Holy One sent him three angels, in visible form, to enquire of his well-being. You may, perhaps, wonder how angels can ever be visible, since it is written, 'Who makes his angels spirits' (Ps. 104.4). Abraham, however, assuredly did see them, as they descended to earth in the form of men. And, indeed, whenever the celestial spirits descend to earth, they clothe themselves in corporeal elements and appear to men in human shape. Now Abraham, although he was in great pain from his wound, ran forward to meet them so as not to be remiss in his hospitality (*Zohar* I.101a).

Abraham is in pain but he is still zealous in greeting guests. Note also that the angels have clothed themselves in corporeal form so that again there is no doubt that Abraham's hospitality is truly practised. The angels will truly eat and drink what Abraham offers them. Therefore, his hospitality is genuine and, thus, the merit that Abraham derives from such practice is ensured.

The *Zohar* explains the significance of Gen. 18.16 – 'Then the men looked out from there, and they looked toward Sodom; and Abraham went with them to set them on their way' – to make a final point about the rewards of hospitality. Seeing the angels on their way is a precondition for the deity consulting with Abraham about Sodom because 'when a man escorts a departing friend, he draws the Shekinah to join him and to accompany him on the way as a protection' (*Zohar* I.104a-104b). Hospitality is crowned by seeing off one's guests safely. Abraham's example shows that all the elements of hospitable practice place the host in the company of the Divine. He demonstrates that the hospitable person is a friend of the Divine and that the Heavenly Court is made present when guests are made welcome.

For subsequent Jewish tradition, the visitation at Mamre remains a narrative supremely illustrative of the virtue of hospitality and Abraham, the exemplar of hospitable practice. The thirteenth-century *Encyclopedia of Torah Thoughts*, by R. Bahya ben Asher, invokes the events at Mamre in the chapter on hospitality. Bahya states that Abraham 'would go in search of wayfarers and bring them to his house' (Bahya 1980: 43). The visitation is evidence that a person who consistently practices hospitality and 'meticulously honours and serves his guests is worthy of praise and great reward' (Bahya 1980: 46). Three centuries later, Isaiah Horowitz declared that Abraham's hospitality at Mamre lies behind the *Talmud*'s dictum that the entertaining of guests is of more account than the welcoming of the divine presence. Abraham asked the deity to wait for a moment while he attended to the needs of his guests. By emulating Abraham's hospitality one is actually emulating the deity. The whole of creation is an act of hospitality on the part of the deity and all 'creatures are His guests, we are all like strangers vis-a-vis G'd' (Horowitz 1992: 92). This Divine hospitality serves as a strong contrast to what will occur in Sodom where, far from seeking out guests, the inhabitants shun them and abuse them. In so acting, they will summon Divine hostility.

b. *Lot*

Abraham has emerged as a role model, a friend of the deity who, as we will see, stands in contrast to the Sodomites. However, Abraham also stands in contrast to Lot who is more often presented negatively even as a type of apostate. When Lot is portrayed favourably, it is always with qualifications. Everything Lot does in Genesis 12-19 gives rise to negative appraisals of his character. However, it is the events of Gen. 13.5-13, his separation from Abraham, along with the events of Genesis 19 that give rise to the most negative portraits of Lot.

Lot might be Abraham's companion on the journey to Palestine but this fact does not count in his favour. Instead, *Genesis Rabbah*, in a midrash on Gen. 12.4, says that was Lot 'a lot of extra baggage for' Abraham (*Gen. R.* 39.13.1). Rashi, commenting on Gen. 13.14, declares that '(a)ll the time that the wicked (Lot) was with him (Abram) the word (of God) was departed from him (Abram)' (Rashi 1949: 113). Sforno notes that it is only after Lot has departed from Abraham that the deity appeared to renew the promise of the land with Abraham (Sforno 1997: 68). Yitzchaq Arama goes as far as saying that the deity engineered the strife between the shepherds of Lot and Abraham to bring about their separation because 'Abraham's spiritual growth had been impeded by the proximity of Lot' (Arama 1986: 110).

As for the reason for the strife between the herdsmen of Lot and Abraham, *Targum Pseudo-Jonathan* adds this gloss to the account in Genesis 13, 'the herdsmen of Lot allowed (their cattle) to go about freely and to eat in the fields of the Canaanites and the Perizzites who were still dwelling in the land' (*Targ. Ps.-Jon.* Gen. 13.5-7). In other words, Abraham is concerned about respecting the rights of his neighbours and has given instructions accordingly, whereas Lot is not concerned with respecting such rights and rather turns a blind eye to the unscrupulous behaviour of his herdsmen. A reason for such disregard is provided in *Genesis Rabbah*, in which the herdsmen of Lot declare

> So has the Holy One, blessed be He, said to Abraham, 'To your seed I will give this land' (Gen. 12.7). Now Abraham is a barren mule. He is not going to produce an heir. So Lot will inherit the land. Accordingly the cattle are eating what belongs to them (*Gen. R.* 41.5.1).[1]

Not only do the herdsmen show an arrogant disregard for the rights of other people in the land but they also compound it by their presumption on the divine promise to Abraham. They act as if their master is Abraham's heir and has even already inherited the promise. The midrash immediately presents the deity rebuking their presumption (and Lot's complicity in it), by re-affirming the promise to Abraham. Possibly this midrash lies behind Sforno's observation that the deity renewed the promise with Abraham after he separated from Lot to forestall Lot and his men becoming

---

1.   The *Sefer ha-Yashar* is even stronger in portraying this conflict. Abraham accuses Lot of ordering his herdsmen to graze the cattle in the fields of others and of making Abraham 'despicable to the inhabitants of the land'. Abraham quarrels daily with Lot over this but Lot refuses to listen, so eventually Abraham implores Lot to separate from him (*SY* 15.39-43).

more arrogant and seizing land for themselves without consideration for the inhabitants or for Abraham (Sforno 1987: 68-9).

A lengthy midrash on Gen. 13.5 extends the negative portrait of Lot by alluding to his role as progenitor of the Ammonites and Moabites, enemies of Israel (*Gen. R.* 41.3.3). Lot owed everything to Abraham, including his life, because the midrash, while foreshadowing that Lot will be saved from Sodom's destruction, tells the reader that Lot is saved not on his account but Abraham's. The greater part of the midrash focuses on condemning Lot through his progeny, Moab and Ammon, by listing all their evil actions against Israel. By looking forward to Moab and Ammon, we are reminded that Lot decided to move to Sodom when he left Abraham. This fact more than any other is counted as definitive of his character. *Targum Pseudo-Jonathan* portrays his choice thus, 'And Lot lifted up his eyes with lustful desire and saw that the whole plain of the Jordan was all irrigated...' (*Targ. Ps.-Jon.* Gen. 13.10). Lot is greedy and only concerned for himself much like the Sodomites will soon be revealed to be.

Lust figures prominently in the midrash on Gen. 13.10 onwards, the separation of Lot and Abraham, in which Lot's choice to settle in Sodom is used to compare him unfavourably to Abraham (*Gen. R.* 41.7.1). In fact a pun on the word for lust and Lot's name is used to illustrate why Lot chooses Sodom. While it is one of few early rabbinic references associating sexual sin with Sodom and Gomorrah, it does so through linking sexual sin with Lot not Sodom. It opens with a reference to incest clearly alluding to Lot's fate of being raped by his daughters, and then links Gen. 13.10 inter-textually with several biblical accounts of sexual sin. Lot lifts up his eyes to Sodom like Potiphar's wife when she lusts after Joseph in Genesis 39. The Plains of the Jordan evoke the bread that is the prostitute's fee in Proverbs 6. Being well watered the Plains evoke the waters of bitterness used to test a wife's fidelity in Numbers 5. Finally and ominously the reference to Sodom's destruction evokes the story of Onan in Genesis 38. Onan is not merely a sexual sinner. Like Lot and, as will be seen, the Sodomites, his sin is much more one of callous disregard for the rights of others[2] as it is a sexual sin.

But *Genesis Rabbah* is not content with impugning Lot on the basis of sexual sin alone. It continues, invoking the image of apostasy, by portraying Lot as saying when he departs for Sodom, 'I want no part of Abraham or of his God' (*Gen. R.* 41.7.4). Lot's apostasy is also central to the *Zohar*'s comment on his departure from Abraham, 'That Lot actually did revert to idolatry we know from the words AND LOT JOURNEYED FROM THE

---

2. In Onan's case, of Tamar, his brother's widow, and of his dead brother.

EAST: the word *mi-qedem* (from the East) is equivalent to *mi-qadmono* (from the Ancient One) of the world' (*Zohar* I.84a). The Lot of the *Zohar* is an apostate *converso* who abandons his people, his uncle and the Most High.

When we meet Lot in Genesis 19, Genesis Rabbah is again concerned to portray him as negatively as possible. Lot sits at the city gate because he has been appointed chief justice that day. A Talmudic reference to the evil judges in Sodom[3] is expanded to declare 'Lot was chief justice of them all!' (*Gen. R.* 50.3.5). Lot is negatively contrasted to Abraham when the angels initially reject his hospitality – 'People may decline hospitality of an ordinary person, but they may not decline the hospitality of a great person' (*Gen. R.* 50.4.3). Lot's tardiness in fleeing Sodom is attributed to his unwillingness to part with his great wealth of 'silver and gold and precious stones and pearls' (*Gen. R.* 50.11.1), a point with which Rashi agrees (Rashi 1949: 171). Lot in *Genesis Rabbah* refuses to flee to the hills because there he will be with Abraham, against whom all his moral weaknesses will be clearly apparent, unlike in Sodom where even a reprobate like Lot looked good (*Gen. R.* 50.11.5). Another midrash makes Lot a type of evil Jonah. Explaining the reference to the deity destroying 'the cities in which Lot had settled' (Gen. 19.29) it says, 'The sense is that Lot had lived in all of those cities' (*Gen. R.* 51.6.2). Thus all five cities are destroyed because Lot had lived in each of them.

There are only two consistently sympathetic portraits of Lot in rabbinic literature. One is found in *Pirke de Rabbi Eliezer* although even here Lot suffers in comparison to Abraham. Abraham intercedes with the deity to spare Sodom especially on behalf of Lot, who, like Abraham, proclaims the truth of monotheism in Sodom. He also welcomes strangers and the needy in contravention of Sodom's laws. However, for fear of the Sodomites, Lot only does so by night (*PRE* XXV: 184). As will be seen the *Pirke* also stands alone in Jewish commentary in clearly endorsing Lot's offer of his daughters to the Sodomites.

The other sympathetic portrait is found in the commentary by the great thirteenth-century figure, Nahmanides (Ramban). The reader first meets Lot where he and Abraham separate. Ramban disputes both Rashi and *Genesis Rabbah*, as he is not convinced by their blaming Lot's greed for

---

3.   *Sanhedrin* 109b: 'There were four judges in Sodom (named) Shakrai, Shakurai, Zayyafi, and Mazle Dina.' The translator, H. Freedman, footnotes that the names mean Liar, Awful Liar, Forger and Perverter of Justice. In *Genesis Rabbah* there are now five judges: 'False-Principles, Lyings-Speech, Cad, Justice-perverter and Man-Flayer' (*Gen. R.* 50.3.5).

what transpires. He argues that, from the plain meaning of the text, 'the quarrel concerned pasture as the land could not support them both' (Nahmanides 1971: 178). Key to his argument is that the text points out that the Canaanites and Perizzites were also in the land. Ramban imagines ancient Canaan as a land of nomadic pastoralist peoples. Abraham and Lot had herds in abundance and were both strangers and sojourners in the land. Abraham feared that the other inhabitants of the land (the Canaanites and Perrizites), seeing these vast herds, would either drive them out of the land or slay them and take all their cattle and wealth, hence the need to separate. While Lot is not to be condemned for leaving Abraham, Ramban accepts that the reference in Gen. 13.13 to the wickedness of the Sodomites is meant to accuse 'Lot for not restraining himself from dwelling with them and also speaks of the merit of... (Abraham) whose lot did not fall in the place of wickedness' (Nahmanides 1971: 180).

In his discussion of Genesis 19, Ramban's Lot emerges as a complex character, who can be both praised and condemned. Strong condemnation is only elicited by Lot's offering of his daughters to the mob, which will be discussed later in this chapter. Thus, he argues that the form of Lot's invitation to the angels in 19.2 is an expression of pleading and supports his argument by citing similar usages in Ruth 4.1 and Judg. 4.18. Lot's invitation, saying that the angels will rise early, also stresses that they should not stay in the city in the morning because of the wickedness of its inhabitants. Ramban observes that Lot thought the angels were merely transients adding that 'urging them was meritorious on the part of Lot, and he indeed had a sincere desire to welcome wayfarers' (Nahmanides 1971: 249). The angels refuse Lot at first, both to increase his merit and because he 'was not a perfectly righteous man' (Nahmanides 1971: 249). On Lot's flight from Sodom, Ramban agrees with Ibn Ezra that the angels grabbed Lot by the hand to lead him out because he was paralysed by fear. Lot is warned not to look back because of his merit, for which Zoar is also spared. What does Ramban mean by this merit of Lot? Lot had been obedient to Abraham and went with him from Haran at Abraham's command. His obedience was in fact a 'kindness' to Abraham and it was on Abraham's account that Lot was now living in Sodom (Nahmanides 1971: 261). As will be seen, Ramban stands alone in not holding Lot responsible for his daughters raping him at the end of Genesis 19.

With these two exceptions, the rabbinic portrait of Lot is generally unfavourable. He is a covetous, greedy and lustful figure. While his uncle, Abraham, is a friend of the Most High, consorting with angels and the Shekinah, it is not so with Lot. If Abraham is a model for Israel to follow then Lot becomes a model of the *converso*. By opting for Sodom, Lot typifies those Jews who renounce their people and the Holy One of Israel. If it was a bad day for Lot when he opted for Sodom, perhaps it was a worse day for the cities of the Plain. Lot's character might have been such that it tipped the scales of Sodom's descent into evil and subsequent destruction.

c. *The Sins of Sodom and Gomorrah*

So what are the sins of Sodom and Gomorrah? As has been seen, sexual sin was used in *Genesis Rabbah* to defame Lot. Similarly, sexual sin will some-times be seen to be associated with Sodom and Gomorrah, but it is not a predominant motif and certainly not the cause of the divine intervention. Indeed, the character of Lot is a pointer to Sodom's sin in that what counts most against Lot is his covetousness and greed. Similarly, Sodom and Gomorrah are sites of covetous greed and arrogance. Lot allows his herds-men to trample on the rights of others and so, too, the cities will be seen as places where the rights of the poor and weak count for nothing and where cruelty is a way of life. Lot is an apostate who rejects the Most High and the cities of the Plain are places of idolatry. Lot leaves his uncle's tent, which is a place of hospitality where even angels and the Most High come as guests. Rapacious, abusive and greedy, the people of Sodom and Gomor-rah know nothing of the heavenly ways of hospitality.

Sodom in the *Talmud* is very much a byword for 'dog in the manger' attitudes, smugness, selfishness and generally vexatious behaviour (*Erubin* 49a, *Kethuboth* 103a, *Baba Bathra* 12a, 59a, 168a, *Aboth* V.10). It is not, as Christians might expect, a name connoting sexual difference or sexual sin. There are also references in the *Talmud* to Sodom as a place of unspecified wickedness (*Abodah Zara* 19a, *Baba Bathra* 20b). One Talmudic reference compares Sodom to Jerusalem before the exile, specifically citing Ezekiel 16.49 that Sodom's sins were pride, greed and not helping the needy (*Sanh.* 104b). Another Talmudic reference compares Sodom to Jerusalem using sexual references. However, the sexual sin is adultery and is underscored by the image of leopards which were reputed to be unfaithful to their mates (*Kiddushin* 70a).

The most extensive treatment in the *Talmud* is found in *Sanh.* 109a–109b, which details the nature of the wickedness of Sodom and Gomorrah. Their crimes are portrayed as exploitation of the poor and abuse of strang-ers combined with the corruption of justice to favour the rich and power-ful. The Sodomites are haughty and, because their land is rich and they are well provided for, they resolve, 'why should we suffer wayfarers, who come to us only to deplete our wealth...let us abolish the practice of travelling in our land' (*Sanh.* 109a). Wealthy travellers are particularly targeted and subjected to violence, even being killed, so that their wealth can be stolen. The poor, on the other hand, are mistreated, and denied any aid or assistance so that they starve in the midst of a wealthy city. One particular cruelty depicted is a bed on which strangers are made to lie – '(i)f he (the guest) was too long, they shortened him (by lopping off his feet); if too short, they stretched him out' (*Sanh.* 109b). No reason is given for such behaviour. It represents a particularly gratuitous form of cruelty on the part of the Sodomites.

Justice is corrupted in Sodom to favour wrongdoers and the powerful while the poor are defrauded. Sodom's courts were presided over by four judges whose names mean Liar, Awful Liar, Forger and Perverter of Justice. Abuse of the poor and strangers and the perversion of justice come together in the story of a woman who gives food to a poor man. When she is found out, she is smeared 'with honey and placed...on the parapet of the wall, and the bees came and consumed her' (*Sanh.* 109b). It is her death, which causes the outcry prompting the deity to act against the cities of the plain.

While in the *Talmud* there is no association of Sodom's evil with same-sex desire, in the Minor Tractate, *Abot de Rabbi Nathan* Version B, there is this curious commentary on Genesis 13.13

> HATRED OF MANKIND. This means that God uproots from the world everyone who hates his neighbour. We found that this was the case with the men of Sodom, that God uprooted them only because they hated one another, as Scripture says: 'Now the men of Sodom were evil, great sinners against the Lord' (Gen. 13.13). 'Evil' to one another. 'Sinners' by incest. 'Great' by shedding blood. Another Interpretation. 'Great' by homosexuality (*ARN*[B] 30, p. 64).

Does this passage indicate that same-sex desire was the sin that caused Sodom's destruction? Saldarini comments on his translation here that the last line in this passage is unusual and appears to refer to the siege of Lot's house. The English word 'homosexuality' is little more than a century old and Saldarini has used it to translate the phrase, *mshkb zkwr* (personal email from Anna Urowitz-Freudenstein, 13 February 2002). This term, *mshkb zkwr*, echoes the phrase used to describe male-male anal sex in Lev. 18.22 and 20.13. As already seen, Rashi employed it tersely to clarify the meaning of 'know' in Judges 19 and does so again in his commentary on Genesis 19 (Rashi 1949: 168-69). If Saldarini sees here a reference to the siege of Lot's house then the word 'homosexuality' is a particularly misleading choice to translate the phrase used in this context. In referring to the siege, this phrase reflects the heavily nuanced style of such shorthand references in these texts. In rabbinic literature, the Sodomites' intentions are generally understood to be the sexual intimidation and degradation of Lot's guests, rather than same-sex eros *per se*. Such an understanding would work quite well in this passage and is supported by the parallel passage in *Abot de Rabbi Nathan* A, 'greatly, that they sinned through malice' (*ARN*[A] 12.4.1). The Sodomite mob is motivated primarily by malicious intentions towards Lot's guests not lust. Another midrash on Gen. 13.13 in *Tanna debe Eliyahu* declares that there are eight sins, which together incur the destruction epitomized by Sodom's fate. These include '(1) miscarriage of justice; (2) idolatry; (3) incest; (4) bloodshed; (5) profanation of God's name; (6) lewd speech; (7) arrogance; and (8) slander' (*T. d. Eliyy.* ER 74). It goes on to say that covetousness is sometimes added but makes no reference whatsoever to same-sex desire.

Genesis 13.13 is similarly glossed in the Targumim to list Sodom's crimes. *Targum Pseudo-Jonathan* is the most explicit, 'evil towards one another with their wealth, and sinful with their bodies through sexual immorality, by shedding innocent blood, and by the practice of idolatry, and rebelling grievously against the Lord' (*Targ. Ps.-Jon.* Gen. 13.13). Non-specific sexual sin is included but it is not outstanding. Likewise, *Genesis Rabbah* includes fornication together with idolatry and murder, and unspecific wickedness in their dealings with each other in its gloss on this verse (*Gen. R.* 41.7.6). It goes on to employ a pun on the names of the kings of the five cities in Genesis 14 to highlight greed and lust for money as typical Sodomite traits (*Gen. R.* 42.5.1).

The 'outcry' of Sodom's sin in Genesis 18, is elucidated in *Genesis Rabbah* by a version of the *Talmud*'s story of the woman executed for her charity. She gave food to a poor woman she met at the city well. When her charity is detected by the Sodomites, 'they took the girl (who had shared the food) and burned her' (*Gen. R.* 49.6.3). The deity resolves 'Even if I wanted to keep silent, the requirement of justice for a certain girl will not allow me to keep silent' (*Gen. R.* 49.6.3). So whatever the range of sins might be in Sodom, the deity acts in response to injustice and oppression. The issue of hospitality arises in the midrash on Gen. 19.3, in which Lot invites the angels firstly to stay overnight and then to wash their feet: 'It was so that when they went forth in the morning, there would be dust on their feet, and people would not say, "Where did they spend the night?"' (*Gen. R.* 50.4.2).[4] There is a touch of menace, here, implying that it is

---

4.   cf. the Minor Tractates of the *Talmud, Kallah Rabbathi* 54a: 'Lot surely spoke with the wisdom of the wise. If (the men of Sodom) see them with their face, hands

unwise to shelter strangers in Sodom. Most surprising is the midrash on the siege of Lot's house. The Sodomites demand Lot's guests because they resolved 'any wayfarer who comes here, we shall have sexual relations with him and take away his money' (*Gen. R.* 50.7.2). Sex is combined with theft to make clear that the Sodomite's main intent is abuse of strangers.

In *Pirke de Rabbi Eliezer*, the Sodomites' crimes are injustice and hatred of outsiders rather than sexual sins. Sodom is a city of great wealth with an abundance of gold, silver, precious stones. Even their garden beds contain gold dust. This wealth is the root of their downfall because they 'did not trust in the shadow of their Creator, but (they trusted) in the multitude of their wealth' (*PRE* XXV: 181). For *Eliezer*, the prime sin of Sodom is miserliness, a complete refusal to share their bounty with others, even the birds of the air:

> Rabbi Nathaniel said: The men of Sodom had no consideration for the honour of their Owner by (not) distributing food to the wayfarer and the stranger, but they even fenced in all the trees on top above their fruit so that they should not be seized; (not) even by the bird (sic) of heaven... (*PRE* XXV: 181-82)

The system of justice in Sodom and its fellow cities is designed to oppress every stranger passing through, to fleece them of everything so that, if they are lucky enough to leave, they leave literally naked. Furthermore *Eliezer* cites Ezek. 16.49 – 'Behold, this was the iniquity of thy sister Sodom; pride, fullness of bread and prosperous ease was in her and her daughters; neither did she strengthen the hand of the poor and needy' – to portray Sodom as a city that oppressed the poor to the point of expelling them.

This evil behaviour is exemplified in *Eliezer* by an extensive account of the young woman executed for helping the poor. Here, the woman is not anonymous but is Lot's eldest daughter, Peletith.[5] Despite being the wife of a city magnate she defies a newly-enacted city law, forbidding citizens to feed and assist the poor and needy. Apprehended she is tried and condemned to suffer the only prescribed penalty, to be burnt alive. The account concludes:

and feet washed they would kill him and his children; but if they see the dust on their feet (they would conclude) that they had only just arrived from their journey.' Also *Derek 'Erez Rabbah* 56b.

5.   In various other texts, as will be seen, she is called Paltit or Pelotit. Pelotit's name is derived from the Hebrew *plt* which can mean 'escape', 'bring to safety', and, in other forms, 'what has survived', 'fugitive/refugee' and she is named by Lot to honour his delivery by Abraham from the captivity following the battle of the kings of Genesis 14 (bin Gorion 1976: 54; Brown, Driver and Briggs 1907: 812).

> She said: Sovereign of all the worlds! Maintain my right and my cause (at
> the hands of) the men of Sodom. And her cry ascended before the Throne
> of Glory. In that hour the Holy One, blessed be He, said: 'I will now
> descend, and I will see' (Gen. 18.21) whether the men of Sodom have done
> according to the cry of this young woman, I will turn her foundations
> upwards, and the surface thereof shall be turned downwards, as it is said, 'I
> will now descend, and I will see whether they have done altogether accord-
> ing to her cry which is come unto me' (Gen. 18.21) (*PRE* XXV: 183).

The outcry of Sodom's sin is Peletith's demand for justice and vengeance.
Her execution crowns Sodom's cruelty and stirs the deity's intervention.
As if to underscore this portrait of Sodomite cruelty and selfishness, *Eliezer*
then recalls Abraham's hospitality. It states that he had settled opposite
Haran and received all travellers to and from there, giving them food and
drink. Friedlander notes here that Luria argued Sodom should be read
instead of Haran. If this reading is accepted, Sodom's evil is put in stark
relief by comparison with Abraham's hospitality at Mamre, opposite
Sodom.

According to the *Zohar*, Peletith's fate explains why Lot only offered
hospitality by night (*Zohar* I.106b) but it offers s a different explanation of
the outcry that moves the deity to act. It gives a harrowing picture of Sodomite cruelty and oppression together with the outrage and anguish of their
victims. The Sodomites had outlawed giving food and drink to strangers.
Anyone who did so would be drowned in a nearby river along with the
recipient of their hospitality. If any stranger came to Sodom, 'as no food
and drink was given to them, their bodies became so emaciated that they
scarcely looked any more like human beings' (*Zohar* I.105b-106a). So
hostile were the Sodomites to outsiders that even the birds avoided it. In
response to such cruel hostility:

> (a) universal outcry therefore went up against Sodom and Gomorrah and
> all the other towns that behaved like them... When the voices of all of
> them are clear they unite into one. Then a voice ascends from below and
> mingles with them, and the combined cry keeps on ascending and clam-
> ouring for justice, until at last the Holy One appears to investigate the
> accusation (*Zohar* I.105b-106a).

This strong image of the evil plight of the outsider rejected by a cruel
society perhaps echoes the Jewish experience of being the outsider in Christendom. Such experience might account for the Jewish sensitivity, recurring throughout rabbinic texts, to the plight of the outsider in the biblical
story of Sodom (in contrast to Christian fixations on sexual outrage). The
absolute evil of Sodom's cruelty and injustice prompts an absolute and

total judgement on the part of the deity by which the *Zohar* clearly outlines how integral these sins are to Sodom's fate:

> R. Isaac then said to him: 'Observe that just as the soil of their land was
> destroyed to all eternity, so were the inhabitants themselves destroyed to
> all eternity. And observe how the justice of the Holy One metes out meas-
> ure for measure: as they did not quicken the soul of the poor with food or
> drink, just so will the Holy One not restore them their souls in the world
> to come. And further, just as they neglected the exercise of charity which
> is called life, so has the Holy One withholden from them life in this world
> and in the world to come. And as they closed their roads to their fellow
> men, so has the Holy One closed to them the roads and paths of mercy in
> this world and in the world to come (*Zohar* I.108a).

This image of divine inhospitality to the Sodomites in return for their
inhospitality towards others is a strikingly powerful way to foreground
abuse of hospitality as the primary evil of the Sodomites.

Jewish texts go into great detail in their portraits of Sodomite cruelty
and injustice, but show little interest in elaborating the few references to
Sodom's sexual sins. In the *Sefer ha-Yashar* there is such an account, but it
is not a story of homoeroticism. Instead, heterosexual adultery and wife-
swapping serve to typify Sodom's sexual excesses. The account begins
describing a lush well-watered valley near the city. Four times a year the
men of Sodom went there with their wives and children. It continues,

> they would all rise and lay hold of their neighbours' wives, and some, the
> virgin daughters of their neighbours, and they enjoyed them, and each
> man saw his wife and daughter in the hands of his neighbour and did not
> say a word. And they did so from morning to night, so they always did four
> times a year (*SY* 18.12-15).

Nowhere does the *Sefer ha-Yashar* associate homoeroticism with Sodom.
Apart from this short account of sexual communism, it repeats in even
greater detail all the stories of Sodomite cruelty and injustice seen so far.

There are also further accounts of Sodomite mistreatment of outsiders
and of how Sodom's laws are designed specifically to defraud the poor
and the outsider. Travelling merchants are set upon by the Sodomites
who rob them of all their goods. If the merchants complain, the Sodomites 'approach him one by one, and each would show him the little
which he took and taunt him saying, I only took that little which thou
didst give me' (*SY* 18.17). In another account, a travelling merchant is
robbed by a certain Hedad under the ruse of hospitality. Not only does
Hedad steal the goods but, when the merchant asks for them, Hedad
claims the merchant is dreaming, gives an interpretation of the dream

and then demands payment for the interpretation. The merchant takes the case to court, but the judge does not grant justice and drives him from the court (*SY* 18.18-43). Abraham's servant, Eliezer, uses the clever ways of Sodomite justice to outsmart it. Sent by Abraham to ensure Lot's welfare, Eliezer intervenes to protect a stranger being robbed by the Sodomites and is struck by a stone. The assailant seeing the blood gush demands payment for cupping. Eliezer refuses and is taken to court. When the judge rules against Eliezer, he throws a stone at the judge's forehead drawing blood. Eliezer then says that the money owing him for cupping the judge can be paid direct to his assailant in lieu (*SY* 19.11-22). The point of all these stories is that Sodomites are not just thieves or gangsters but take special delight in vexatious harassment of their victims.

References to sexual sin occur in Rashi's commentary, too, but inhospitality, exploitation and idolatry remain Sodom's defining sins. Commenting on Gen. 13.10 Rashi explains Lot's decision to settle in Sodom by citing an Aggadic interpretation that the people 'were carried away by lewdness' (Rashi 1949: 111). The word translated as 'lewdness', *zimmāh*, has a range of meanings pertaining to licentiousness, adultery, and incest. Because of these associations, I believe Rashi is more influenced here by Lot's fate at the hands of his daughters than by any sins of Sodom and Gomorrah. Rashi makes a vague allusion to sexual sin by glossing v. 13 that the Sodomites were wicked with their bodies and sinners with their money. He continues commenting: ' "Against the Lord exceedingly" – They knew their Master and intended to rebel against Him' (Rashi 1949: 112). Sexual sins are, thus, part of a greater pattern in Sodom of exploitation (money) reflecting a deliberate apostasy from the deity. Apostasy and hatred of humanity are the central focus of Rashi's comments on the names of the kings of Sodom and her allies in Genesis 14 (Rashi 1949: 114). By naming these kings for their hatred of and rebellion against the deity, Rashi makes them representative of their cities and of the evil found there and indicates the sins he considers worthy of divine vengeance. None of the kings are associated with sexual sin, let alone homoeroticism. On the outcry of Sodom's sin, Rashi explains that it is the outcry of the land, but then cites the *Talmud* to point out that traditionally the outcry was understood to be 'the cry of a certain girl whom they killed by a strange (unnatural) death because she had given food to a poor man' (Rashi 1949: 159).

When Rashi 'enters' Sodom in Genesis 19, the theme of hospitality becomes paramount. He injects a note of urgency into Lot's speech by portraying him as meaning, '(b)ehold now, you must pay attention to these wicked people that they should not recognize you; and this is proper counsel' (Rashi 1949: 165). Rashi's Lot urges the angels to make their way to his house in a 'roundabout' way so that no one will notice they are sheltering there. Lot does not first invite the angels to wash their feet but offers shelter and food because he thought,

> 'It is better that they remain here with dust of their feet, that they should appear as though they had come (just) now.' Therefore, he said first, 'Tarry all night', and afterwards, 'Wash' (Rashi 1949: 166).

Lot's anxiety that his hospitality might be witnessed is well founded. This consideration for outsiders is what enrages the mob in Rashi's commentary on the siege of Lot's house.

> because he spoke in defense of the guests (they said) 'This one fellow came in to sojourn', an alien man, the only one, you are among us, who have come to sojourn, – 'and he will play the judge' – and you have become one who rebukes us (Rashi 1949: 168-69).

Lot's own outsider status is also emphasized here. The Sodomites' demand to know the angels draws the terse comment, *běmiškab zākār*, to explain the meaning of 'know' in the context of the Sodomites' demand. Rashi addresses the question of idolatry when commenting on the final destruction of the cities. Echoing earlier midrashim, he notes that the cities were destroyed 'when the moon stands in the heaven with the sun' because 'there were some that worshipped the sun and others the moon' (Rashi 1949: 175-76). Thus, the deity demonstrated that neither sun nor moon had power to prevent the destruction.

Sodom's abuse of hospitality is most prominent in later commentaries. Sforno states that, when in Gen. 18.16 Abraham and his guests look down on Sodom, Sodom is here being contrasted to Abraham's house and the hospitality he practices. To reinforce his argument Sforno cites Ezek. 16.49 on Sodom's failure to feed the poor and needy (Sforno 1987: 86). Similarly, Alshech highlights the contrast between Abraham, the epitome of hospitality, and the Sodomites who epitomize the negation of that virtue (Alshech 1988: 90). According to Sforno, the deity plans to investigate the outcry against Sodom in the form of a test. The angels are sent to test whether the Sodomites will attempt to prevent Lot's hospitality (Sforno 1987: 87). Sodom will be spared if 50 righteous men protest such an attempt (Sforno 1987: 89). Sforno further notes that Lot offers the angels hospitality because, not only will no other household in the city do so, but that not even the safety of travellers who stay overnight in the public square is guaranteed (Sforno 1987: 90).

For both Ramban and Arama, Sodomite society represents structured injustice. Sodom is not just a city of individuals who collectively share a taste for evil, but rather the whole society has been structured so as to maintain evil. Taking the cue from Ezek. 16.49 and the subsequent tradition, the evil is identified as the abuse and exploitation of the outsider and the poor. Ramban declares that the outcry of Sodom's evil 'is the cry of the oppressed, crying out and begging for help' (Nahmanides 1971: 244). Explaining the Sodomites' demand to 'know' Lot's guests, Ramban states that their intention 'was to stop people from coming among them...for they thought that because of the excellence of their land...many will come there, and they despised charity' (Nahmanides 1971: 250). Sodom is destroyed not for sexual or even homosexual sin but because:

> they continued provoking and rebelling against Him with their ease and the oppression of the poor... In the opinion of our Rabbis, all evil practices were rampant among them. Yet their fate was sealed because of this sin – i.e., that they did not strengthen the hand of the poor and needy – since this sin represented their usual behaviour more than any other...there was none among all the nations who matched Sodom in cruelty (Nahmanides 1971: 250).

Lot escapes from Sodom 'in honor of hospitality for it is the ethical way of messengers to save their host and all that belong to him' (Nahmanides 1971: 250). He underscores this point citing the example of Rahab (Josh. 2, 6.22-25) who was spared along with her family, in reward for her sheltering the Israelite spies, when the Israelites took Jericho.

It is this inability to give, share or extend help to others that Arama sees as intrinsic to Sodomite society. Sodom passed laws designed to prevent help being given to the weak and the outsider. If 'someone were to...extend help to outsiders, he would be in defiance of their laws and face death, even if it involved offering benefits to a third party at no cost or inconvenience to the donor' (Arama 1986: 146). Sodom's laws were designed to 'frighten off would be visitors, and ensure an UNDISTURBED life for its inhabitants' (Arama 1986: 147). Citing *Genesis Rabbah*, Arama argues that the Sodomites had resolved to rape and rob every stranger to give their city the evil reputation and deter travellers coming there. Linking Ezek. 16.49 with the events outside Lot's house, Arama asks why Ezekiel makes no mention of sexual crime but focuses instead on economic injustice. The answer he gives would, no doubt, surprise those used to homophobic readings of Genesis 19.

> Their (the Sodomites) main concern was their unwillingness to share their wealth. Their / '*chet*', criminal act, as distinct from their wickedness '*raah*', namely the raping of strangers was incidental and not basic to their character. We can then understand Ezekiel, who proclaimed that the sin of Sodom was that they would not help the poor and destitute... Ezeqiel (sic)

does not bother to mention that sin (rape of strangers), since it was not
endemic to their character, and could have been atoned for (Arama 1986:
147).

In other words, sexual misdeeds alone, such as the Sodomites threatened
upon Lot's guests, do not constitute an evil warranting divine intervention
in Sodom. It is Sodom's sanctioned use of violence including sexual violence to maintain a cruel, oppressive and selfish social system that incurs
the divine wrath.

d. *Offered Daughters*

Curiously many early rabbinic texts, such as *Genesis Rabbah* and the
Targumim, simply note the incident of Lot's offering his daughters without
comment. The *Pirke de Rabbi Eliezer* compares Lot to Moses, stating, 'Just
as Moses gave his life for the people, so Lot gave up his two daughters
instead of the two angels...' (*PRE* XXV: 185). But *Eliezer* stands alone in
Jewish commentary with this clear endorsement of Lot. If silence is consent, does the lack of comment on this incident in other earlier rabbinic
texts mean that no problem is seen with Lot's behaviour and is thus
endorsed? An alternative perspective, based on the complete excision of
the incident from such texts as the *Zohar* and the *Sefer ha-Yashar*, would
understand the offer by Lot as an unpleasantness best ignored. But a problem, then, would be the fact that, apart from the *Pirke de Rabbi Eliezer*, all
of the texts hold Lot in fairly low regard. Such an outrageous action would
be yet more proof of Lot's perfidy. Perhaps such an act speaks for itself and
needs no further commentary. It is, of course, a typically Sodomite thing
to do.

   This perspective is what one finds in the brief reference to the incident
in the *Tanna debe Eliyahu* (*T. d. Eliyy.* ER 158). Braude and Kapstein
mistranslated the passage rendering it:

> Thus when Lot offered them natural sexual intercourse with his own
> daughters (in order to divert them from unnatural intercourse with his
> male visitors) they said, *Stand back* (Gen. 19.9); but when he argued with
> them against such unnatural intercourse with his visitors, they mocked
> him saying, *This one fellow came in to sojourn, and he will needs play the
> judge* (Gen. 19.9) (*T. d. Eliyy.* ER 158).

The term that Braude and Kapstein mistranslated as natural/unnatural
intercourse is *derekh eretz* or the 'way of the land/earth'. Birnbaum points
out that this term is used to signify 'local custom, good behaviour, cour-
tesy, politeness, etiquette' (Birnbaum 1979: 147). According to Ulrich Berzbach, *derekh eretz* is a major structuring principle and underlying theme of

this substantial section of the *Tanna debe Eliyyahu* (for a detailed argument of this position see Berzbach 1999).[6] What might have misled Braude and Kapstein is the fact that the negative form of *derekh eretz* can also have the meaning of unusual, irregular or not the standard way. Consequently its negative form is used as shorthand in rabbinic texts to denote anal sex, generally in cases between a man and a woman, husband and wife. In other words, anal sex is not a standard, regular or customary use of the anus. However, the issue in this passage is not about anal sex, whether inside or outside of marriage, but the customs/mores of the land (*derekh eretz*) of Sodom. Lot offers his daughters to the mob, behaviour in keeping with the ways (*devarim she-hen be- derekh eretz*) of Sodom. By so describing Lot's offer, the text clearly registers strong disapproval. The only mitigating factor in the whole incident might be that Lot is interceding on behalf of his guests, something which is the complete opposite to the normal ways (*devarim she-einan be- derekh eretz*) of Sodom. But the offering of his daughters is considered typical Sodomite behaviour.

Not only does this passage register disapproval of Lot but it also damns him by highlighting the brazenness of the Sodomites. Braude and Kapstein point out that *Eliyyahu* understands that the Sodomites' reply commands Lot to lead the women out to them not merely to stand back. In other words they accept his offer, a reading with which Rashi later concurs. He says, 'Concerning that which (Lot) said to them regarding the daughters, they said to him "Stand back" – a gentle expression' (Rashi 1949: 168). Rashi contrasts this gentleness with the Sodomites' rebuke of Lot for interceding on behalf of his guests. He observes that 'Stand back' can also mean step aside, which, if it is a 'gentle expression', connotes acceptance of Lot's daughters, without relinquishing the demand for his guests. Thus, not only does Lot engage in typical ('natural') Sodomite behaviour, by offering his daughters, but Lot's action was also foolish and ill-considered because the Sodomites accepted it without being deterred from their original intent.

Even Ramban, who gives the most sympathetic treatment to Lot, condemns offering the daughters to the mob in no uncertain terms. For Ramban, this action represents Lot's disgrace showing that he has 'an evil heart'. The offer reveals that Lot is ready to appease the men of the city by abandoning his daughters to prostitution... it shows that the prostitution of women was not repugnant to him, and that in his opinion he would not be doing such great injustice to his daughters (Nahmanides 1971: 251).

---

6. I want to thank Ulrich Berzbach and the following people for their advice on the Hebrew text of this passage: Yoel Kahn, Admiel Kosman, Israel Sandman and Jonathan Schofer.

He reinforces his condemnation by quoting *Tanchuma Vayeira* 12, which states that a man should fight to the death to protect his wife and daughters. What is surprising is that some later rabbis, despite viewing Lot negatively, attempt more generous explanations of the intentions behind his offer. Noteworthy is that none of these explanations employ comparisons between the supposed 'naturalness' of the rape of women vis-à-vis the 'unnaturalness' of male rape as is found in Christian interpretation. Sforno suggests that Lot made the offer, certain that his daughters' fiancés would rise up to defend them from the crowd. The ensuing uproar, Lot hoped, would deter the mob from their original purpose (Sforno 1987: 91). Arama argues that Lot wanted the mob to recognize that he was the one who had breached the city's laws by offering shelter to the angels and that the angels, his guests, were unaware of the import of his action. Therefore Lot 'offered his daughters as expiation for his own disloyal conduct, not as substitute for the strangers' (Arama 1986: 150). However, Arama does not say in what way Lot's daughters were meant to expiate his conduct, that is was he handing them over to be raped, to be punished in his place or as hostages?[7]

e. Lot's Wife

The treatment of Lot's wife, Edis/Edith,[8] in the texts is more ambivalent than that of her husband. Some regard her in a similarly hostile way to her husband, but in others she receives a far more sympathetic treatment. In the *Targumim*, there is disagreement about her character. *Targum Neofiti* is ambivalent, almost sympathetic. It glosses her being turned to salt by pointing out that she was a native of Sodom and looked back to see the fate of her relatives (*Targ. Neof.* Gen. 19.26). Lot's wife is a Sodomite but she looks back out of concern for her family and friends. Such care and concern for others, even kin, is remarkably untypical behaviour for Sodomites in these Jewish texts. On the other hand, *Targum Pseudo-Jonathan* is more hostile to Lot's wife and glosses her fate thus:

> His wife looked behind the angel to know what would be the end of her father's house. She was one of the daughters of the Sodomites, and because she had sinned through salt by publicizing (the presence) of the afflicted ones, behold she was made into a pillar of salt (*Targ. Ps.-Jon.* Gen. 19.26).

7. Some Islamic commentators accept the last option to explain Lot's offer (e.g. Muhammad Ali 1951: 515)

8. Different commentaries employ variant spellings of her name. These spelling variations derive from the different ways of representing Hebrew in Sephardic and Ashkenazic traditions. In my discussion of Lot's wife I will alternate between these variants, employing the form found in the particular text under discussion.

In other words her fate was due recompense for an earlier sin, one involving salt. Nevertheless, the *Targum* gives no details of this incident and how it pertains to salt, nor does it reveal the identity of these 'afflicted ones'. This incident will have particular significance for my discussion, in the following chapter, of Christian readings of Sodom.

This sin of salt recurs in *Genesis Rabbah* (Neusner's translation) where, in three different accounts, Lot's wife is consistently portrayed negatively to typify Sodomite selfishness and inhospitality. In the first account, Lot's wife refuses to offer salt to the angels, the offer of salt being the ritual for welcoming of a guest and extending hospitality. In fact, she is portrayed as quarrelling with Lot over his hospitality to the angels saying '(e)ven that lousy practice (that you learned from Abraham) do you want to teach here?' (*Gen. R.* 50.4.7). Thus, she becomes representative of the inhospitality of Sodom. The second brief account is in the context of the siege of Lot's house. When Lot tells the mob that the angels have come under the shelter of his roof (Gen. 19.6), the midrash explains, 'This (reference to the shelter of *my* roof, thus *mine* and not my wife's) teaches that (Lot's wife) had split up the house on their account, saying to him, "If you want to receive them, receive them in your half"' (*Gen. R.* 50.6.3). Lot's wife thus typifies Sodomite hospitality. When she is turned to salt *Genesis Rabbah* appears to agree with *Pseudo-Jonathan*. It is 'because she sinned through the argument about salt' (*Gen. R.* 51.5.1). Here, salt represents her inhospitable attitude to Lot's guests, the angels, but none of these accounts repeat *Pseudo-Jonathan*'s claim that Lot's wife sinned specifically through publicizing the presence of the 'afflicted ones'. It is apparently unknown to Rashi who draws on *Genesis Rabbah* to build his negative portrait of Lot's wife. For Rashi, Edis is representative of the meanness of spirit that infects the cities of the plain. He declares that Edis is turned to salt because 'by salt she sinned' (Rashi 1949: 177) and cites the midrash in which Lot asked her to give salt to the angels, their guests. He continues that she rebuked him complaining, '(t)his evil custom too you come to institute in this place' (Rashi 1949: 177).

However, in a footnote to the Soncino translation of *Genesis Rabbah* the following account is found:

> On the night that the angels visited Lot, what did she do? She went about to all her neighbours and asked them, 'Give me salt, as we have guests', her intention being that the townspeople become aware of their presence. Therefore, SHE BECAME A PILLAR OF SALT (*Gen. R.* [Soncino] LI, footnote 1).

In other words, then, it is the inhospitality of Lot's wife that triggers all the events of that night. She alerts the townsfolk to the fact that Lot was entertaining guests, a breach of Sodomite law, so that the Sodomites lay siege to Lot's house demanding the angels be brought out to them. As Rashi's commentary shows, this story, relegated to a footnote in the Soncino edition of Genesis Rabbah, was not originally found there. In the Jewish tradition, the story only appears in written form in the Venice printed edition of *Genesis Rabbah* in 1544 and in two midrashic compilations from the thirteenth century, *Yalkut Shimoni* and *Midrash Aggadah* (personal email from Ben Begleiter, 2 December 2001, and E. Pellow, 2 December 2001). The story is not related in any of the commentaries of the other great medieval rabbis after Rashi. In the following chapter, a version of this story will be found to occur in a ninth-century Syriac Christian commentary. The fact that, with the exception of *Targum Pseudo-Jonathan*'s allusion, this Jewish story possibly first appears in a Christian text will prove important for my argument concerning the relationship of Jewish and Christian readings of Genesis 19.

In contrast to this negative portrait of Lot's wife, her treatment in other Jewish texts is neutral and even positive. The *Zohar* neither defames nor justifies her. Instead, it argues that by turning back she saw the face of the destroying angel, who was following them behind. Therein lay the reason for her being turned to salt because 'as long as the destroying angel does not see the face of a man he does not harm him; but as soon as Lot's wife turned her face to look at him she became a pillar of salt' (*Zohar* I.108b). Ibn Ezra merely notes that her 'bones were burned by brimstone and she was encrusted by salt, for it is written, "brimstone and salt...like the overthrow of Sodom and Gomorrah, Admah and Zeboiim" (Deut. 29.22)' (Ibn Ezra 1988: 208). Ramban combines both positions to argue that Edith's fate was not a punishment, but rather shows that looking upon the process of destruction was potentially lethal. He says,

> Looking upon the atmosphere of a plague and all contagious diseases is very harmful, and they may cleave to him... It was for this reason that Lot's wife turned into a pillar of salt for the plague entered her mind when she saw the brimstone and salt which descended upon them from heaven, and it cleaved to her...when G-d destroyed these cities the destroying angel *stood between the earth and heaven* (1 Chron. 21.16), appearing in a flame of fire. Therefore he prohibited them from looking (Nahmanides 1971: 259).

Sforno agrees saying that by looking back the destructive power overtakes and cleaves to the person, as was the case with Edis (Sforno 1987: 92).

In both the *Sefer ha-Yashar* and the *Pirke de Rabbi Eliezer*, Lot's wife is treated more sympathetically and no defamatory moral is drawn from her fate. Indeed, her fate is the tragic result of her maternal concern:

> ...the wife of Lot looked back to see the destruction of the cities, for her compassion was moved on account of her daughters who remained in Sodom, for they did not go with her. And when she looked back she became a pillar of salt, and it is yet in place unto this day (*SY* 19.52-3, see *PRE* XXV: 186).

Edith looks back out of concern for her married daughters who remain in Sodom, in the hope that they might be following behind. As in the *Zohar*, her fate is not a punishment so much as something that would happen, to anyone good or bad, like getting wet when standing in the rain. In that sense hers is a maternal tragedy. Ramban makes this point in his sympathetic account of Edith's fate. Citing *Pirke de Rabbi Eliezer*, he explains that she looks back out of compassion, which 'welled up for her married daughters who were in Sodom' (Nahmanides 1971: 259), to see if they were following behind.

f. *The Rape of Lot*

There is a good narratological reason for Lot's wife being turned to salt. If she had not escaped Sodom then her daughters would not have raped their father and had children by him. Through those children they become foremothers of Ruth and Naamah and through them the royal Davidic lineage and ultimately the Messiah. These messianic implications predominate in rabbinic interpretations of the closing scene of Genesis 19 and will be the main focus of my discussion. However, this incident also provides an opportunity to further denigrate Lot.

Crucial to such denigration is a feature of the Hebrew text of Gen. 19.33, that Lot did not know when his elder daughter lay down or arose. As *Genesis Rabbah* explains, 'There are dots written over the word 'when she arose' meaning that while he did not know when she lay down, he did know when she got up' (*Gen. R.* 51.8.3). The implication is that, while Lot was at first unaware what was happening, he knew when his daughter arose. As he did not let on that he knew of their plan and take efforts to stop the younger daughter, he becomes complicit in what happens. On this basis, *Genesis Rabbah* says, 'it is clear that Lot lusted after his daughter' (*Gen. R.* 51.9.2). Subsequent tradition mostly concurs with *Genesis Rabbah* as Rashi's commentary shows. He cites the point concerning the dots on the word saying that Lot lusted after his daughters (Rashi 1949: 178). Ramban, alone, stands out for his support of Lot. While he acknowledges that rabbinic tradition holds Lot culpable for the incident and condemns him, Ramban argues that Lot's daughters were responsible, not their father. Neither does he condemn them, but argues that they acted thus because they thought that the whole world was destroyed. The older said to the younger, 'Let us do what we can, so that G-d should have mercy, and we shall give birth to a boy and a girl from whom the world shall be sustained, and it is not in vain that G-d has saved us' (Nahmanides 1971: 262-3). They get Lot drunk because 'they were modest and did not want...their father to marry them' (Nahmanides 1971: 263). Furthermore, Ramban points out that 'as a Noachide' Lot 'is permitted his daughter' (Nahmanides 1971: 263). Therefore no wrong was done by any of the actors in this situation.

Ramban might stand alone in his attitude to Lot, but not so with the daughters, as the tradition is far more ambivalent about their role. In *Genesis Rabbah*, while the incest-rape is condemned, at issue is whether the daughters acted out of lust. If not, they are apparently exonerated, and the point is made that 'the girls imagined that the entire world had been destroyed, just as in the generation of the flood' (*Gen. R.* 51.8.1). In that case, theirs is a noble act to preserve the human race as a whole, but the question is left unresolved. *Genesis Rabbah* continues by condemning the elder for unashamedly acknowledging her deed by naming her son, Moab. The younger is not condemned because in naming her son, Ben-Ammi, 'she treated with regard the honour of her father' (*Gen. R.* 51.11.1). This argument is repeated by Rashi who is similarly ambivalent about Lot's daughters. However, while sympathetic to the younger, he clearly does not countenance their actions and refers to the daughters' act as adultery. Nevertheless, he acknowledges that Lot's daughters believe the whole world to have been destroyed, leaving them the only survivors. He adds further that the women break their hymens before raping their father in order to readily conceive as it is difficult for virgins to conceive when they first have sex (Rashi 1949: 179). Such an act demonstrates their good intent in that the sex was purely for procreative purposes. Rashi even accepts that the wine 'was prepared for them in the cave to bring forth two nations' (Rashi 1949: 178) but he doesn't answer the obvious question, prepared by whom? Unlike Rashi, Alshech endorses the daughters who acted 'to maintain the human race' (Alshech 1988: 94). They gave their father a lot of wine because his age required it to give him extra strength to ensure they could conceive. He points out that they experienced no pleasure at all and acted without 'thought of physical gratification' (Alshech 1988: 94). However, Lot became aware of what they were doing on the first night and enjoyed it so much that that he didn't try to stop them on the following night. Instead, he pretended to be overcome by wine. Thus, Alshech defends the women by defaming their father.

The ultimate defence of the daughters is not their motivation but the ultimate results. Through their action, the daughters become the foremothers of Ruth and Naamah and hence the Davidic line and ultimately the Messiah. *Genesis Rabbah* declares, 'What is written is "so that we may preserve offspring through our father" (Gen. 19.31) the king-messiah, who will come from another source' (*Gen. R.* 51.8.2). To underscore this link, *Genesis Rabbah* shares two blocks of text with *Ruth Rabbah*, pertaining to Sodom and Lot's daughters, which elaborate Gen. 14.1-2/Ruth 1.2 and Gen. 19.37/Ruth 3.6 respectively. The latter links Moab's conception with the incident in Numbers 25 where the Israelites take up idolatry through intermarriage with Moabite women. The latter event was one of fornication and gross idolatry whereas 'the conception of Moab…was not for the sake of fornication but for the sake of heaven' (*Gen. R.* 51.10.1, *Ruth R.* 55.1.1). The daughters of Lot acted to preserve the human race and thus become foremothers of the messiah. Another midrash in *Ruth Rabbah* links Obed's birth with both the rape of Lot and the birth of David to reveal the messianic conclusion of each, 'What is written is not "a son" but "seed" and that is "seed" (Gen. 19.32) that comes from another source… (t)he messiah' (*Ruth R.* 81.1.3). Lot's daughters act not for the short-term interest of raising sons for their father but for a more distant objective, raising up the messiah, through a womb (source) yet to come.

In the *Zohar*, the dotted Hebrew word in Gen. 19.33, by which *Genesis Rabbah* argues Lot's complicity, is given a striking messianic twist, 'the word *b'qumah* (when she arose)…is written *plene*, i.e. with the letter *vau*, which moreover, is provided with a dot…to signify that heaven…was an accomplice to the act which ultimately was to bring about the birth of the Messiah' (*Zohar* I.110b). Rather than signifying Lot's complicity, the Hebrew is dotted to show it to be heaven, implying the deity, that was responsible. Of Lot's older daughter, the text goes on to say, citing Ruth 3.4, 'it was on that day that Lot's daughter could be said to have risen to the height of her destiny in that Boaz became attached to one of her lineage, by means of which there were raised from her all those kings and the elect of Israel' (*Zohar* I.110b–111a). The Messiah is the crown of those elect of Israel. Both daughters are praised in the *Midrash ha-Gadol* to Numbers, 'Three were promiscuous, and on their account the world survived; they are Tamar and Lot's two daughters' (*Midrash ha-Gadol*, in *Yemenite Midrash* 4.22). The link to Tamar in Genesis 38 connects the daughters to the messianic lineage. Ostensibly, Lot's daughters acted immorally, promiscuously, but in so doing their actions saved the world.

Even more startling is the comment by the German Kabbalist, Isaiah Horowitz, on the messianic implications of Genesis 19:

> Although what the daughters of Lot did appears as brazen, G'd knew that their motivation was pure. It was…a sin performed for the sake of G'd. If prompt performance of such a dubious act brings such reward in its wake, how much more must one hurry to perform those מצות promptly that are clearly means of sanctifying oneself (Horowitz 1992: 126).

I can think of no stronger endorsement of Lot's daughters than holding them up as emulatory models of Torah observance for all Jews.

g. *Sodom and Gibeah Compared*

As I have observed, references to Gibeah in early rabbinic texts are sparse and it is only from medieval times that the story receives more detailed treatment. Two of these later rabbis, Ramban and Arama, go so far as to compare the two stories and explain at great length why, despite the similarities, there are such radically different outcomes. The answer these rabbis give is surprising for those used to Christian homophobic interpretations. In Gibeah, the men there act solely out of lust and not to intimidate outsiders into staying away. In Sodom's case, the deity acts precisely because the attempted rape of the angels is not just a crime of excessive lust, but is designed to intimidate and oppress outsiders, thus being representative of a deeper systemic cruelty. It is this oppressive and cruel system that arouses the deity's vengeance.

Ramban discusses at length the events of Judges 19 while commenting on the Sodomites' siege of Lot's house to show that the wickedness of Sodom is quite different to that of Gibeah. He argues, first, that all the men of Sodom gathered at Lot's house whereas in Gibeah it was only 'certain base fellows' (Nahmanides 1971: 252). Secondly, deriving from this fact, the Sodomites' siege of Lot's house is representative of the broader systemic evil of Sodom. Ramban stresses,

> Those wicked ones of Gibeah had no intention of stopping people from coming among them. Rather, they were steeped in immorality and desired sexual relations with the wayfarer, and when he brought his concubine out to them, they were satisfied with her (Nahmanides 1971: 252).

> In contrast, the Sodomites acted not out of lust but miserliness 'to stop people from coming among them, as our Rabbis have said, for they thought that because of the excellence of their land…many will come there' (Nahmanides 1971: 250).

Misogyny figures strongly in Ramban's portrait of the concubine and she is blamed for her fate while both the old man and the Levite are exonerated. Thus, the old man offers his virgin daughter because he 'knew that they would not want' her 'and...would not harm her' (Nahmanides 1971: 252). The old man is concerned to save his guest and both he and the Levite hand over the concubine because she did not have 'the status of a man's wife' (Nahmanides 1971: 252). Furthermore, 'she had already played the harlot against him (the Levite)' (Nahmanides 1971: 252). Ramban further repeats the charge that she was a harlot in order to mitigate the actions of the men of Gibeah. Furthermore,

> They did not intend her death, nor did she die at their hands for *they let her go at the approach of dawn* (Jud. 19.25), and she walked from them to her master's house and after that she died, weakened perhaps by her numerous violations, and chilled while lying at the door until it was light (Nahmanides 1971: 253).

Consequently, according to Torah, the men did not deserve the death penalty because all they did was 'torture' the concubine!

Like Pseudo-Philo and the *Talmud*, Ramban understands the resulting war and its progress as a divine punishment of Israel. In Ramban's account, Israel sins by failing to follow the proper procedures laid down by the Torah. Believing that Gibeah had become as bad as Sodom, the Israelites resolved to wipe it out without fully investigating the incident or consulting the tribe of Benjamin, whose responsibility it was to carry such investigation and subsequent awarding of punishment. By not attempting to punish or even rebuke the culprits, Benjamin sinned while 'Israel sinned by making war not in accordance with the law' (Nahmanides 1971: 254).

Arama discusses the events at Gibeah in the context of elucidating the sins of Sodom. He shares Ramban's understanding that the Sodomites are not lustfully motivated but employed rape as a weapon to deter travellers from their land. This abusive behaviour targeting outsiders typified a systemically evil society grounded in cruelty and selfishness. Nevertheless, comparing Gibeah and Sodom, Arama is concerned because

> ...the Benjaminites perpetrated their crime on a fellow Jewess, not against aliens like the men of Sodom in our Parshah. Also, whereas the men of Sodom never had a chance to carry out their evil designs, the men of Givah did in fact execute the heinous deed. Clearly then, Israel sinned more grievously than did Sodom (Arama 1986: 145).

Why then was there no divine intervention with Gibeah when it behaved similarly if not in a worse fashion to the Sodomites? The rapists certainly warranted the severest punishment but, unlike the Sodomites

...they did not deserve a rain of sulphur and brimstone... The men of Givah
...were quite different in that their laws were perfectly good, only they failed
occasionally to live up to the standards of those laws, and gave vent to their
passions (Arama 1986: 147).

Gibeah is subject to the Law of Moses and therefore not a society deliberately structured on injustice as in Sodom. Consequently, Gibeah's crime is
simply one of sexual excess and a breakdown of the Law's application,
unlike Sodom's structured injustice, and therefore not a crime warranting
divine intervention.

4. *Conclusion*

In the Jewish tradition, Sodom's crime is constantly associated with oppression, injustice, greed and hostility towards strangers. These crimes are
often augmented with idolatry and sexual misbehaviour, especially adultery, but these remain secondary and could be expected in a place so
totally evil that it incurs divine retribution. In fact, Sodom is a byword for
selfish, cruel behaviour and not same-sex desire or a penchant for anal sex.
Indeed, it is the judicial murder of young women for the crime of feeding
beggars that prompts the deity to act. In contrast to the Sodomites' attitude towards strangers, Abraham's hospitality is regarded as paradigmatic.
Abraham and the Sodomites are polar opposites with Abraham's hospitality highlighting the crimes of Sodom crying out for divine judgement.

There is great ambivalence towards Lot and his family, with Lot faring
worst of all. He is negatively compared to Abraham and is even said to
impede Abraham's spiritual progress. Lot's choice to settle in Sodom is
seen as an act of apostasy, rejecting both Abraham and the deity. This
separation is necessary for Abraham to fulfil his spiritual destiny. While
some commentators tend to a more generous evaluation of Lot, the most
sympathetic, Ramban, strongly condemns Lot's offering his daughters to
the mob. Similarly, Lot's wife receives an ambivalent treatment. Where
Lot's wife is portrayed negatively such portrayals draw on her fate and make
her symbolic of the evil of Sodom. However, there is a strong counter-
tendency to see her fate as an unfortunate accident. In particular, her fate
is held to be due to her maternal compassion. She looks back to see if her
other daughters are following behind.

On the other hand, there is a strong tendency to endorse Lot's daughters because of the messianic overtones of the rape of their father. Indeed,
in having no qualms to act for the survival of the race, they become models
to be emulated by all Jews in the observance of Torah. Indeed, the daugh-

ters work with heaven and the deity to fulfil their destiny through this sexually transgressive act. This positive understanding comes from awareness
of this incident's place in the overall narrative structure of the Hebrew
Bible. Ruth, of course, is from Moab, the elder daughter's son, and she is
the great-grandmother of David the king and thus foremother of the messiah. Therefore, by raping their father, Lot's daughters initiate the line of
David and Israel's kings that will culminate in the coming of the messiah.

On the outrage at Gibeah, there is a general lack of sympathy for the
concubine. The *Talmud*, alone, softens the story so that she leaves the
Levite due to quarrels with him, suggesting that he was a tyrannical or
abusive husband. The most common position, however, is that she left
to commit adultery and thus her subsequent fate can suggest that 'loose'
women deserve rape. Israel is also condemned for going to war over the
outrage at Gibeah rather than over the incident of Micah's idolatry – for
putting the honour of a concubine above that of the deity. Because it
could be argued that these ensuing events result from the concubine's
adultery, the danger of 'loose' women to the community is reinforced.
Indeed, so disgraceful are these events that the deity has even changed
the order of scripture, putting the story at the end of the book of Judges
instead of at the beginning, where it should be located chronologically, to
mitigate Israel's shame. Concerning the mass rapes in Judges 21, Rashi
brings in an obscenely grotesque image, echoing the wine used to rape
Lot. He also introduces the anti-messianic image of the failed king Saul
amongst the Benjaminite men abducting the virgins at Shiloh, in contrast
to the messianic overtones closing Genesis 19.

Most importantly, two commentators compare the events in Sodom
and Gibeah and each city's fate. They make this comparison questioning
why is there divine intervention in Sodom and Gomorrah but not in
Gibeah, where there no such intervention but a disastrous civil war. The
answer given must come as a surprise to most Christians used to a homophobic reading of Genesis 19. Sodom and Gomorrah had constructed a
social system institutionalizing the abuse and oppression of the poor and
outsider. The attempted rape of the angels was meant to enforce this systemic cruelty. However, the men of Gibeah were not acting out of such
cruel and selfish motives, but were merely carried away by their lust.

It must be remembered that many of these rabbinic commentators lived
and wrote in the broader world of Christendom. I find it noteworthy that,
despite being a minority in a Christian world, they opted not to import the
Christian homophobic interpretation of Genesis 19, even though Jewish
tradition contained some associations of Sodom and Gomorrah with sexual excess. While it is clear that the rabbis do not approve of male-male

sex, it is not behaviour warranting divine intervention. The deity is only moved by structured injustice and divine retribution is only visited upon societies that abuse the poor and outsider. Perhaps it should come as no surprise that this concern for proper treatment of the weak and the outsider should be the primary message Judaism gained from Genesis 19. Christians have always read their Bibles at home, whereas Jews have had to read Torah as outsiders in exile.

In contrast, Christians will use Genesis 19 to create a whole new class of outsiders based on sexual orientation. In the remaining chapters, I will outline how Christians turn Sodom's abuse of the poor and outsiders into a sex crime. It will be important to bear in mind two points as we proceed. First, early Christians shared these Jewish understandings of Sodom and Gomorrah. The Christian homophobic reading marks a shift in interpretation that takes place over many centuries. As the homophobic reading becomes dominant some Christian exegetes remained aware of these Jewish readings but opted to ignore them. Eventually no Christian voices dissent from the homophobic consensus. Secondly, and with tragic irony, given these Jewish readings, medieval Christian phobic fantasies of an organized underground of sexual outlaws, the Sodomite counter-society, will be derived from Christian anti-Semitic constructions of the Jewish Other, the counter-culture within Christendom.

Chapter 5

TOWARDS SODOMY:
SODOM AND GIBEAH IN THE CHRISTIAN ECUMEN

1. *Rehearsing Sodomy*

Having surveyed the literature of the Second Temple period and of rabbinic Judaism, I now turn to the world of Christianity. In this chapter I will discuss a wide variety of texts from the Ecumenical Church of the first Christian millennium. Most of these texts come from the first six Christian centuries with the exception of some later eastern Christian material, including a ninth-century Syriac exegete. I must remind the reader that my analysis of the interpretation of Genesis 19 and Judges 19–21 is focused on the role homophobia plays in that interpretation. I am not studying the acceptance or rejection of same-sex desire and homoerotic relationships, *per se*, in early Christianity (or rabbinic Judaism, for that matter). In Christianity, the story of Sodom becomes caught up with the history of homophobia through the development of what I term the homophobic reading of the narrative. This reading emerges by the fourth century and eventually gives birth, in the eleventh-century Latin West, to the word/concept of *sodomy* (cf. Jordan 1997). In the history of homophobia, this is an event of profound consequences, under the shadow of which we still live. Nevertheless, the medieval invention of sodomy is an event rehearsed on a number of occasions in this earlier period. The name of Sodom is used to denote a type of person who is not a resident of the city, or an abstract behavioural pattern, understood to be exemplified by the city. This chapter is partially structured around four such rehearsals. While only one of these clearly anticipates the homophobic intent of the final medieval achievement, all represent Christian reading processes that will culminate in the medieval birth of sodomy.

2. *The Evil City, Strange House Guests, Spiritual Models*

I will begin with a number of Christian texts that do not specifically associate Sodom with sex. I have ordered my discussion around three themes in order to identify certain processes in these texts. The first deals with Sodom as the archetypal evil or ruined city cursed by the deity for its misdeeds. The second theme I call 'strange houseguests': just who is staying the night with Lot? Does Lot entertain angels, or something more Awesome? Finally, I explore a number of texts that read the characters of the story, particularly Lot and Lot's wife, as exemplars for the faithful and, more pertinently, for monastics. Husband and wife represent contrasting behaviours, one positive, one negative. Of course, implicit in these discourses is a third exemplar, Sodom itself. The evil city, which attacks and rejects messengers from heaven, exemplifies the life of sin and ungodliness. Consequently, its inhabitants represent those who embrace such a life. In such contexts the very name of Sodom and its inhabitants can be used figuratively to signify the ungodly life, resulting in sodomy's first rehearsal – to denote not homoeroticism, but arrogant self-indulgence and luxurious living.

Given the spectacular nature of its demise, it should not come as a surprise that various Christian apocryphal apocalypses in the first three centuries contain references to Sodom. In these texts the city appears mostly as a place of unspecified wickedness. Thus, in the *Ascension of Isaiah* 3.10, Isaiah is accused before King Manasseh of comparing Jerusalem to Sodom and Gomorrah. To defame David's city in such a way is a capital offence, and Isaiah's trial is presented to foreshadow the trial of Jesus and his own condemnation of Jerusalem. Similar themes are found in *5 Ezra*. Here Israel is presented as the people rejected by the deity in favour of Christians. Israel has been cursed and scattered among the nations and Sodom serves as a sign of such abjection. In *5 Ezra* 2.7-9, Sodom and Gomorrah, in Jewish tradition the cities destroyed for rejecting and abusing the outcast, are inverted to serve as a warning to any who would give shelter and succour to outcast Israel. Sodom is employed in a similar anti-Jewish fashion in *Christian Sibyllines* 6.20-25 where Jerusalem is likened to Sodom for rejecting Christ.

The theme of hospitality possibly occurs in a further reference found in the *Acts of Paul*, in a passage that only exists in damaged form. It is part of a speech Paul gives in Sidon:

> ...(after) the manner of strange men. Why do you presume to do things that are not seemly? Have you not heard of that which happened, which God brought upon Sodom and Gomorrah, because they robbed... (*Acts of Paul* 5).

The Sidonians are warned by Paul that they are behaving similarly to the Sodomites in their reception of the Apostle. The references to 'strange men' and unseemly behaviour initially seem to be sexual references. It also appears that Sodom and Gomorrah are condemned because of theft. If the theme here were theft, this would echo the rabbinic stories of the Sodomites as robbers of travellers. The rest of this section gives no further clues except that Paul and his companions are seized by the crowd and imprisoned in the temple of Apollo. So perhaps there is a theme of hospitality here, the Sidonians violently rejecting the apostle. Perhaps, too, there is an allusion here to the references in Lk. 10.1-17 and Mt. 10.5-15 where Jesus sends the disciples out on a preaching mission and charges them to warn those towns that refuse them that they will fare worse than Sodom and Gomorrah. In none of these references is sex associated with the story, but it is clear that, however they will develop the story, the new Christian movement is morbidly entranced by the disaster story of Sodom, the city destroyed by the deity for its sins.

Sodom can be used in Christian polemics, not only to prefigure Jerusalem and the Jews but also to 'prove' Christian trinitarian claims as well. In so doing, something strange happens to Lot's guests such that the reader is left wondering whether it is merely angels that Lot receives or whether both he and his uncle entertain the Trinity or the pre-existent Christ. One implication of such readings is that when the Sodomites attack Lot and his guests they are actually attacking the deity in the form of the pre-existent Christ.

This process can be clearly identified in Justin Martyr who uses the Sodom story to score points against the Jews. One example occurs in his *First Apology* where Justin holds up Sodom and Gomorrah as a type of Israel rejecting its Messiah, except for a remnant represented by Lot and his daughters: 'All the Gentiles were desolate of the true God...but the Jews and Samaritans, having been given the word of God by the Prophets, and having always awaited the coming of Christ, did not recognize Him...except a few...' (*First Apology* 53 [1948: 91]).[1] Using Jer. 9.26 and the reference to Sodom in Isa. 1.9, Justin Martyr develops his theme that the embrace of Christianity by the Gentiles and its rejection by the Jews was foretold in the Jewish scriptures themselves (*First Apology* 53). However, he does not detail the nature of the 'impiety' of Sodom and Gomorrah and, despite the reference to Lot's daughters, neither does Justin Martyr discuss the events of Gen. 19.30 following.

In his *Dialogue with Trypho*, Justin Martyr twice uses the story of Sodom and Gomorrah as part of his anti-Jewish polemic. In the first instance, in chapter 19, he argues against the necessity of circumcision citing Abel, Enoch, Noah, Melchizedek and Lot as examples of men pleasing in the sight of God who were uncircumcised. He says of Lot that the 'Lord and His angels led Lot

---

1.   Many of the patristic translations that I cite, as in the case of Justin here, do not provide number and line/verse identification. Citations will be by title and chapter of the work followed by date and page number of the translation cited.

out of Sodom; thus was he saved without circumcision' (*D. Try.* 19 [1948: 176]). However, in this text, Justin is also concerned to develop a scriptural basis for trinitarian theology and to show how the pre-existent Christ, Son of the Father, is revealed in the Hebrew scriptures. In so doing he ventures into some strange territory concerning the question of just who it was Lot received as guests that night. In ch. 56 of *Dialogue with Trypho*, Justin uses the deity's appearance to Abraham at Mamre to argue that the divinity and pre-existence of Christ are revealed in the Jewish scriptures. Trypho states traditional Jewish interpretation that the deity appeared to Abraham before he saw the three visitors. In response to Trypho's challenge, Justin Martyr proceeds to directly quote Gen. 18.13-14, 16-17, 20-23; 18.33–19.1; 19.10, 16-26 and concludes:

> Do you not see...that one of the three, who is both God and Lord, and ministers to Him who is in heaven, is Lord of the two angels? When they went on to Sodom, he stayed behind and talked with Abraham... Then He went His way after His conversation... And when He came to Sodom, it was no longer the two angels, but He Himself, who talked with Lot... (*D. Try.* 56 [1948: 237]).

It is not clear from Justin Martyr when this Lord enters Sodom and whether or not he was in Lot's house when the mob made their assault. However, given that Justin nowhere specifies the crime of Sodom, it can be argued that if the Lord is in the city and in Lot's company, then, when the Sodomites attack Lot's house, they are attacking the deity in the form of the pre-existent Christ. This understanding can be further developed into an anti-Jewish reading of Sodom in which it prefigures the rejection of the human Christ in Jerusalem and his handing over to the Romans for execution.

This trinitarian reading of events in Genesis 18–19 emerges also in Prudentius' poem, *The Divinity of Christ*. For Prudentius, Gen. 19.24, 'the Lord rained fire from the Lord', is a clear indication of the plural nature of the deity. Sodom is destroyed by the joint action of the Father and the Son, the Son making manifest the will of the Father. Athanasius makes the same point both in his *Discourses against the Arians* (*Contra Arianos* 2.15.13) and in *De Synodis* (*De Synodis* 27.18; 49). Novatian repeats this theme in his work on the Trinity going so far as to say that it was God the Son Abraham entertained at Mamre (*Trin.* 13-14), a point repeated by Paulinus of Nola (*Letter* 23.40). Caesarius of Arles in his 83rd Sermon reads the three angels who appeared to Abraham as a type of the Trinity whom Abraham 'adored... as one' (83.4). He extols Abraham's hospitality and warns 'listen to this, brethren, if you are unwilling to exercise hospitality and to receive even your enemy as a guest' (83.4). He compares Abraham to Lot in a way that recalls Philo's divine triad/dyad dichotomy in his own commentary on Genesis. However, Caesarius views Lot more favourably than Philo and states that the deity descended to Sodom 'not in order to know what they are doing, but to make them worthy if I find any of them just, repentant, or such as I should know' (83.7). Lot was the only such person and Caesarius concludes with a prayer that his congregation similarly earns such divine attention and recognition.

Caesarius' prayer for his congregation to be found as worthy as Lot of divine recognition represents a final theme, the use of the story to develop exemplary models for Christian behaviour. This use focuses particularly around the dyad of Lot and his wife as positive and negative exemplars, a process identified in the New Testament writings themselves (Lk. 17. 26-32). The oldest such example outside the New Testament is found in *1 Clement* 11. Here, a summary of the events of Genesis 19, focusing on Lot as exemplar, occurs amongst a list of exemplary models for Christians from the Old Testament narratives. The list includes Noah, Enoch, Abraham and Rahab.

> Lot, for his hospitality and his piety, was brought safely out of Sodom, when fire and brimstone were raining down in judgement on all the region round about. Moreover, on that occasion the Lord made it plain that, while He never forsakes those who place their hopes in Him, He visits pains and penalties on the rebellious; and as a sign of this, Lot's wife, who had accompanied him in his flight, but later changed her mind and fell out with him, was turned into a pillar of salt to this day (*1 Clem.* 11).

This passage contains two themes that will recur in other texts. Lot is rescued from Sodom 'for his hospitality and piety' and is held up as an example of those who place their trust in the deity, while Lot's wife becomes a pillar of salt because she 'changed her mind' in 'doubt and distrust of God's power'. Clement's list of Old Testament exemplars, gives priority to the virtue of hospitality, as he does here with Lot. Only Noah and Enoch are not associated with this virtue. Clement says of Abraham that it 'was because of his faith and his hospitality that a son was given him in his old age' (*1 Clem.* 9). Rahab, the prostitute in Jericho, 'owed her preservation to her faith and hospitality' (*1 Clem.* 12). Apart from his reading of Lot's wife, Clement's stress on hospitality rewarded and the identification of hospitality as one of Abraham's main virtues all appear in subsequent rabbinic exegesis, as we have seen. Furthermore, the medieval rabbi Nahmanides cites the case of Rahab in a similar context. As *1 Clement* is dated to the first century CE, the appearance of these rabbinic themes here would indicate that they have a very ancient basis indeed.

Reading Lot as a positive model, of course, can have quite dubious moral effects, as evidenced in the *Apocalypse of Paul*, where Lot is twice presented as a worthy model of hospitality (*Apoc. Paul* 27 and 49). In the second instance, Lot's offer of his daughters to the Sodomites is particularly cited as an example of his righteous hospitality. Lot has no qualms about this and actually boasts, 'I offered to them my two virgin daughters who had never known men, and gave to them saying: Use them as you wish, so long as you do nothing evil to these men' (*Apoc. Paul* 49). Lot's offer is here justified simply by the demands of hospitality. Similarly, Paulinus of Nola can declare 'Lot, Abraham and Job' to be 'examples of how such men put no love of property or relatives before the love and teaching of the Lord' (*Letter* 24.2).

However, it is his rescue and flight from Sodom, not the offering of his daughters, that forms the basis of most of the positive evaluations of Lot. Conversely the fate of Lot's wife establishes her as the negative pole of this exemplary dyad. Thus, Leander of Seville, in *The Training of Nuns*, compares the nun to Lot who was taken by the deity out of Sodom. Lot's wife, on the other hand, is held up as a warning for nuns who have not fully committed themselves to the religious life but keep looking back to the life they left behind (*Inst. Virg.* 31). Similarly John Cassian, in his *Conferences*, twice refers to Lot as a model for monks, both for his hospitality (*Conferences* 8.23) and his persistence in entreaty (and thus prayer) when he pressed his hospitality on the angels (*Conferences* 17.25). Athanasius, in his *Life of Antony*, presents Lot's wife and her fate as an example of those who look back from the spiritual life to the ways they left behind (*Vita Antoni* 20). Cyprian cites Lk. 17.31-32, along with the Genesis account of her fate, to use Lot's wife as a warning against backsliding in face of persecution (*Ad Fortunatus* 5.7).

These images recur in Prudentius' other poem, *Origin of Sin (Hamartigenia)*, which contains an extensive account of the destruction of Sodom. Lot's wife is presented as a 'fickle woman' who 'clung to her dear Sodom's luring charms' (*Ham.* 739-40) while Lot is described as a man of 'resolution firm' (*Ham.* 757). What is also striking is that, while Prudentius gives extensive treatment to Sodom, going into most lurid detail on the destruction of the city and the fate of Lot's wife, he nowhere makes any sexual allusions in his account. I can only conclude from Prudentius and the other texts discussed in this section that not all the early Christians understood the story of Sodom as one primarily concerning sexual sin.

Of all the early Christian writers, Irenaeus is the most idiosyncratic in his reading of the story, both in his positive reading of the rape of Lot and his positive reading of Lot's wife and her fate. On the rape of Lot, Irenaeus recognizes that scripture does not condemn what takes place. He is also concerned that latter day moralists should not condemn what scripture does not condemn, while ensuring that this lack of condemnation does not lead to libertinism. Irenaeus points out that Lot had no control over the events and did not will or plan what happened with his daughters. Lot's daughters, on the other hand, acted with the best of intentions out of 'simplicity and innocence... for the preservation of the human race' (*Adv. Haer.* 4.31.2). He then proceeds to read the rape of Lot as a type of the Christ event with Lot's daughters representing the two 'synagogues' of Jews and Gentiles and Lot himself representing Christ. He does so in a manner resembling Jewish midrash, weaving Lot and the Christ event together, employing Mt. 11.19, Ps. 3.6 and Jer. 31.26. Irenaeus reads Gen. 19.30 following as a seduction scene or an erotic waking dream where the boundaries of reality and fantasy blur. Lot represents Jesus, the incarnate Word, who comes eating and drinking with humanity. The daughters are read as types of Gentile and Jewish humanities (the two churches or assemblies). The Christ event is then interpreted as a type of human seduction of the Divine from which are generated Christians, 'living sons to the living God'. And while Irenaeus' erotic interpretation of the Christ event might surprise many Christians, we have already seen in Jewish midrash the recognition, that through raping their father, Lot's daughters inaugurate the line of the Messiah.

However, Irenaeus' reading of the fate of Lot's wife is more surprising still, considering how negatively she has been read by Christians, for he understands her as a type of the Church:

> ...his wife remained in (the territory of) Sodom, no longer corruptible flesh, but a pillar of salt which endures for ever; and by those natural processes which appertain to the human race, indicating that the church also, which is the salt of the earth, has been left behind within the confines of the earth, and subject to human sufferings; and while entire members are often taken away from it, the pillar of salt endures, thus typifying the foundation of the faith which maketh strong, and sends forward, children to their Father God (*Adv. Haer.* 4.31.3).

There is a tradition that the pillar of salt that was Lot's wife remains in the region of Sodom. Josephus (*Ant.* I.203) claimed to have seen it himself and similarly in *1 Clement* it is said that the pillar remains 'to this day' (*1 Clem.* 11). Irenaeus links this tradition to the gospel saying from the Sermon on the Mount in Mt. 5.13 where Jesus calls his disciples 'salt of the earth'. Thus, rather than being a sign of disgrace, Lot's wife, the pillar of salt, represents the Church constantly enduring in the world. Lot's wife is not dead but is still alive and fertile, because, although a pillar of salt, she still menstruates. Like her, the Church is fertile and, like her, the Church is left behind by her children. But the Church is greater than she because the Church still produces children that 'go on to the Father'. However, the menstruating pillar of salt that is Lot's wife attests to the fertility and fecundity of the Church.

Irenaeus is the only Christian to give any sort of positive reading of Lot's wife. While he stands very early in Christian interpretive trajectories, such priority does not privilege his reading of her in subsequent traditions. Ultimately, she is the one who looks back on cities cursed by the deity. So for Christians, if her husband is the model of one who flees evil, she will stand as the one who cannot quite let go of the sinful life and therefore perishes. But Lot's wife and her husband are not the only models in the story. Implicit in such exemplary readings is the idea that the Sodomites themselves represent another category: those who have embraced the ungodly life and ignore any exhortations to abandon it. In a monastic setting, the godly life is the ascetic life and Sodom represents the antithesis, a life of indulgent ease. It is precisely in such a context that the first semantic move is made to employ the name Sodom figuratively to represent something other than the city destroyed in Genesis 19 or its inhabitants. Nilus is indicative of a process in early Christianity by which names and characters from the Hebrew Scriptures come to figuratively represent abstract concepts and thus make the Hebrew Bible a Christian one. Writing briefly to a deacon, Tapiscus, the fifth-century abbot, St Nilus, invokes the Sodomites as the archetype of those who pursue a worldly life of self-indulgence and ease. He cites Ezek. 16.49, saying that Sodom grew proud and arrogant through its indulgence and fullness of bread. He draws a contrast to those nourished on the bread of knowledge. The sodomitic soul – *sodomoumenē psuchē* – rejects them and finds them hard to bear (*PG* 79: 424B). The word, *sodomoumenē*, which I have rendered as 'sodomitic', is, according to Lampe's *Patristic Greek Lexicon*, a form of *Sodomeomai*, which he translates as 'be lapped in luxury' (Lampe 1968: 1244) and so Lampe would translate the phrase as 'the soul lapped in luxury'. The Latin translation of Nilus renders *sodomoumenē* as 'quae aeque ac Sodoma' (*PG* 79: 423B) or 'living just as did Sodom'. While Nilus might be the first to coin a word that could be translated 'sodomitic', it is important to note that this word does not signify sexual sin but rather arrogant self-indulgence and luxurious living. He demonstrates that a Christian word, sodomy, did not necessarily have to have a sexual meaning and clearly didn't in the fifth-century Greek Christian world.

3. *Sodom the Sexual City, Developing Sodomy*

Although in the fifth century Nilus can employ a word derived from Sodom, *sodomoumenē*, with no specifically sexual meaning, a process is already under-

way in his day for Christians to read the story primarily for its sexual significance. The first such explicit sexual associations with the story of Sodom are
found in Christian writings of the third and fourth centuries CE and will come
to predominate in Christian readings. We have already seen the characters of
Lot, Lot's wife and the Sodomites themselves being used to represent various
aspects of the godly and ungodly life. In the monastic world, especially,
Sodom comes to represent the old corrupt life that one leaves behind, a trope
that might also have had a broader resonance in early Christianity, being a
minority missionary religion for which conversion was a regular experience.
For the novice monastic especially, the old life left behind includes sexuality,
something precluded in the new celibate life. It is not a big step, then, to read
the story of Sodom as an example of divine displeasure at sexual misconduct.
Hand in hand with this process comes a growing identification of a specific
form of sexual misconduct meriting severe divine condemnation, namely
male to male sex. Because the story of Sodom is a disaster story, there is also a
growing tendency to regard homosexual behaviour as something that invites
disasters on human society. What is striking, in reading these texts, is that
homosexual behaviour is not seen as aberrant or deviant but as a potentiality
within everyone. It arises when people give themselves over to rich indulgent
living, something with which Sodom is already primarily associated, and
the resulting excessive pleasure and passion. Thus, there is a further impera-
tive for curbing sexuality, preferably through following the celibate life.

Most of these elements are found in Clement of Alexandria's *Christ the
Educator*, which represents the earliest Christian use of Sodom in a sexual
context. Clement regards the story as an educative model for all time,
particularly about the need to keep control of sexuality. He says that the
Sodomites

> were people driven headlong upon the shoals of immorality through much
> self-indulgence, for they committed fornication without restraint, and were
> continually inflamed by their frenzied passion for the objects of their lust.
> The all-seeing Word…inflicted punishment upon these sinners, lest…their
> sin turn into a torrent of unbridled licentiousness (*Christ. Ed.* 3.8.43-44).

While Clement does not specifically mention homoeroticism, he regards the
incident outside Lot's house as due to free rein being given to sexuality latent
within everyone. Such behaviour is highly offensive to the deity and so Sodom
is rightly destroyed, both as an example to others and to check the disease of
unbridled passion.

Other references to Sodom as the city destroyed because of its lust are
found in Gregory of Nazianzus (*Rebus* 480-1) and Pseudo-Titus (*NT Apoc.* 2:
150). In his treatise, *On Virginity*, Gregory of Nyssa cites the fate of Sodom

and Lot's wife as warning exemplars for those monastics who do not master their passions (*On Virginity* 4 [1967: 25]). John Cassian, in his *Institutes*, uses Sodom as a warning against a life of pleasure and gluttony because he sees these as giving rise to unrestrained lust.

> The cause of the overthrow and wantonness of Sodom was not drunken-
> ness through wine, but fulness of bread… And because through fulness of
> bread they were inflamed with uncontrollable lust of the flesh, they were
> burnt up by God with fire and brimstone from heaven (*Institutes* 5.6).[2]

Cassian here clearly demonstrates the association, in early Christian thought, of sexual excess with a rich and indulgent lifestyle.

All these texts I have referred to so far mention lust and sex in general. However, from the fourth century, references occur that explicitly cite male to male sex as prominently or primarily implicated in Sodom's fate. The *Apostolic Constitutions* declares that 'the sin of Sodom is contrary to nature' (*Apost. Const.* 6.18) and cites Lev. 18.22 in support, the first occasion when the Levitical proscriptions on male-male sex are linked to the story of Sodom. In the *Apocalypse of Paul*, the seer, on a tour of hell, sees a group of people caught in a river of fire, tar and brimstone: 'And I asked: Who are these, sir? And he said to me: They are those who have committed the iniquity of Sodom and Gomorrah, men with men' (*Apoc. Paul* 40). Thus, male-male sex is identified as the sin of Sodom.

Similarly, Paulus Orosius states that Sodom and its fellow cities had an abundance of blessings, which gave rise to luxury and 'out of luxury grew such disgraceful passions that men rushed upon men committing base acts' (*Against the Pagans* 1.5). This situation arouses divine wrath resulting in the destruction of the cities. But Orosius goes further and compares the fate of Sodom to the invasion of Rome by the Goths seeing both as equivalent divine punishments for sin. He concludes: 'I warn these of this very fate of the people of Sodom and Gomorrah, that they may be able to learn and understand how God has punished sinners, how He can punish them, and how He will punish them' (*Against the Pagans* 1.6). Sodom and Gomorrah are the archetype of cities and societies suffering divine punishment for sin. Divine intervention in Sodom is a pattern recurring throughout

---

2.   Boswell cites the first part of this text as evidence that Cassian 'rejected or ignored the supposed homosexual import of Sodom's fall and claimed that it was occasioned by gluttony' (Boswell 1980: 98). Whether or not Cassian saw a homosexual import to Sodom's fate it is clear that he does see unbridled sexuality as causing Sodom's fall. Gluttony led to unrestrained lust, which called down the wrath of God. Therefore I must disagree with Boswell on his reading of Cassian.

history and explains the fate of Rome, which was punished for allowing the same sins as were practised in Sodom.

Salvian the Presbyter makes a similar politico-historical application in his treatise, *The Governance of God*. He states that Sodom and Gomorrah were destroyed because of their obscene lusts (*Gub. Dei* 1.8). Further on in the treatise he compares Rome to Sodom particularly because of homo-eroticism: 'effeminacy had long been considered a virtue rather than a vice by the Romans' (*Gub. Dei* 7.20). He focuses on the fate of the province of Africa. The Africans who were 'never able to conquer the Romans in power and greatness, have now surpassed them in impurity' (*Gub. Dei* 7.17). Salvian clearly refers to homoeroticism because he speaks of turning men into women, adding that 'the abominable mixture of a few effeminate men infects almost the greatest portion of the population' (*Gub. Dei* 7.19). Thus, like Sodom, Rome has been punished by the barbarian invasions. In Africa's case, it was particularly felicitous that they were occupied by the Vandals because: 'The great and particular merit of the Vandal people is not only that they themselves are not stained by pollution, but that they have made provision that not even others are ever polluted' (*Gub. Dei* 7.21). The Vandals are not only the agents of divine retribution but they also act as restorers of purity and morality. It is important to note here that Salvian (like Orosius) does not associate homoeroticism with the Other, the barbarians. It is something endemic to the Romans, almost like a disease, which can infect an entire population.

These gathering themes around the story of Sodom have a civil impact in the reign of Justinian, who issued two *novellae* against homosexual behaviour. The first, issued in 538, condemns homosexual behaviour to ensure 'that the city and the state may not come to harm by reason of such wicked deeds' because the scriptures say 'that because of like impious conduct cities have indeed perished, together with the men in them' (*nov.* 77, cited Bailey 1955: 73, 74). The second *novella* in 544, the year following a great plague that struck Constantinople, similarly declares,

> ...instructed by the Holy Scriptures, we know that God brought a just judgement upon those who lived in Sodom, on account of this very madness of intercourse... If, with eyes as it were blinded, we overlook such impious and forbidden conduct, we may provoke the good God to anger and bring ruin upon all... (*nov.* 141, cited Bailey 1955: 74, 75).

Same-sex desire and homosexual behaviour caused the destruction of Sodom and Gomorrah by arousing the divine anger. In Justinian's day, as Orosius and Salvian testify, the fall of the western Empire to the barbarians was understood to be due to the divine anger being aroused against the free expression of homoeroticism permitted in Old Rome. As emperor in the east, Justinian is determined that Constantinople, the New Rome, will not suffer the fate of the old, let alone that of Sodom.

Finally, in Old Rome itself, in the years after Justinian, Gregory the Great, administrator, monk, politician, pope and Doctor of the Church entrenches for the western tradition the sexual and homophobic associations of the story. For Gregory, Sodom clearly represents sexuality unbound. Citing Lot's example, he declares in his *Pastoral Care (Regula Pastoralis)* that to 'flee burning Sodom is to shun the sinful fires of the flesh', while 'the mountain height is the purity of those who are continent' (*Reg. Past.* 3.27). Lot in Zoar represents those who, in marriage, are 'not proceeding as far as the mountains' but 'relinquish a reprehensible life' and 'do not attain to perfection in conjugal continence' (*Reg. Past.* 3.27). In his *Dialogues*, he declares that the very means of Sodom's destruction, fire and sulphur, signify that it was sexual sin that incurred the divine wrath: 'Because they were consumed with carnal lust, they perished in fire and fumes…the fire burned them while the fumes of sulphur killed them' (*Dialogue* 4.39). Sulphur and fire represent the sins of the flesh. In his *Moralia in Job*, Gregory explains why they are appropriate. He argues that fire is fuelled by sulphur and is fed by the most noxious fumes. What else can sulphur represent but sins of the flesh, which render souls noxious and noisome? A soul filled with perverse (*perversis*) thoughts is a soul filled with the most noxious fumes and is, thus, ready to feed eternal fire. He continues:

> Sulphur signifies well the stench of the flesh, to which the very history in Sacred Scripture testifies, when it relates that the Lord poured down a rain of fire and sulphur upon Sodom. He had decided to punish her (Sodom) for sins of the flesh and the very nature of his vengeance designates the filth for which she is accused. Obviously sulphur has the foulness and fire, the burning torment (*Mor. Job* 14.19.23).

Gregory's argument is that the nature of the punishment matches, and reveals, the crime. Sulphur shows how foul are sins of the flesh and Sodom committed such sins of the flesh because it was destroyed by sulphur. Fire is also appropriate because it represents the burning of uncontrolled desire. This argument really reveals that for Gregory and his audience, that Sodom was destroyed for sexual iniquity is taken for granted.

Gregory never gives any specific details of these sins of the flesh, but his language uses terms such as 'unlawful' and, most frequently, 'perverse' and 'depraved' (*perversa* and *pravae*). He points out that the Sodomites are possessed by depraved (*pravae*) thoughts and perverse (*perversa*) pleasures of the flesh have dominion in their souls. The souls of such people are constantly giving off sulphur (*Mor. Job* 14.19.23). By employing the language of perverse excess to describe the sins of Sodom, Gregory most likely denotes same-sex desire. Certainly, that is how subsequent tradition has understood his meaning. In one of his letters, Gregory addresses the issue of a subdeacon charged with idolatry and a sexual crime. He says, in identifying the latter, that the subdeacon has committed a crime no different in evil from idolatry for he has stained himself with the sin of the Sodomite – *sodomitae illum scelere maculatum* (*Regist. Epist.* 10.2). Jordan points out that scribal error in later centuries will render 'of the Sodomite' as 'of Sodomy' so that some dictionaries will 'record Gregory's letter as the first appearance of the abstract term 'Sodomy'… (i)n fact it is not' (Jordan 1997: 36).

The invention of Sodomy will not occur for several centuries, but it is already implicit in Christian interpretations of Genesis 19. The previous section has shown that combining the paradigm of the city destroyed for its sins with a tendency to read the characters in the story as representing types of behaviour can generate the notion of the sodomitic soul. This soul represents the contrasting Other to whatever good a writer or community aspires to as an ideal. In the monastery it is the simple austerity of the ascetic life that Nilus elevates and promotes by contrasting it with the Sodomite lapped in luxury. The application of erotophobia and homophobia to this process will lead eventually to Sodomy as we understand it today.

4. *From Inhospitality to Homoeroticism*

Judaism understood Sodom's crime to be inhospitality and abuse of outsiders. References to Lot's paradigmatic hospitality in *1 Clement* and elsewhere indicate that early Christians originally shared this perspective. Here I will chart the shift from the focus on inhospitality, primarily represented by Origen, to one where Sodom is paradigmatic of the evil of same-sex desire. Even in this sexualizing process, the homophobic interpretation was not inevitable. Tertullian, for example, uses Sodom to warn against (re)marriage and to advocate the celibate life. Basil uses Sodom's example to caution his monks to adhere to celibacy and to restrain their same-sex desire, but believes Sodom's homoeroticism was a consequence of a deeper disorder, gluttony, which gives rise to excessive and self-indulgent living. John Chrysostom first clearly expounds the homophobic reading by grafting it on to the traditional concern for hospitality. Same-sex desire represents a fundamental spiritual disorder that gives rise to all manner of personal and societal evil. This reading is rapidly taken up in the Latin West and Augustine finally makes the story paradigmatic of uncontrolled sexuality. Sexual desire itself is an evil and must always be subject to control, personal and social. Augustine will also demonstrate some of the fundamental moral quandaries underpinning the homophobic reading. I will finally consider the literary world of Syriac Christianity as it is crucial to my subsequent discussion of Gibeah. Syriac exegesis will be shown to retain the focus on inhospitality and abuse of outsiders in reading Genesis 19.

a. *Tertullian*

Tertullian refers to the story of Sodom in several writings. He was a polemicist, and the references to Sodom, Lot, the angels, Lot's wife and so on serve to underscore and illustrate his points in debates with others. Nowhere does he specify the sin of Sodom. Occasionally he employs the image of Sodom in discussions of sex, but his point is to stress the virtue of celibate life over and against marriage, not sexual excesses or same-sex desire. Reading Tertullian, one gets the impression that even marriage itself is a thing of Sodom.

In his use of Sodom, Tertullian evinces most of the main Christian themes seen so far, except for homophobia. Thus, he knows Sodom and Gomorrah as cities destroyed on account of their wickedness. Because of their sins, Sodom and Gomorrah are now ashes and the sea and soil about them continue to experience 'a living death' (*Pall.* 2.4, 44). Their devastation shows what happens to those who do not repent (*Ieun.* 7.282, 20) and they have been burnt up 'with a tempest of fire' (*Adv. Marc.* 4.29.523). He also draws on Isa. 1.10 to remind his readers that the Jews and their rulers were compared to Sodom and Gomorrah (*Adv. Marc.* 3.13.398; *Adv. Iud.* 9.94). In a similar vein, Lot's delivery from Sodom 'was for the merits of righteousness, without observance of the law' (*Adv. Iud.* 2.90) thus demonstrating that the Law of Moses is not necessary for salvation.

Tertullian uses the story to make a variety of theological and Christological points. The deity does not descend to Sodom and Gomorrah (Gen. 18.21) out of ignorance[3] but rather the words, 'I will go down', express the force of the divine wrath and are meant to awaken the fear of the hearer (*Adv. Marc.* 2.25.371). Tertullian employs Gen. 19.24 ('And the Lord rained on Sodom and Gomorrah sulphur and fire from heaven from the Lord') Christologically to show that Christ, as pre-existent Word distinct from the Father, is known in the Old Testament (*Ad. Prax.* 13.247, 21). Furthermore, it was the Son who rested with Abraham under the oaks at Mamre (*Ad. Prax.* 16.256, 21). That the divine Word became truly human in the flesh is shown by the fact that the angels lead Lot by the hand. They had been transformed into human form, in human flesh, when they came to Sodom: 'will you deprive God, their

---

3. Such ignorance not being the quality of true deity.

superior, of this faculty, as if Christ could not continue to be God, after his real assumption of the nature of man' (*Carn. Chr.* 3.41).

In *Exhortation to Chastity*, Tertullian engages with sexual themes, using Sodom to attack the worthiness of married life. He invokes the fate of Sodom and Gomorrah as an image of the suddenness of the last day that will come to the ruin of people who are living a married life (*Exhort. Cast.* 9.42). This image is also graphically employed in *To His Wife* where marriage is said to divert people from 'divine disciplines', and Tertullian continues by exhorting his audience not to be caught in such an ungodly state 'on the day of fear' as were Sodom and Gomorrah (*Uxor.* 1.5.24). In *On Monogamy*, Tertullian invokes the image of Lot's wife to condemn remarriage.

> What if a man thinks on posterity, with thoughts like the eyes of Lot's wife…if men believe that, at the bar of Christ as well (as of Rome), action is taken on the principle of the Julian laws; and imagine that the unmarried and childless cannot receive their portion in full, in accordance with the testament of God. Let such (as thus think), then marry to the very end; that in this confusion they, like Sodom and Gomorrha (sic), and the day of the deluge, may be overtaken by the fated final end of the world (*Monog.* 16.24-25).

In this extraordinary passage, Tertullian compares widowers who remarry to Lot's wife who looks back on Sodom. However, while ostensibly condemning remarriage, Tertullian's argument tends to compare married life in general to life in Sodom. It is quite remarkable that his employment of the Sodom story against marriage is the only sexual issue he raises in connection with the story. This fact must surprise contemporary Christians who read the story homophobically but regard marriage as divinely ordained and highly esteemed in Christianity from the time of Christ. Clearly, for Tertullian and other early Christians, marriage itself was regarded as a kind of Sodomitic estate.

b. *Origen*

Leaving Carthage behind, I move east to Alexandria and the figure of Origen, one of the great early Christian theologians and probably the first real Christian biblical commentator. Origen discusses the story of Sodom in his fourth and fifth *Homilies on Genesis*. Like Tertullian, Origen is not interested in pursuing homophobic interpretations of the story. Indeed, he does not pursue any sexual themes at all in his reading, which strikingly betrays many features found in Jewish midrash. Thus, in his fourth homily on Genesis, Origen unfavourably compares Lot to Abraham both on the basis of hospitality and on the number of visitors they both receive. Two men come to Lot, for he was 'far inferior to Abraham' and they come in the evening for, unlike Abraham, 'Lot could not receive the magnitude of the midday light' (Origen, *Hom. Gen.* 4.1 [1982: 103]). The meal Abraham serves to his guests is far more sumptuous than Lot's. Origen is explicit that if Lot 'had not been inferior, he would not have been separate from Abraham...the land and habitation of Sodom would not have pleased him' (Origen, *Hom. Gen.* 4.1). Origen does not read the events at Mamre as evidence for trinitarian theology but, instead, echoes rabbinic readings that the deity appeared to Abraham together with the two angels. And like the rabbis, Origen counts this against Lot, who 'received those who would give destruction' not 'him who would save' whereas 'Abraham received both him who saves and those who destroy' (Origen, *Hom. Gen.* 4.1). As in Jewish exegesis, Origen also stresses that Abraham, unlike Lot, is concerned that his guests wash their feet before they dine (Origen, *Hom. Gen.* 4.2).[4] Origen regards Abraham as a model of hospitality, but he also reads Abraham's behaviour as prefiguring New Testament themes. Washing the feet of the guests foreshadows Christ washing the feet of his disciples at the Last Supper. Washing of the feet also anticipates Christ's words to his disciples to shake off from their feet the dust of the towns that don't welcome them (Origen, *Hom. Gen.* 4.2; cf. Mt. 10.14; Lk. 9.5, 10.11; Mk 6.11). In both Mt. 10.15 and Lk. 10.12, the text goes on to say that the fate of those towns that reject Jesus' disciples will be worse than that of Sodom and Gomorrah. Origen has linked these gospel accounts with Genesis 18–19 to highlight hospitality as the crucial theme common to all.

Hospitality will be the focus again in his fifth homily on the events of Genesis 19 but in the meantime Origen turns to the question of the deity's expressed intention to go down and investigate Sodom. Here Origen is primarily concerned to protect divine omniscience and to use the passage to explain the relationship between the deity and sinners. Origen plays on the nuances of what it means to know, citing the scriptures that the deity does not know sin and, hence, sinners. Those 'whose activity is considered unworthy of God are also considered to be unworthy of knowledge of God... God does not deign to know him who has turned away from him' (Origen, *Hom. Gen.* 4.6). Thus, the deity descends to Sodom, not out of ignorance of its crimes, but so that any virtuous people there might be made worthy. How-

---

4.   Origen likewise compares Abraham and Lot, in his *Homilies on Leviticus*, this time on the quality of the bread they serve their guests. Abraham 'excelled in merits' and 'set forth loaves' made from 'fine wheat flour', whereas Lot 'set out loaves from regular flour', thus 'the difference of each one's merits is designated by these signs' (Origen, *Hom. Lev.* 13.3, 4). In his commentary on Leviticus, Origen betrays little concern for sexual issues and none whatsoever for same-sex desire.

ever, Origen does not attempt to explain the details of Sodom's evil, and it is an issue in which he shows little interest. In his *Homilies on Jeremiah*, Origen refers twice to the evil of Sodom but again only in very general terms. He goes no further than to describe it as general injustice, adding that the sins of Jerusalem in the days of the monarchy were worse (Origen, *Hom. Jer.* 8.3, 7). So it would appear that Origen does not know Sodom as a city of sexual transgression but rather as a place of general injustice, again a primary rabbinic theme.

In his fifth homily Origen deals with the events of Genesis 19, but his main focus is on what happened between Lot and his daughters in Gen. 19.30 following. At the outset, however, Origen stresses the virtue of hospitality:

> Lot was living in Sodom. We do not read of other good deeds of his. The hospitality alone occurring at the time is mentioned. He escapes the flames, he escapes the conflagration for this reason alone: because he opened his house to strangers. Angels entered the hospitable house; fire entered the houses closed to strangers (Origen, *Hom. Gen.* 5.1).

Lot is saved through his practice of hospitality, but the Sodomites refused to open their doors to strangers and so are taken by the fire. Origen has nothing to say about the incident outside Lot's house, proceeding to comment on the flight from Sodom. He focuses on Lot's request to take shelter in Zoar rather than flee to the mountains as he was initially instructed. Although Lot's request is granted, Origen counts this fact against him arguing that it shows Lot to be 'somewhere in the middle between the perfect and the doomed' (Origen, *Hom. Gen.* 5.1) since he did not go directly to the mountains. The fate of Lot's wife is given a purely allegorical reading. She represents the flesh, which 'looks backward and seeks after pleasures', while Lot represents 'rational understanding and the manly soul' (Origen, *Hom. Gen.* 5.2). Origen continues that salt represents prudence, a quality shown by her actions to be lacking. She is cited again, in *Homilies on Jeremiah*, as a warning to Christians against looking back to the old life of sin (Origen, *Hom. Jer.* 13.3, 3.2). So, while Origen does not share Christian esteem for Lot as a spiritual model to be imitated, he does concur with negative Christian appraisals of the character of Lot's wife.

The rest of the homily deals with Lot and his daughters. Again echoing Jewish perspectives, Origen does not regard Lot as blameless in the incident. Instead Lot was 'so senseless from wine' (Origen, *Hom. Gen.* 5.3) that he was trapped and, thus, at fault. Lot's fate stands as a warning against drunkenness and confirms, once more, that Lot stands between the sinners and the just. Indeed, 'that he escaped from Sodom…belongs more to Abraham's honour than to Lot's merit' (Origen, *Hom. Gen.* 5.3). But Origen is not so harsh on the daughters themselves. He presumes that they must have known something of the end of the world by fire and did not know that only the region of Sodom had been devastated. Origen concludes, 'nevertheless their impiety would have appeared more serious if, in preserving their chastity, they had abolished…the hope of human posterity' (Origen, *Hom. Gen.* 5.4). He is actually disturbed by this conclusion 'lest the incest of these women be purer than the chastity of many women' (Origen, *Hom. Gen.* 5.4).

As if to counter such a position he then proceeds to give allegorical readings of the story that downplay more blatant sexual themes and put the whole incident in a more negative light. He begins by telling us that there are those who have read Lot and his daughters as representing Jesus and the two Testaments (Origen, *Hom. Gen.* 5.5). Origen is not happy with this reading and gives two alternative allegorical readings. Origen argues that Lot represents the Law while his daughters represent Judah and Samaria. Their children, Moab(ites) and Ammon(ites), represent those Jews who rejected Christ and will, thus, stay outside the Church until all the Gentiles have been saved. There is an irony here in that Jesus, the Christian Messiah, is himself descended from Lot and his daughters through Ruth and Naamah. But Origen does not seem to recognize this fact (and neither do any ancient Christian commentators). His alternative second reading echoes Philo in that Lot represents rational understanding and the 'manly soul' while his daughters are 'vain glory and pride' (Origen, *Hom. Gen.* 5.6). The offspring of the union with pride and vainglory are not qualities that will be found in the church of the LORD.

Origen, therefore, not only shares Jewish discomfort with Lot's character, but also goes out of his way to downplay any positive reading of the rape of Lot. Given that Origen was an ascetic who castrated himself as a young man, it should not be a surprise that he would highlight negative understandings of such sexual transgression. However, it puts in stark relief the complete absence, in Origen's reading, of any sexual associations with Sodom and its people. He appears to know Philo's reading of the story, but he has opted for rabbinic readings that highlight hospitality and hostility to outsiders as the evils exemplified by Sodom.[5]

c. *Basil*

Hailing from the Anatolian heartland of Byzantine Rome, Basil is a leading figure of fourth-century Christendom and considered the foremost Greek Doctor of the Ecumenical Church. In his writings, Basil clearly knows Sodom's

---

5.   It is worthwhile to consider that, having castrated himself, Origen had made himself a eunuch. Philo, as we have seen, abhorred eunuchs as sexual outlaws.

association with homoeroticism but it is only one of several aspects that concern him in his use of the story. These homoerotic associations with Sodom's doom do not appear to be his major issue and, indeed, neither does same-sex desire itself, except insofar as it is a threat to celibate same-sex community. Basil is most interested in using the story to remind people of past divine interventions to either save or destroy, and to exhort them to either take heart or learn accordingly from such examples. Thus, he urges monks, facing Arian persecution, to take heart from 'Lot in Sodom' that 'the Lord will not abandon his holy ones' (*Ep. Basil* 257). Both Babel's Tower and Sodom and Gomorrah testify to the power and vigilance of the deity in attending to human evil (*Hom. Pss.* 15.8) Basil concludes his letter to Amphilocus by warning that divine punishment for sinners is not just in the next life, but in this one too. He cites Gen. 19.17 – 'flee for your life' – as a maxim for all Christians living in the world of sin (*Ep. Basil* 217.84). The letter itself is a form of penitential, listing a variety of sins and the penances for them, but homoerotic behaviour is not included.

However, Basil addresses same-sex desire, warning of Sodom's fate, in the following passage from *De renuntiatione saeculi.*

> If you are youthful in body or mind, fly from intimate association with comrades of your own age and run away from them as from fire. The Enemy has, indeed, set many aflame through such means and consigned them to the eternal fire, casting them down into that loathsome pit of the five cities on the pretext of spiritual love... At meals take a seat far from your young brother; in lying down to rest let not your garments be neighbor to his; rather have an elderly brother lying between you. When a young brother converses with you, or is opposite you in choir, make your response with your head bowed lest, perchance, by gazing fixedly into his, the seed of desire be implanted in you by the wicked Sower and you reap sheaves of corruption and ruin (*Ren. Saec.* [1962: 23-4]).

Not only is same-sex desire associated with Sodom and Gomorrah but, for Basil, it is an ever present potential in everyone and can be triggered in a monk by the mere presence of a young man. While there is an obvious anxiety here about same-sex desire, it must be recalled that this treatise is directed at a monastic audience. Basil's main concern is that his monks adhere to celibacy.

Furthermore, because the treatise moves immediately from the erotic perils of cohabitation for young males to discuss the evil of gluttony, it soon becomes clear that Basil's main anxiety is not homoeroticism but gluttony. His argument here confirms my observations concerning John Cassian's attributing gluttony to be the chief cause of Sodom's doom. For Basil, gluttony is the fundamental source of evil because a gluttonous person is completely controlled by their appetites. Gluttony

> ...delivered Adam up to death; by the pleasure of the appetite consummate evil was brought into the world. Through it Noah was mocked, Cham was cursed, Esau was deprived of his birthright... Lot became both his own son-in-law and father-in-law, by marrying his own daughters...thus making a double mockery of the laws of nature. Gluttony, also, made the people of Israel worshippers of idols and strewed the desert with their bodies (*Ren. Saec.* [1962: 25]).

Here, Basil links sexual and other sin with gluttony (and incidentally reveals his strong disapproval of Lot). All sin arises from gluttony, gluttony being the root of all evil. The gluttonous person is liable to commit the most monstrous sins. If Lot married his daughters because of his gluttony, it is clear that the sexual excesses of Sodom must likewise be due to gluttony, just as John Cassian would later declare. It could also be easily argued that Sodom's injustice and abuse of outsiders were caused by gluttony or are symptomatic of gluttony. As will be seen the developing homophobic interpretation of Sodom will replace gluttony with same-sex desire as the root cause of all evils.

With this understanding in mind, I am struck by one other feature of Basil's tirade against gluttony. He appears to anticipate the role of the closet in the subsequent history of Christian homophobia. Basil's concern is for the hidden glutton. He declares that the problem of gluttony is not that of people who eat great quantities of food when dining. Gluttony is not a matter of indulging in 'a great quantity of food' but lies in the persistent 'appetite for a little taste' (*Ren. Saec.* [1962: 25]). He continues,

> I have seen many who were slaves to vice restored to health, but I have not seen this happen in the case of even one person who was given to nibbling in secret or gluttonous. Either they abandon the life of continency and are destroyed by the world, or they attempt to remain undetected among the continent and fight in league with the Devil by leading a luxurious life (*Ren. Saec.* [1962: 25]).

As far as Basil is concerned, then, beware the secret nibbler. Basil's tirade against gluttony and the closet glutton makes a strong contrast with both his treatment of same-sex desire and his use of Sodom in that context. Basil is aware of the readings of the story of Sodom that place homoeroticism as a primary sin of the city. This reading suits his own purposes of maintaining celibate community in a same-sex environment. In a same-sex environment the homoerotic is the only possible sexual temptation. Basil recognizes this fact and so Sodom's fate, understood as pertaining to homoeroticism, serves Basil's purpose well as a cautionary device to keep his celibates on the path of chastity. Basil uses the story and its characters in a variety of ways so that using it to underscore his warning of the risks of same-sex desire to adherence to celibacy is just another usage. However, the paranoia and obsessive panic aroused by the homoerotic in the later homophobic interpretation of Sodom, is, in Basil's case, only reserved for gluttony.

d. *Ephrem*

Ephrem is the great classical writer of the Syrian tradition, writing both poetry and prose, and is the only Syrian counted as a Doctor of the Ecumenical Church. As a prolific Syriac author, his work has been important for both the east Syrian Church of the East tradition and the west Syrian Monophysite Syrian Orthodox tradition. His prose includes a commentary on Genesis, while his poems and hymns contain some references to Sodom, one hymn being about Lot and his daughters. His reading of Genesis 18–19 clearly develops an interpretation focusing on the sexual nature of Sodom's sin although hospitality and other Jewish ideas are also present. Ironically, given his importance for Syriac Christianity, his sexual interpretation of Sodom will not be taken up by later Syriac exegesis.

His commentary on Genesis 18 is rather brief compared with that on Genesis 19. Ephrem does not adhere to trinitarian readings of the apparition at Mamre, stressing a more Jewish notion that 'the Lord…appeared to Abraham clearly in one of the three' (*E. Comm. Gen.* 15.1.1). Abraham's hospitality is further presented as more an act of worship of the deity than the appropriate reception of guests. While Sarah is faulted for laughing at the news of her imminent pregnancy, she is not told of the mission to Sodom so that her joy is not turned to sorrow. Ephrem does not comment on the nature of Sodom's evil whose outcry moves the deity to action, but the reader is directed to the events outside Lot's house for an explanation. The main point of Ephrem's discussion of Gen. 18.21 is to argue that the deity does not descend to investigate Sodom's evil out of ignorance. Instead the deity intends to set an example to judges not to prejudge a case and 'not effect a judgement before the case is heard' (*E. Comm. Gen.* 16.1.2).

The events of Genesis 19 are presented as a series of tests by which people are found worthy. Lot passes his test by pressing his hospitality on the angels and defending them from the Sodomites. The Sodomites are themselves tested by the 'favourable aspect' of the angels (*E.Comm. Gen.* 16.2.2). It is almost as if the angels deliberately tempt the Sodomites since Ephrem goes on to say of the Sodomites that

> (i)f they had not run after the vision they saw with such rabid fury, even though their former sins would not have been forgiven, they still would not have received the punishment they were about to receive (*E. Comm. Gen.* 16.2.2).

Indeed, the angels keep stalling on Lot's offer of hospitality 'so that the Sodomites come and be tested by them' (*E. Comm. Gen.* 16.3). It will be the events of this night that lead to the destruction of the Sodomites and not any earlier sinfulness on their part. And lest the lure of angelic beauty seems an unfair test he points out that the angels came by night to be obscured by darkness so as to make the test more 'manageable' (*E. Comm. Gen.* 16.4). Elsewhere, in one of his hymns on the Nativity, Ephrem states categorically that the Sodomites 'perverted nature' (*Nat.* 1.26) and it is clear from his commentary that Ephrem would understand same-sex desire as determining Sodom's fate. Indeed, the angels in Ephrem's reading are very much engaged in deliberate entrapment of the hapless Sodomites.

Next to be tested are the women of Lot's household and the command not to look back on Sodom's doom is the vehicle of the test. Lot's wife fails and therefore 'doubled the trial of Lot and of his two daughters' (*E. Comm. Gen.* 16.7.2). However, the latter do not succumb and remain obedient to the angels' command. It is not clear whether the rape of Lot is also a test that the daughters fail because Ephrem's major concern is to vindicate Lot. Lot and his daughters take refuge in Zoar which, although spared the conflagration, was empty because it had 'swallowed up its inhabitants' with only its goods left behind to console Lot who had lost everything in Sodom (*E. Comm. Gen.* 16.8). Those goods left behind include the wine. Ephrem acknowledges that the daughters thought they were the only three people left in the world and that they had a duty to repopulate it. In his portrayal of how the daughters get their father to drink, Ephrem gives a harrowing portrait of survivor trauma. Lot's daughters plead with their father that they are unable to sleep because of their nightmares.

> Our mother comes and stands before us like a pillar of salt and we see the Sodomites burning with fire. We hear the voices of women crying out from the midst of the fire and young children writhing in the midst of the conflagration appear to us (*E. Comm. Gen.* 16.9).

While, in his commentary, Ephrem tends to portray the daughter's complaints as more of a ruse to get Lot to drink, in his 38th hymn to Virginity he portrays both Lot and the daughters as suffering very real survivor trauma. Ephrem says that Lot used wine to get to sleep 'since sleep fled from fear' and goes on to graphically describe the aftermath of Sodom's destruction, 'the bellowing... from the depth, roars and thunderclaps from the height (*Virg.* 38.3-5)

Both Lot and the daughters are portrayed as terrified and grief-stricken and their refuge as surrounded by the smoke of the destruction blocking anything else from sight. They are also grieving for Lot's wife. Thus, they drink to console themselves and Ephrem implies that the daughters decide their course of action when influenced by wine. The poem stresses that the daughters thought there was no one else left in the world and thus vindicates them even though they are often called foolish. The poem strongly infers that, following the horror of the events they witnessed, blame cannot be apportioned to anyone, and concludes, '(w)ine consoles old age; conception consoles youth' (*Virg.* 38.17).

Ephrem's commentary on Genesis 19 closes by addressing the issue of how the daughters explain their pregnancies to their father. Lot clearly believed his daughters to be virgins because he offered them to the Sodomites as women who had not known men. However, Lot cannot but help noticing day by day that 'the stomachs' of his daughters 'confirm the suspicion of adultery I have concerning you' (*E. Comm. Gen.* 16.11). The older daughter again takes the initiative and lies to her father to the effect that she and her sister had been raped by their prospective husbands. She claims that they kept this from their father on their mother's advice that 'they were your betrothed and not adulterers; you have received the seed of your ploughmen even though you were, in all truth, raped' (*E. Comm. Gen.* 16.11.2). This explanation satisfies Lot because 'it was nothing that those who had assailed both each other and angels on high would rape and disgrace, before the time of marriage, those to whom they were betrothed' (*E. Comm. Gen.* 16.12). Consequently, Ephrem's story stresses the sexual nature of the sins of the Sodomites as much as it addresses how Lot accepted his daughters' pregnancy, but by downplaying the specifically homoerotic dimension of Sodomite sexuality.

e. Jerome

Jerome straddles both east and west. Although a Latin, he spent considerable time in the east including the last half of his life as a monk in Bethlehem. Most famous for his Latin translation of the scriptures, he also wrote a number of commentaries, including one on Genesis. This commentary gives only a brief treatment of Sodom's story but Jerome makes references to the story in other commentaries and in his letters. In one of his letters, Jerome refers to a person as a sodomite (*sodomita*). While Jerome is quoting his correspondent's description of a third party, the word, *sodomita*, is clearly not referring to a resident of Sodom. The context is possibly sexual, since the person is called an adulterer as well. However, as will be seen, neither in the letter nor in any other text does Jerome's writing offer clear homophobic associations with Sodom nor does it appear to be particularly interested in developing such associations.

Jerome's commentary on Genesis is more an explanation of the Hebrew text, sometimes in comparison to various translations, and he gives only a very brief discussion of Genesis 18–19. His most extensive discussion is on 19.30 following, the rape of Lot (*QHG* 19.30, 35, 36-8), and it is only here that he engages with the narrative in a more than linguistic way. To clarify Jerome's understanding of Genesis 19, it will be necessary, therefore, to examine references to Sodom elsewhere in his work. Unsurprisingly, he cites the example of Lot's wife when advising Eustochium that in pursuing the celibate life, she is 'fleeing from Sodom and...should take warning from Lot's wife' (*Ep. Jerome* 22.2). Similarly, he commends, to Rufinus, his friend Bonosus, as someone who in taking on a spiritual life 'does not look back' (*Ep. Jerome* 3.4). General references to Sodom in his correspondence (*Ep. Jerome* 21.39.2, 46.7) or in homily 60 on Psalm 10 (1966: 12 ditto) indicate that Jerome has Ezekiel 16 in mind, not the story in Genesis 19. Turning to Jerome's commentary on Ezek. 16.44-58, one discovers that Jerome twice identifies the sins of Sodom. Commenting on v. 48, Jerome declares that the first sin of Sodom and her daughters is pride, the primary sin of the devil (*Comm. Hiez.* 5.16.48-51). There follows a more detailed description of Sodomitic sin, beginning with pride and listing bloatedness, abundance of all things, ease and delicacies[6] in consequence of which they were cast into oblivion by the deity.

Shameless pride is the focus, too, of Jerome's reference to the siege of Lot's house in his commentary on Isa. 3.8-9, where the princes of Jerusalem are called 'rulers of Sodom'. Jerome states that Isaiah prophesies the behaviour of the chief priests who cried out to Pilate that Jesus was not their king and demanded his crucifixion because Caesar alone was king. Jerome then compares the chief priests to the Sodomites demanding Lot bring out his guests so that they might have sex with them. The chief priests and the princes of Judah, before them, are like the Sodomites in that they publicly proclaim their sin without any shame (*Comm. Es.* 2.3.8-9). While citing the siege of Lot's house, Jerome betrays no obsessive paranoia about homoeroticism in connection with it. His main concern and primary focus is the public proclamation of sin by the Sodomites, together with the princes and later priests of Jerusalem – a strong contrast to the subsequent homophobic interpretation. Despite the same-sex nature of the threat of male rape, it is striking that Jerome does not take the opportunity to condemn same-sex desire here. Indeed, it is possible to concur with Jerome's point about public sin without reading this incident homophobically. In other words, in a reading of the incident as illustrating inhospitality and abuse of outsiders, Jerome's point is still valid. Perhaps, given his identification of Sodom's primary sin as pride,

---

6. I acknowledge here my indebtedness to Jordan's translation of this passage (1997: 33).

Jerome's point only makes its full impact where Sodom's sin is primarily regarded as inhospitality and abuse of outsiders.

With this thought in mind, Jerome's reading of the rape of Lot in his commentary on Gen. 19.30 following takes on a new significance, because he here demonstrates a clear knowledge of Jewish readings, where Sodom is destroyed because of inhospitality and abuse of outsiders. That Jerome accepts many aspects of these readings suggests that he concurs with Jewish readings of the whole Sodom story. He quickly exonerates the daughters of wrongdoing and puts the argument that they thought the human race had been destroyed. They acted therefore to preserve humanity. However, he holds Lot responsible in two ways. First, Lot's decision to flee Segor/Zoar for the mountains, even though he had been promised it would be preserved, was an act of 'faithlessness' on his part (*QHG* 19.30). He should have trusted the promise of the deity. Through this faithlessness, Lot enabled the situation to occur, possibly by further heightening the panic and desperation of the daughters. Secondly, Jerome holds Lot complicit in his daughters' action. He says, 'Consequently, the Hebrews put dots above what follows, *And he did not know when he slept with her and when she rose up from him*, as if it were unbelievable, and because nature does not allow any man to have sexual intercourse without knowing it' (*QHG* 19.35) – in other words, Lot was aware of what was happening.[7] Jerome thus follows rabbinic midrash in Genesis 19, though, as a Christian, he is more understanding of Lot.

Nevertheless, a sign of later Christian reading is seen in the use of 'sodomite' in an extended sense in one of Jerome's letters. At issue in the letter is whether a woman whose husband is 'an adulterer and a sodomite' (*viro adultero et sodomita*) (*Ep. Jerome* 55.4.3) can regard the marriage as dissolved and take another husband. It is clear that the term is not Jerome's but belongs to his correspondent, Amandus. On the first occasion, Jerome quotes Amandus. He states that he has found a piece of paper attached to Amandus' letter on which was written:

> It is necessary to ask him – that is to say myself – whether a woman who has left her husband, an adulterer and sodomite, and has accepted another man by virtue of that fact, can share in the communion of the church without doing penance, while the man she left is still alive (*Ep. Jerome* 55.4.3).

Jerome's answer, after a long discussion in which there is no reference to Sodom or to homoeroticism, is in the negative. On the second occasion,

---

7.   In his letters Jerome refers to this event and, while he doesn't hold Lot completely responsible for what happened, he understands Lot's paternity of Moab and Ammon to be a punishment of him, nevertheless (*Ep. Jerome* 22.8.4).

Jerome himself uses the word 'sodomite' in his conclusion, but reflecting Amandus' original question:

> as long as the husband lives, be he adulterous, a sodomite, immersed in all that is shameful (*flagitiis omnibus coopertus*), and even though she has left him because of these crimes, he is always regarded as her husband, and the woman is not allowed to take another man (*Ep. Jerome* 55.4.3).

So, whatever is meant by 'sodomite', the original word belongs to Amandus not to Jerome. As Jordan points out, an adulterer is here different from a sodomite (1997: 33), but there is nothing in this letter to indicate what that difference is. While Jordan considers it to be a sexual reference, I will conclude my discussion of Jerome by suggesting a different meaning. I referred above to Nilus' use of sodomitic to describe a type of person. As was seen, Nilus uses the word, *sodomoumenē*, to refer to a person leading an excessively indulgent life. Nothing Jerome has written would contradict applying that same meaning to the use of 'sodomite' in this letter. Of course, whether or not that is Amandus' meaning is impossible to tell. But Nilus demonstrates that a person can be called a sodomite without any specific sexual meaning being intended. Jerome himself appears closer to Nilus, and even the rabbis, in what he says about Sodom, than to the subsequent homophobic tradition.

f. *John Chrysostom*

If for Basil, Sodom's underlying sin was gluttony and for Jerome, pride, for John Chrysostom it is clearly same-sex desire and homoeroticism. His commentary on the story, in his *Homilies* 41–44 on Genesis, specifically attempts to blend a homophobic reading of the story with the more traditional emphasis on inhospitality and rejection of outsiders as the sins of Sodom. Chrysostom seems to suggest that such hatred of fellow humans is a natural result of surrendering to same-sex desire. Elsewhere in his literary corpus, the sins of Sodom are regularly identified with same-sex desire. In his treatment of Genesis 18, Chrysostom extols Abraham as a model of piety and hospitality. In his exposition of Genesis 19, however, he is determined to do the same for Lot. I will start with Chrysostom's account of Sodom's sins, which he describes in relation to the outcry in Gen. 18.20-21.

Chrysostom's description of Sodomite sins clearly attempts to link traditional understandings of Sodom as a city of abusive injustice with a new homophobic understanding of the Sodomites as sexually disordered. The outcry of Sodom's sin 'means that in addition to that unspeakable iniquity they were giving evidence also of many other offences, the powerful oppressing the weak, the rich the poor' (*Chrys. Hom. Gen.* 42.11). But what is that 'unspeakable iniquity'? The Sodomites

> had invented monstrous and illicit norms of intercourse, the frenzy of
> their wickedness was so powerful that all were infected with total defile-
> ment, and far from giving evidence any longer of good behaviour they
> called for utter destruction (*Chrys. Hom. Gen.* 42.12).

Thus, it is their unspeakable sexual iniquity that causes the Sodomites to
practise gross injustice and tips the balance against them. For Chrysostom,
sexual iniquity is akin to pride (*Chrys. Hom. Mt.* 6.9) or a type of luxury or self
indulgence (*Chrys. Hom. Mt.* 57.5) that results in social injustice. However, he
underscores sexual iniquity, rather than injustice and hatred of outsiders, as
the cause of Sodom's fate.

> ...since they had overturned the laws of nature and had devised novel and
> illicit forms of intercourse, consequently he (the deity) imposed a novel
> form of punishment, rendering sterile the womb of the earth on account
> of their lawlessness and leaving a perpetual reminder to later generations
> not to attempt the same crimes... (*Chrys. Hom. Gen.* 42.21).

And in his *Homilies on the Statues* he points out the appropriateness of a
fiery doom for a people who 'burned in their lust towards one another'
(*Chrys. Hom. Stat.* 19.7). Indeed, Chrysostom's attempt here, to link same-
sex desire with social injustice, stands out in its novelty, even within his own
writings. The references to Sodom in his other homophobic polemics highlight the monstrousness of same-sex desire itself. Commenting on Rom. 1.26-
27, Chrysostom invokes Sodom's fate as a historical warning for those engaging in homoeroticism and who 'utterly disbelieve the things to come after the
resurrection' (*Chrys. Hom. Rom.* 4.1.26-27). If these people do not believe in
the fires of hell, they should be instructed by the blasted wasteland that was
Sodom. In *Against the Opponents of the Monastic Life*, he denounces same-
sex desire as a 'new and lawless lust...a terrible and incurable disease... a
plague more terrible...a great abomination' (*Adv. Oppugn.* 3.8). He warns that
those 'who dare to commit the sins of Sodom' and have not learned from
Sodom's fate are 'worthy of a greater punishment' (*Adv. Oppugn.* 3.8).

Chrysostom's linking of same-sex desire as an evil that results in social
injustice and inhospitality enables him to read Genesis 19 as a text about the
virtue of hospitality with Lot as its exemplar. Lot is Chrysostom's hero and is
referred to throughout as the just man or the good man, whose association
with Abraham led him to the 'pinnacle of virtue' particularly in his 'practice
of hospitality' (*Chrys. Hom. Gen.* 43.2). Lot is presented as someone who
habitually waits at the city gates to welcome strangers and his goodness demonstrates that believers do not have to leave the city but can remain there as a
'yeast to the others and lead many to imitation of them' (*Chrys. Hom. Gen.*
43.5). Chrysostom comments that Lot prostrated himself before the angels

because he was giving 'thanks to God for being found worthy to welcome the visitors' (*Chrys. Hom. Gen.* 43.10) and underlines this point by declaring that Lot did not know the strangers were angels. He commends Lot to his audience because Lot, a 'man of good name and reputation, enjoying great prosperity, a householder, addresses as master these travelers' (*Chrys. Hom. Gen.* 43.10). The angels initially refuse the hospitality to give Lot an opportunity to demonstrate his virtue more clearly 'and to teach us all the extent of his hospitality' (*Chrys. Hom. Gen.* 43.12). Furthermore, Lot's behaviour demonstrates the need for persistence in the spiritual life. When the angels relent and take shelter with Lot, Chrysostom takes the opportunity to portray Lot as a felicitous host busily occupied in attending to his guests.

In discussing the outrage at Lot's house, Chrysostom develops his themes of the goodness of Lot and the virtue of hospitality. The Sodomites are portrayed as frenzied, lawless, insolent and shameless, but mainly to allow Chrysostom to extol Lot, who is likened to a physician placed in Sodom by the deity to cure its ailments. Even though Sodom ultimately proves incurable, Chrysostom plays on his metaphor, saying that an incurable condition does not deter a good physician from continuing to care for a patient. All this medical imagery is derived from Lot's confronting the mob, which elicits further praise for Lot as longsuffering and extraordinarily humble (*Chrys. Hom. Gen.* 43.16). Most surprising is Chrysostom's attitude to Lot's offering his daughters to the mob. It is not condemned, but praised as yet another proof of Lot's virtue.

> What marvellous virtue in the just man! He surpassed all the standards of hospitality! I mean, how could anyone do justice to the good man's friendliness in not bringing himself to spare even his daughters so as to demonstrate his regard for the strangers and save them from…the Sodomites (*Chrys. Hom. Gen.* 43.18).

Lot can do no wrong and Chrysostom draws a further moral from this incident by condemning those who 'are content to see our brothers brought to the very depths of impiety…without troubling to…counsel them…and guide them towards virtue' (*Chrys. Hom. Gen.* 43.18). True Christians should be like Lot and intervene when their neighbours fall into the ways of sin. Returning to the story, Chrysostom argues that the angels intervene both because Lot had fully demonstrated his virtue and in reward for his hospitality. The whole exposition of this incident demonstrates the moral quicksand underpinning Chrysostom's argument. His homophobic interpretation of the story relies on holding up Lot as a worthy figure in contrast to the Sodomites. Consequently Chrysostom has been led to endorse offering the daughters up for rape, an act of which he would not normally approve.[8] He seems surprisingly unaware of this moral contradiction but others, like Augustine, will attempt to resolve it without any ethically credible result.[9]

In the destruction of Sodom and Gomorrah Chrysostom continues his theme of Lot's virtue. There is no fault in Lot wanting to flee to Zoar instead of the mountains. Rather, the incident is further evidence of his merit. Indeed, Chrysostom says that Lot's virtue 'averted the catastrophe from that city' (*Chrys. Hom. Gen.* 43.30), and he concludes by exhorting his congregation to practise hospitality unreservedly. Abraham and Lot

> were even found worthy to welcome angels and the Lord of the angels…let us welcome strangers in this fashion…if…we give evidence of the practice of hospitality in such a spirit, we too will be found worthy to welcome such guests (*Chrys. Hom. Gen.* 43.32).

Such statements indicate that, despite his homophobic agenda, Chrysostom still defers to the priority of hospitality and the right treatment of outsiders as the issues central to the story of Sodom.

In homily 44 Chrysostom turns to the incident of Lot and his daughters. He again extols Lot as a model of virtue but, surprisingly, endorses the action of the daughters. He points out that scripture exonerates them all of any wrong. Lot was plied with wine because he would in no way have consented if sober. He succumbs to wine 'not so much from incontinence as from depression' (*Chrys. Hom. Gen.* 44.20). His daughters act this way because, believing the rest of humanity has been destroyed, they want to 'leave a succession of progeny' (*Chrys. Hom. Gen.* 44.19). That they name their children so openly shows that their intent was virtuous. Chrysostom declares, '(s)crutinize their intent, and acquit them of any crime…let no one ever presume to condemn the just man or his daughters' (*Chrys. Hom. Gen.* 44.19, 21).[10]

Chrysostom's is probably the first detailed Christian account of the events of Genesis 18–19 that highlights same-sex desire as the primary evil of Sodom and responsible for its fiery doom. However, he still preserves a tradition that associates the sins of Sodom with inhospitality and abuse of the poor and outsiders. Chrysostom attempts to link such social injustice and structural oppression to same-sex desire – they are the natural outcome for societies

---

8.   Robert Hill, who translated the text, comments in a footnote 'Chrysostom's congregation must have wondered if he spoke with tongue in cheek in commending Lot's behaviour in this incident' (Hill, footnote 19 in 1990: 445).

9.   Only Augustine recognizes this failure on his part.

10.   Again, in a footnote, Hill comments 'Chrysostom's defense of these two women runs counter to his usual pattern, and is all the more surprising considering the conduct involved' (Hill 1990: 465, fn 32).

that embrace the homoerotic. Chrysostom's reading valorizes Lot as a heroic figure resisting and trying to cure the rampant homoeroticism of the city. Doing so, however, leads him into the moral contradiction of accepting the appropriateness of handing over women to be raped in place of men. This contradiction is a fundamental flaw in all such homophobic readings of the story.

g. *Ambrose*

Ambrose of Milan does not often refer to the story of Sodom and the only extensive treatment occurs in his untranslated treatise, *De Abrahamo*. Here Ambrose, like Chrysostom, links the homophobic interpretation of Sodom with the more traditional focus on hospitality. While he does so in a more abbreviated way, Ambrose is important because he features prominently in my later discussion of Gibeah.

Other references to Sodom can be found in Ambrose's letter to Irenaeus (*Letters* 79) and in his treatise, *Flight from the World*. In both of these, Ambrose is more concerned with expounding biblical models of virtue than in discussing the story itself in any detail. Thus, in his letter to Irenaeus, Ambrose commends Lot as a model who 'left behind the sins of Sodom' and urges Irenaeus not to be like Lot's wife 'who looked back and could not reach the higher ground' (*Letters* 79 [1954: 446]). Similarly, in *Flight from the World*, Lot is held up as a model of someone winning salvation by fleeing the lures of the world (*Flight* 5.31). Lot is 'a holy man' who 'chose to shut his house to the men of Sodom and flee the contagion of their offences' (*Flight* 9.55). His flight from Sodom symbolizes the life of the 'man who renounces the vices and rejects the way of life of his countrymen' (*Flight* 9.55). Those, who still yearn for their old life, are like Lot's wife who 'looked back in womanly fashion and lost her salvation' (*Flight* 5.31). Sodom, for Ambrose, symbolizes evil and the Sodomites 'were overcome by…a blindness of depravity' (*Flight* 4.23) Clearly, Ambrose refers here to the siege of Lot's house because he adds that blindness prevented the Sodomites finding Lot's door. While he is not more specific about this Sodomite evil, this allusion shows it to be clearly sexual.

It is in *De Abrahamo* that Ambrose clearly indicates same-sex desire to be Sodom's crime. As he does so in the context of justifying Lot's offer of his daughters, Ambrose falls into the same moral contradiction as Chrysostom. The treatise presents a quite brief version of the story, dealing mainly with the siege of Lot's house, the flight from Sodom and the rape of Lot. The story is introduced with the deity revealing Sodom's impending doom to Abraham, without elaborating on the nature of Sodom's sin. Ambrose's main point is to reject the notion that the deity plans to go down to Sodom out of ignorance (*Abr.* I 6.46-47). On the events in Sodom, Ambrose stresses that it is all the men who surround Lot's house, from the infants to the old men (*Abr.* I 6.52). Scripture records this fact to show that no one in Sodom was righteous or blameless. The old men were not there to prevent the outrage. Instead 'while worn out with age, their minds were full of lust' (*Abr.* I6.52). Thus, by offering his daughters' virginity to protect his guests, Lot was offering the Sodomites something that accorded with nature. While it was a shameful impurity it was the lesser evil than to have sex in a manner contrary to nature. The rape of the daughters is shameful and impure, but at least 'natural'.

For Ambrose, Lot's offering of his daughters shows his determination to uphold the hospitality of his house. The virtue of hospitality was a matter of reverence in Lot's house, a virtue still held inviolable among barbarian peoples. This last point accuses the Sodomites of being worse than barbarians. They have become so because of their predilection to same-sex desire.[11] Ambrose here, like Chrysostom, links his homophobic reading with the tradition of Sodom's sin as lack of hospitality. Furthermore, the image of Lot as a paragon of hospitality serves to counter any doubts about him by the offer of his daughters to the mob. Certainly, for Ambrose, Lot is a worthy model and is always referred to as 'holy Lot'. He is not to be condemned, either, for what happens with his daughters. Nor are the daughters: they acted to preserve the human race, not knowing that only the region of the cities had been destroyed (*Abr.* I 6.56-8). His only moral point from this event is to highlight the dangers of drunkenness.

Thus, Ambrose, like Chrysostom, attempts to graft homophobia onto inhospitality. In so doing, he falls into the same moral contradiction of defending the offer of Lot's daughters to the mob. He attempts to resolve the problem by introducing notions of the preferability of 'natural' sex to the abomination of 'unnatural' sex between men.

h. *Augustine*

There can be little doubt that Augustine considers same-sex desire and homoeroticism to be the main evil of Sodom and Gomorrah. He makes references to the story in a number of his works and detailed discussion is found in *City of God* and in his untranslated commentary, *Questiones in Heptateuchum*. Two of his works are particularly significant for a history of Sodom. In the first, *Against Julian*, Augustine's argument hinges on the sin of Sodom, and reveals a possible clash between a new sexual and homophobic reading and

11. This point may lie behind Salvian's later praise of the Vandal occupation of Africa as rescuing the people from the homoerotic ways of old Rome.

an older non-sexual understanding of the story. In *Against Lying*, Augustine gives a detailed discussion of the siege of Lot's house and the offering of Lot's daughters to the Sodomites. At issue is the ethics of using lesser sins to avert greater ones. Augustine's discussion rehearses some basic elements of the Christian homophobic reading of Genesis 19 and very tellingly exposes the moral contradictions on which it is based.

In his argument with Julian, Augustine is maintaining the fundamental evil of lust and concupiscence in response to two of Julian's points. Augustine has apparently originally argued that Sodom's fate was due to sexual desire being given free rein, leading to the city being taken over by homoeroticism, and hence her fiery doom. Julian has apparently responded by, first, citing the deity's determination to see if there are any in Sodom who are worthy of being saved. If all are concupiscent by nature and therefore sinful there would be no need for such a fact-finding mission (*Against Julian* 3.20, 39). Julian has then used Rom. 1.27 to argue that heterosexual desire is good and only same-sex desire is disordered. Augustine's response to these points is to condemn all desire as evil, whether for the natural or unnatural, and therefore must always be subject to restraint (*Against Julian* 3.20, 40). The deity is seeking out those who have applied such restraint. It is important to note here Julian's use of Paul in relation to same-sex desire rather than Genesis 19. Julian's second point is to state that 'the Sodomites also sinned in the creature of bread and wine' (*Against Julian* 3.20, 41). In other words, Julian is citing as common knowledge that the Sodomites were destroyed for gluttony, not sex. Augustine condemns that argument, saying that 'the creature of bread and wine does not lust against the spirit' (*Against Julian* 3.20, 41). He continues,

> This creature enters the body from outside... The reason it should be used sparingly and with restraint is that the concupiscence which is an evil within us and part of us may not rise up more vehemently and invincibly against us (*Against Julian* 3.20, 41).

Augustine acknowledges the excessive living of the Sodomites but, for him, it was not this that was the evil of Sodom. Instead it was through excessive living that the Sodomites lost control of their sexual desires and succumbed to same-sex desire. Here, Augustine has established a fatal continuum. Sexual desire must be constantly controlled, otherwise it will lead humans into the homoerotic chaos of Sodom, which, for Augustine, incurred the divine punishment. Sodom 'was a place where the practice of unnatural lust'[12] was 'much sanctioned by custom' (*City of God*, Book XVI [1952: 543]). They were

---

12. *Stupra in masculos.*

destroyed because they had 'filled out the measure of their sinning' (*The Christian Life*, chapter 4 [1953: 17]).

Augustine declared sexual desire itself to be an evil but, unlike Tertullian, did not see marriage *per se* as a thing of Sodom. He associates Sodom with homoerotic chaos but does not mandate celibacy for all, seeing in marriage an arena where sexual desire can be appropriately employed. What gives legitimacy to such usage is the requirement to reproduce, and Augustine argues that such procreative employment of desire is a natural usage and thus legitimate. The homoeroticism of Sodom is thoroughly unnatural and hence illegitimate. This dichotomy of natural and unnatural concretizes a fundamental moral flaw underpinning the Christian homophobic reading of Genesis 19. If the point of the story is, as such readings allege, that there is no greater sexual evil than sex between men, then is such male homo-eroticism more abominable than the rape of women? Is it even legitimate to offer women to be raped if it will prevent such sexual activity? Contributing to the problem is the Christian tradition of reading Lot as a positive model.

Augustine confronts this moral dilemma in the ninth chapter of *Against Lying*, one of the few Christians to consciously engage with it. While he attempts various justifications for Lot, Augustine appears to realize that they are all morally untenable. However, he resolves to leave the matter unresolved rather than critique the fundamental assumptions on which it is based. At issue for him is the question of compensatory or justifiable sin: whether it is right to commit a lesser sin to forestall a greater one. The focus of the discussion is the siege of Lot's house and his offer of his daughters to the mob. Augustine commences by asking if anyone doubts that it is sinful 'for a father to prostitute his daughters to the fornication of the impious' (*Against Lying* 9.20). Yet, he points out, this was exactly the situation of Lot in Sodom. Surely the intent of the Sodomites towards Lot's guests would merit whatever action could be taken to avert it? Lot was undoubtedly a just man and justice recognizes that it is 'less evil for women to suffer violation than men' (*Against Lying* 9.20). Augustine rejects that argument saying that if it were accepted the enemy would tempt people into sin by threatening them with a greater sin.

Augustine then raises the question of consent to sin. Even if the Sodomites had violated the angels, as no consent was involved the angels would not be spiritually defiled. The focus on consent at this point suggests an understanding of the importance of a person's consent in determining an ethical evaluation of these events. His argument almost enables a reading that recognizes rape in a way that no other text has done. He says

> But, do not let your fears compel you to do that which, if done to your daughters with their consent, will make you a pander to their profligacy with the Sodomites, and, if done without their consent, will make you a betrayer of their innocence to the Sodomites (*Against Lying* 9.22).

However, while Augustine has some sense of the importance of consent in these events it seems beyond his capacity to initiate or articulate a Christian moral theology of rape. But, then, Augustine's main focus is on the men, in particular Lot. Does Lot provide a worthy emulatory model in this instance? Augustine concludes that Lot cannot here be regarded as a model for Christians. Through the confusion and panic of the moment, Lot has been made to fall into sin.

Nevertheless, Augustine considers another possible defence of Lot, on the grounds that it is better to suffer a wrong than inflict it. Lot's guests were the potential victims of a wrong. Augustine argues that maybe 'the just man ...preferred his daughters to suffer the wrong instead of his guests, in view of his authority over his daughters' (*Against Lying* 9.22). Once again the question of consent takes on a central importance in Augustine's argument. He points out that Lot cannot offer himself because in doing so he would then give consent to having sex with the Sodomites. By offering his daughters instead,

> the women...did not offer themselves to be defiled...lest the consent of their own will, not submission to someone else's lust, make them guilty... Against his daughters, moreover, who were free from sin he did not sin either, for he did not make them sin, if they were subdued against their will, but merely put up with sinners (*Against Lying* 9.22).

However, this argument raises the whole question of power and authority. In a revealing analogy, Augustine then raises the question of whether a master sins by offering a slave to be killed so as to protect the guests of his house. Augustine refuses to pursue the answer to this question in detail but concludes, 'we should not make part of our manners everything that we read has been done by righteous or just men' (*Against Lying* 9.22).

I am both frustrated and fascinated by Augustine's arguments. Frustrated because, as I noted above, the importance of consent in considering the ethics of these events could have opened up an important moral discourse on rape in Christianity. However, Augustine's homophobia and erotophobia ultimately preclude that possibility. What is fascinating is that Augustine's arguments reveal the misogyny that is a fundamental basis of homophobia – it is better that women be violated than men – and which, together with homophobia, is a crucial element of the sexual violence being threatened in the Genesis narrative. Despite Augustine's clear perception that there is something very wrong in what Lot does, his own homosexual panic renders him ultimately complicit in the sins of the father against the daughters and thus complicit in the sexual power politics of the Sodomites' own behaviour.

Augustine's moral failure is graphically illustrated in the ancient Christian poem, *Sodoma*, which, in its graphic account of the destruction of Sodom and the delivery of Lot, contains all the fundamental elements of the Christian homophobic reading of Genesis 19 developed in this period.[13] Once wrongly ascribed to Tertullian, the poem is of uncertain authorship and date, though Jordan attributes it to an unknown author from the fifth-century Gaul (1997: 35). The poem presents same-sex desire as the determining factor of Sodom's doom, and the poet couches this homophobic account in a dichotomy of natural versus unnatural that becomes crucial for the siege of Lot's house. In the poem, Lot is a good and noble man and praised for his wisdom, piety, and righteousness. When the Sodomites besiege his house, Lot valiantly confronts them. Addressing the mob, he sets up a dichotomy of the natural and the unnatural, appealing to a wide variety of examples from the animal world to show that natural sex is between male and female, not male and male. He then offers his daughters to the mob in lieu of his guests, proclaiming their nubile virginity and desirability. Lot's appeal to the Sodomites is predicated not on the injustice threatening his guests, but on the unnaturalness of the Sodomites' desires. Thus, his daughters are offered not simply to protect his guests but to redirect such unnatural desires into a more natural course. The author of *Sodoma* never questions the appropriateness of Lot's actions and furthermore couches those actions in a sexual dichotomy of the natural and the unnatural within which the hierarchical gender dichotomy of male and female is subsumed.

i. *The Syrian East*

The Syriac world, spanning the frontier between Rome and Persia, lay for the most part outside the Roman Empire during the Persian dominion. Centred in Mesopotamia, it also lived side by side with the great Babylonian centres of rabbinic Judaism. While Ephrem gave prominence to sexual sins in his reading of Genesis 19, the later east Syrian tradition downplays such sexual motifs. Importantly, the east Syrians will be shown to be familiar with Jewish understandings of the story and to employ them in their own exegesis, which foregrounds issues of hospitality and abuse of outsiders. These patterns are

---

13. In English, the poem exists only in Thelwall's floridly Victorian translation in volume 3 of the 1870 edition of the works of Tertullian (also reprinted in Paul Hallam's *The Book of Sodom* [1993]). The Latin text is found with Tertullian's work in the *Patrologia Latina* (*PL* 2: 1159-1162).

found in the work of Aphrahat, Theodore bar Koni, Iso'dad of Merv and an anonymous Syriac exegetical compilation on Genesis.

While the anonymous Genesis compilation contains some parallels to Ephrem's commentary, in its shorter coverage of Genesis 18–19, there are also differences, most importantly the nature of Sodom's sin, which is not here primarily sexual. As in Ephrem, the deity, in the company of two angels, appears to Abraham at Mamre and the deity's decision to investigate the outcry of Sodom's sin is approved; he does not act out of ignorance but because 'He bore with them a long time' (*ESF* 91). But, unlike Ephrem, there is no testing of Lot; instead he is declared righteous, the only such in Sodom. The rape of Lot receives only a brief discussion and the incident is not held against him or his daughters. The text mostly comments on the meaning of the names Moab and Ammon.[14] However, a number of negative evaluations of Lot's wife are recorded. She did not want to leave, as she did not believe the angels. She despised 'the command of God and pitied those who perished', and finally she looked back out of curiosity and a pillar of salt fell, absorbing her whole body (*ESF* 92). The reference to her pity for those who perished echoes a theme that was developed in Judaism in later centuries. This Jewish echo brings me back to the one striking difference from Ephrem: the Genesis commentary downplays the sexual themes of Sodom's sin, echoing instead Jewish concepts of its hostility to outsiders. Sexual violence is a strategy to deter outsiders from sojourning in Sodom:

> It is probable that these Sodomites did not do these things from licentiousness, since they could do this to one another; but as at one time, they fell away from the fear of God, they became very incensed against men, and especially against strangers (*ESF* 91-2).

So not uncontrolled sexual desire, but arrogant disdain for the rest of humanity is the sin of Sodom and Gomorrah.

Ironically, Jewish motifs appear in Aphrahat's 'Demonstrations', a Christian anti-Jewish polemic.[15] Aphrahat draws extensively on biblical material and much of the anti-Jewish rhetorical use of Sodom and Gomorrah already discussed elsewhere in this chapter is found again in 'Demonstrations'. In XI, XII, XVI and XIX, Aphrahat makes only general references to Sodom and Gomorrah as places of desolation and destruction. Demonstration XXI has as

---

14. However, the text says that the incident took place 'after some years, when he had planted a vineyard' (*ESF* 92) which evokes for me the parallel story of Noah who cultivated the vine after the flood and who was exposed, when unconscious from drinking, to his son, Ham.

15. I am using Neusner's translation of the 'Demonstrations' from his *Aphrahat and Judaism: The Christian Jewish Argument in Fourth Century Iran* (1971).

2

its central theme the comparison of Israel and Judaism to Sodom and, there, Aphrahat extensively compares Zion and Sodom as cities punished by the deity. Demonstration XXIII contains a reference to the rape of Lot in relation to the lineage of the Messiah, a Jewish motif not normally found in Christian commentaries.

To develop his anti-Judaic polemic in Demonstration XXI, Aphrahat draws on the prophetic comparisons of Judah and Sodom in Isaiah and Ezekiel. In particular, Aphrahat is determined to counter interpretations of Ezek. 16.55 – 'Sodom and her daughters shall be rebuilt as of old, and you (Jerusalem) and your daughters shall be as of old' – that affirm Jewish hopes for an eventual restoration of Zion. Instead, Aphrahat argues that these prophetic references actually mean that a Jewish Zion shall never be restored. The crucial point for Aphrahat is that a 'wrathful passage is altogether wrath, and there is no peace in it' (XXI: 396). Accordingly, he argues that Sodom was named by the prophets as more righteous than Zion and still awaits restoration, so as to demonstrate that the prophetic verses on Sodom's (and hence, Zion's) restoration are an expression of prophetic wrath and not to be taken literally. He belabours the point by counting up all the years since Sodom's destruction and comparing those many centuries with the short period of Zion's desolation (he counts from the Babylonian Captivity up to 70 CE [XXI: 399]). Aphrahat concludes by comparing Babylon with Sodom and Zion. Babylon, like Sodom, was destroyed and, concerning Babylon, it was prophesied that 'Babylonia shall fall and not rise' (Jer. 51.64). Babylon and Sodom are still in ruins and so Aphrahat concludes with cruel irony, 'It is quite true that he will no longer be angry against her, nor will he ever again rebuke her, for that which is in desolation he does not reprove, nor will she enrage him' (XXI: 402).

In all of his argument, Aphrahat does not identify the sin(s) of Sodom, apart from quoting Ezek. 16.49, 'This is the iniquity of Sodom and her daughters, that they did not take by the hand the needy and the poor' (XXI: 397). However, he makes no comment. The commentary compilation indicates that the East Syrians shared Jewish understandings of Sodom's sin as hostility to the poor and to foreigners, as underscored by Aphrahat's quoting of Ezek. 16.49, the only instance in which he clearly identifies the nature of Sodom's sin.

This shared perspective (or at least strong Jewish influence) is also demonstrated by Aphrahat's sole reference to the rape of Lot by his daughters

> Boaz married Ruth the Moabite, so that Lot might be a partner in the blessing of the righteous. And from the son of Ruth was born the family of the house of David. From their seed was born the king Messiah... God further remembered Lot by the hand of Naama the Ammonite, whom Solomon married, and who gave birth to Rehoboam the king (XXIII: 466).

Of all these ancient Christian texts, Aphrahat stands alone in recognizing the role of the rape of Lot in the messianic lineage. His language echoes that of the Midrash Rabbah (e.g. *Gen. R.* 51.8.2) and he makes the statement as a matter of fact, showing that, east of the Empire, Christians and Jews shared many understandings of the biblical narratives.

Another Jewish theme pertaining to Lot's wife appears in one of the two east Syrian writers who will figure prominently in my discussion of Christian readings of Gibeah. As will be seen in that discussion, Iso'dad of Merv probably has the distinction of inventing a word that can only be translated by 'sodomy'. However, I will be suggesting that Iso'dad's 'sodomy' is nuanced very differently from the meaning of that word in western Christian traditions, probably due to the influence of Jewish traditions.

Iso'dad's commentary on Genesis is as much a compilation as his own work. For example, he quotes this passage from the anonymous Genesis compilation on the nature of Sodom's sin,

> It is probable that these Sodomites did not do these things from licentiousness, since they could do this to one another; but as at one time, they fell away from the fear of God, they became very incensed against men, and especially against strangers (*ESF* 91-2).

This quote introduces his discussion of the siege of Lot's house (*Iso. Comm. Gen.* 2.176), thus subordinating sexual themes to those of violence. Iso'dad's significance, however, lies in his commentary on the fate of Lot's wife. He quotes much of the same material about her that was found in the anonymous Genesis compilation plus further material from the Urmia recension of bar Koni's *Liber Scholiorum* (*LS*[U] 2.139B). Furthermore, he engages in a long discussion as to why Lot's wife was turned to salt as opposed to stone or any other material. When Lot received the angels, Lot's wife went to her neighbours to ask for salt. They realized that the angels were at Lot's house and alerted all the Sodomites, who then gathered to lay siege to it. Hence it was quite fitting that she should be turned to salt (*Iso. Comm. Gen.* 2.179). The significance of this detail is that it is not found anywhere else in Christian tradition, only in Jewish (in the Venice printed version of *Genesis Rabbah* in 1544 and two thirteenth-century midrashim, *Yalkut Shimoni* and *Midrash Aggadah*; none of the great individual rabbis such as Rashi include it in their commentaries). With the exception of a possible allusion in *Targum Pseudo-Jonathan*, Iso'dad's commentary is possibly the oldest written reference to this Jewish story, though he gives no acknowledgement of its Jewish provenance.[16]

---

16. None of the east Syrian commentators acknowledge the Jewish provenance of any of the material they share with rabbinic interpretations.

Its appearance here further demonstrates the strong Jewish influences on east Syrian Christian biblical interpretation.

j. *Summary*

This survey has demonstrated that the homophobic reading of Sodom developed later in Christianity and was not present from the start. Neither Origen, the first Christian exegete, nor Tertullian shows any awareness of it. For them, Sodom is a byword primarily for an arrogantly excessive way of life that pays no heed to others. Such a life can include sexual excess but there is no particular sexual sin associated with Sodom. Tertullian can even liken marriage to the ways of Sodom. The homophobic interpretation becomes established by the end of the fourth century, though Jerome adheres to the older interpretation. To John Chrysostom belongs the credit for systematically developing the homophobic reading by grafting it onto the established reading so that inhospitality is replaced by homoeroticism as the main sin of Sodom. He does so by declaring same-sex desire to be the fundamental disorder in a manner reminiscent of Basil's understanding of gluttony. He is followed in this enterprise by the Western Fathers, Ambrose and Augustine. The latter prefers the homophobic reading as most suited to his own theology of sexuality and marriage, thus entrenching the homophobic interpretation in the Latin West, where notions of natural and unnatural eros are applied to the story, in particular to justify Lot's offer of his daughters to the mob, with serious moral consequences. Also important for my discussion has been the interplay with Jewish traditions, with which both Origen and Jerome are clearly familiar. Similarly in the Syriac east, the shared perspective on the story between Christians and Jews means that the homophobic interpretation of the story does not achieve dominance amongst Syriac Christians.

5. *And Gibeah?*

In contrast to the vast quantity of material on Sodom, very little Christian literature from this period pertains to the events at Gibeah. Some early Christian commentaries on Judges exist, but only a handful of Christian texts that are in any way significant in their treatment of Gibeah. It would seem, nevertheless, that the story aroused as much aversion amongst Christians as amongst Jews. Origen's *Homilies on Judges* (1993) only deals with the first seven chapters of Judges and there is no evidence that he ever wrote on the events of Judges 19–21. An examination of the *Patrologiae Graecae* and the *Patrologiae Latina* shows only nine commentaries on Judges prior to 800 CE, mostly partial or partially preserved. Diodorus Tarsensis survives only on

Judg. 15.14 (*PG* 33: 1587-88), while the commentaries of Theodore Prodomus (*PG* 133: 1145-56), Isidore of Seville (*PL* 83: 390), Augustine (*PL* 34: 324) and that attributed to Bede (*PL* 93: 430) go no further than Samson (Judges 14-16). Two other commentaries, by Theodoret (*PG* 80: 513-16) and Gregory the Great (*PL* 79: 790), discuss the civil war between Israel and Benjamin but ignore Judges 19 and the events at Gibeah. Procopius of Gaza quotes Judges 19.1 but the details of the outrage at Gibeah are ignored (*PG* 87: 1078-80). Procopius's commentary on Genesis is interesting in offering a link between Sodom and Gibeah. In the Latin text/translation, but not the original Greek, one finds the comment that the siege of Lot's house is not unlike the outrage at Gibeah (*PG* 87: 371A). But it is most likely the comment of a later translator.

Athanasius, in his *Encyclical Letter*, uses the events at Gibeah briefly to illustrate his account of the ecclesiastical struggles over the Arian controversy. His main focus is the indignation of Israel at the outrage at Gibeah as recounted in Judges 20 and the resulting civil war. Of the outrage itself all he says is that 'a certain Levite was injured in the person of his wife' (*Encyclical Letter* §1 [1971: 92]). He then develops the story as an analogy of the Church in his day, riven by heresy, likening the concubine to the Church itself, the members of which 'are seen divided from one another, and...sent abroad... bringing word of the insults and injustice which they have suffered' (*Encyclical Letter* §1). However, Athanasius is not especially interested in the biblical account of events at Gibeah nor does he connect them to Sodom or make any homophobic use of the story.

Likewise, Ambrose makes no connection of Gibeah with Sodom, but his account is extremely significant. His theme is the need to honour and protect chastity and he introduces the story in his letter to Syagrius (*Letters* 33), to show that '(o)ur ancestors did not think chastity so to be despised' (*Letters* 33 [1954: 163]). While he gives a detailed account of the events at Gibeah it soon becomes apparent that Ambrose does not use the biblical account but Josephus' version instead. According to Josephus, the concubine herself is the focus of attention of the men of Gibeah, not the Levite, and despite the entreaties of the Levite's host, the men break in to seize the concubine rather than the Levite forcing her out to them to save himself.

Ambrose recounts Josephus' version almost word for word but adds glosses of his own. The Levite is much older than the concubine, thus accounting for the problems in their relationship. Furthermore, the Levite was partially culpable for the quarrels that drove her back to her parents because 'he used to chide her' (Ambrose 1954: 164). Ambrose also stresses the inhospitality of Gibeah. There was no inn in the town and the people were 'unfriendly, harsh, unbearable...who could stand anything but to receive people hospitably' (*Letters* 33 [1954: 165]). In describing the concubine's death, he clearly echoes Josephus.

> She went back to the door of their lodging, where she would not ask to see her husband, whom she thought she must now forego, ashamed at her pitiable condition. Yet, to show her love for her husband, she who had lost her chastity lay down at the door of the lodging, and there in pitiable circumstance came an end to her disgrace. The Levite, coming, found her lying there and thought that she dared not lift her head for shame. He began comforting her, since she had succumbed to such injury not willingly but unwillingly (*Letters* 33 [1954: 167]).

Thus we learn that for a woman to be raped is a matter of shame for her and injury to her husband (as in Athanasius), something that can only be redeemed by her giving up the ghost. But the reader must also wonder about Ambrose passing off Josephus as scripture. It is clear that he is presenting this as the biblical account. He introduces it as 'the sacred lesson' and closes it by saying '(s)cripture proves this not only here, but in many places' (*Letters* 33 [1954: 164, 171]). Like Athanasius, Ambrose does not make any homophobic use of the story, but links the crime of rape with inhospitality. In employing Josephus' version he also obscures that resemblance between the events at Gibeah and Sodom that figure in subsequent homophobic tradition of the West.

With the exception of Ambrose, the only detailed Christian accounts of Judges 19 are found in the east Syrian writers, Theodore bar Koni and Iso'dad of Merv, from the eighth and ninth centuries. Additionally, both writers compare these events to the story of Sodom, in the context of which Iso'dad coins the word 'sodomy' (although he appears to attribute the word to bar Koni).[17] Theodore bar Koni's account is brief. He is attempting to explain what the sin was for which the Benjaminites were condemned (*LS*(S) 3.78), but also accounts for the difference between the fates of Sodom and the Benjaminites. Here, too, it would appear that the Benjaminites are guilty not so much of a crime of unbridled passion but more one that used sex to harass and degrade outsiders.

He begins by saying that the Benjaminites had revived amongst themselves the practices of the Sodomites and used them as a trick to abuse strangers who came among them. In his brief summary of the events at Gibeah, he states that

---

17. These two texts are only translated into French and I would like to acknowledge the assistance of Dr Keith Atkinson in assisting with the finer points of the French translation. I also acknowledge the assistance of Professor Michael Lattke in translating the Syriac to compare with the French.

immediately the Levite entered the old man's house, it was surrounded by the Benjaminites. Rather than allow the man to be abused, the old man handed over his concubine and the Benjaminites pack raped her all through the night until she died. It is not clear, however, what bar Koni means when he says that they used practices of the Sodomites as a trick in order to abuse strangers. He goes on to say that they did not act out of shamelessness and lust, as verified by the fact that they obeyed the old man when he intervened to protect the Levite. The old man forbade them to abuse the Levite, but not to refrain from debauchery. Bar Koni concludes by arguing that because they obeyed the old man they did not merit the punishment of the Sodomites (by which he means extinction, not death by fire and brimstone). He also explains that it would not be good for one of the tribes of Israel to be wiped out.

It strikes me that bar Koni is perhaps trying to reconcile several different answers to his initial question. He clearly states that the Benjaminites had revived the ways of the Sodomites, but does not explain how such ways could be used as a trick to abuse strangers.[18] By saying that the Benjaminites did not act out of lust or shamelessness, bar Koni echoes the explanation of the Sodomites' motives in the anonymous Syriac commentary discussed earlier. However, the Benjaminites obeyed the old man, whereas the Sodomites did not obey Lot. If that fact proves the Benjaminites were not primarily motivated by lust, what then of the Sodomites? As bar Koni does not discuss Genesis 19, there is no point of comparison within his text. Nevertheless, it remains a chilling thought that the concubine's fate hinged on the old man's precision in his use of language.

While I find bar Koni unclear, Iso'dad is quite straightforward. What makes him all the more so is that he quotes from bar Koni as part of his commentary on these events. Iso'dad only relates the sins of the Benjaminites to the Sodomites in his commentary on vv. 19.25, 20.17 and 20.38, each time quoting from bar Koni. The first passage concerns the handing over of the concubine to the mob. Iso'dad says that because he did not want to be treated shamefully himself, the man brought out his concubine to them (*Iso. Comm. Judg.* 19.25). He does not clarify whether he means the old man or the Levite here and perhaps this ambiguity is appropriate, as both are complicit in her fate. However, he then cites bar Koni that the Benjaminites did not act out of shamelessness and lust, but incorrectly makes bar Koni say that the Benjami-

---

18. Several centuries later in the west, Nicholas of Lyra will argue that the men of Gibeah might have pretended to be like the Sodomites and demanded the Levite in order that the concubine, the real object of their desire, be handed over to them in his place (see below, Chapter 6). I can't help but think that maybe some such notion is behind bar Koni's argument. Nevertheless, it remains inconsistent and unclear.

nites acted not out of lust alone but also sheer malice, because the old man had told them not to commit evil but had not forbidden them from committing debauchery. Reading his version of bar Koni alongside Iso'dad's observations on the Sodomites in Genesis, I suspect that Iso'dad is here highlighting a delight in cruelty on the part of the Benjaminites. The old man asked them not to do harm (against the Levite, but only implicitly in Iso'dad's version) but did not ask them to refrain from sex. Iso'dad's version further seems to downplay the erotic in the Benjaminites' threat to the Levite. In other words they were demanding the Levite so as to do evil against him. When appealed to, however, they relented but accepted the concubine to abuse sexually. While the concubine is very clearly the victim here, if the Levite has any feeling for her, then her rape-murder is psychological assault on him as well. The sadistic logic here reminds me of Jewish accounts of Sodomite justice where a person has to be very careful what to request in dealings with the Sodomites. A literal interpretation of a person's request often turns out to be cruelly opposite to what the person really means.

In his discussion of Judg. 20.17, Iso'dad addresses the issue of why, given their outrageous behaviour, the Benjaminites were initially successful in the ensuing civil war. Why did the sons of Benjamin who had revived sodomy, of all behaviours, carry the victory and massacre 40,000 Israelite men (*Iso. Comm. Judg.* 20.17). The first clause of his question quotes the opening sentence of bar Koni's own response to the issue of Benjamin's sin, but with an important alteration. Rather than the phrase, 'practices of the Sodomites', Iso'dad uses the word, *s'doomayootha*, which is an abstract noun formed from *S'doom*: in other words, *sodomy*. Although Iso'dad uses it in a quote from bar Koni, the *Thesaurus Syriacus* indicates that this word first appears here in Iso'dad's own commentary (*TS* 2529). It would appear, then, that to Iso'dad belongs the dubious honour of being the inventor of the word 'sodomy'. But is *s'doomayootha* is the same as *sodomia*? The *Thesaurus Syriacus* is no help here, merely translating the word as 'Sodomia peccatum' (*TS* 2529). But does a ninth-century Nestorian bishop from eastern Mesopotamia intend the same meaning as an eleventh-century Latin Catholic monk from Italy, when he coins the same Latin word?

I suggest that the two words did not have the same meaning.[19] It is clear from Nilus' use of *sodomoumenē* and Jerome's use of 'sodomite' to describe a

---

19. That is not to say that the meaning of the Syriac word does not later get subsumed under that of the later Latin word. I would suggest this happened when, in the thirteenth century (post-Crusades), Bar Hebraeus describes Socrates, in his Chronography, as a lover of beautiful boys who was consequently accused of sodomy, *s'doomayootha* (*Chron.* VI, 35; 12r: 19).

type of person living an excessively indulgent life, that Sodom is used by Christians in late antiquity to categorize a variety of vices or undesirable personality traits. The medieval Latin term *sodomia*, is merely a later and the most successful instantiation of this process, but there is no consistency of meaning in earlier usages: different meanings derive from different contexts. I would argue that Isodad's *s'doomayootha* must be understood from within the context of his own readings and the interpretative tradition to which he is heir. He employs the word as a shorthand way of rendering the phrase, 'the practices of the Sodomites'. The meaning depends on what Iso'dad understands those practices to be. The changes Iso'dad makes in the earlier quote from bar Koni tend to downplay the erotic nature of the threat to the Levite. This impression is heightened when one reads Iso'dad's commentary on the parallel incident in Genesis 19, cited earlier. Iso'dad, like the east Syriac tradition behind him, agrees with the Jewish position that the Sodomites act out of hatred of strangers, not lust. As we saw earlier, Iso'dad seems aware of the Jewish tradition in respect of Lot's wife and her sin of salt.

Iso'dad's own answer as to why the Benjaminites twice won victory in the civil war displays further Jewish influences. He gives two reasons why the deity twice allowed such a victory. First, he says that the concubine had committed adultery and therefore was liable to be stoned to death. However, no one had bothered to uphold the Law of Moses. This omission was further compounded by the Israelites' tolerance of the idolatry of Micah. The Israelites were outraged over the treatment of an adulterous woman, but had not been outraged over the offence to the deity. Iso'dad here echoes Jewish themes I identified in *Sanh.* 103b, where the Israelites are punished by defeat for being outraged for the woman but not for the deity's honour. Indeed, Iso'dad gives a more detailed account than that found in the Babylonian Talmud[20] and one more disturbing to the reader. He is perhaps suggesting that the Benjaminites' treatment of the concubine was a crude fulfilment of the requirements of the Law.

On the basis of all these (unacknowledged) Jewish tropes in his commentary, I would argue that Iso'dad's understanding of the ways of Sodom is very different from that of the medieval Latins. Consequently, I would argue that *s'doomayootha* here is meant to convey the systematically cruel treatment of outsiders, probably, but not necessarily, incorporating sexual violence. I think what is most fundamental to Iso'dad's understanding is the cruel delight taken in the victimizing of others, a delight most strongly manifested in the rape-murder of a woman in accordance with a plea not to do evil to her

---

20. Theodoret of Cyrrhus gives a similar but less detailed account in his brief commentary on Judges 20 (*PG* 80: 515/6C-517/8B).

husband. Iso'dad's final comment on the story, in discussing Judg. 20.38, is to quote without comment bar Koni's explanation of why the Benjaminites were not wiped out like the Sodomites (*Iso. Comm. Judg.* 20.38). Given what he has said about the concubine being liable for death on account of her adultery, the citing of bar Koni to the effect that the Benjaminites were not completely wiped out because they accepted the correction or appeal of the old man, makes the deity itself complicit in the woman's death. The Benjaminites do not suffer extinction because, when they take the woman in place of the Levite, they inadvertently enforce the Law of Moses.

It is clear that, for this period, as far as Gibeah is concerned, most Christians ignore the story and silence predominates in most texts, including the few Christian commentaries on Judges. For most of these commentaries, Judges apparently ends with the story of Samson. Bailey claimed the Gibeah story was partially responsible for shaping Christian attitudes to homosexuality and claims that 'tradition has imposed a homosexual interpretation' (Bailey 1955: 53) on the story. In the first millennium, however, the evidence suggests otherwise. In the Latin and Greek traditions, the commentaries do not read the story homophobically. I have yet to find evidence that the two stories were even linked in any way by any of these commentators. Outside the commentaries, Athanasius is not interested in these aspects of the story, using it, instead, to dramatize the ecclesiastical and doctrinal conflicts of his day. Ambrose does not read the story homophobically and masks the parallels between Gibeah and Sodom such that it will play little part in shaping Christian homophobia in the west. The only clear connection made between the two stories occurs late in this period in the heretical east Syriac tradition. Its significance lies in the fact that *sodomy* is invented to name a shared evil of Sodom and Gibeah. However, this east Syriac *sodomy* does not signify same-sex desire but cruel delight in victimizing others, including sexual violence directed at men and women alike. Nevertheless, this Syriac *sodomy* highlights not only the similarities but also the differences between the two cities. Sodom is Gibeah's archetype, but not completely. Unlike Sodom, the events at Gibeah do not result in complete extinction for the perpetrators. They survive because, in taking the woman in place of the man, they inadvertently carry out the provisions of the Law. Consequently, this Syriac inventor of 'sodomy' makes the deity and himself complicit in the cruel victimization so named.

6. *Conclusion*

It is clear from Christian texts that Sodom is the archetype of the wicked city destroyed for its sins. However, there is no single understanding of what these sins are. Inhospitality, gluttony, opulent self-indulgence, pride and even the married estate are associated with Sodom. With the exception of the last, all of these accord with Jewish perspectives. Over time, however, the homophobic reading emerges, by which Sodom epitomizes the unnatural chaos of unrestrained homoeroticism that results in destruction. Such chaos is an affront to the deity warranting divine intervention and retribution, as Sodom demonstrates. In the west, this argument is used to explain the fall of Old Rome to the barbarians, sent by the deity to cure the Roman world of its menfolk's unnatural predilection to effeminacy. There is nothing inevitable about the homophobic reading, nor is it inherent in the text. That apparent inevitability comes from the fact of living now, on the other side of the invention of sodomy in the eleventh century, an event nurtured by a homophobic matrix. Indeed, this earlier period is marked by several attempts at defining 'sodomy', only one of which, by Gregory the Great, clearly prefigures the sodomy of homophobic invention. Had any or all of the other three become successful instead, then the contemporary Christian understandings of Sodom and Gomorrah would likely have been very different and same-sex desire would not have been framed in the apocalyptic fires of Sodom's doom.

The first of these earlier 'sodomies', Nilus' *sodomoumenē*, clearly contrasts the simple asceticism of the monastic life to the excessive self-indulgence of the opulent worldly life. This sodomy is primarily a sin of the arrogantly rich and powerful and accords in many ways with the understandings of Sodom found in the latter prophets, especially Ezekiel. It is also congruent with rabbinic notions of Sodom, for with the arrogance of wealth can come the vicious meanness that stops at nothing, even sexual violence, to prevent others sharing in the prosperity. Two other attempts, Jerome's almost casual use of 'sodomite' as a type of person, and Iso'dad's Syriac sodomy, have been appropriated under the later Latin sodomy. I have challenged that appropriation by my strategy of locating Christian readings of Sodom in the broader context of rabbinic and earlier readings. I have further broadened this context by including readings of the events at Gibeah, without which I would not have discovered Iso'dad's invention.

The lens of medieval sodomy could be used to harmonize all of these Christian texts with the homophobic interpretation of Sodom. Reading them in the broader context of rabbinic interpretation collapses this harmony. Origen's focus on hospitality, rather than same-sex desire, no longer seems unusual but typical. Chrysostom's, on the face of it, ludicrous assertion that inhospitality and abuse of strangers are the evil results of homoeroticism make better sense when seen as trying to graft a homophobic reading onto a more generally accepted association of Sodom with those two evils. Similarly, Jerome, through his obvious knowledge of rabbinic readings of Sodom,

now appears in a completely different light. Nowhere does he clearly associate same-sex desire with Sodom and Gomorrah, the main sin in his mind is
pride combined with the excessive indulgence of arrogant wealth. This sin
is characterized by its complete shamelessness, typified for Jerome by the
behaviour of the Jewish chief priests in claiming Caesar as their king to
force the execution of Jesus. So, when Jerome refers to someone as an adulterer and a sodomite, he should not be automatically assumed to be referring to homoeroticism. There is nothing in Jerome that would preclude
applying Nilus' definition to his sodomite.

With Iso'dad, these broader contexts take on even more importance,
because the Syriac tradition displays a particularly strong Jewish influence. As
Iso'dad coins his sodomy to highlight how the people of Gibeah were behaving sodomitically in what they did, his meaning depends on how both stories
are read and related to each other. Given the almost complete silence
concerning the events at Gibeah in early Christianity, it is essential to employ
Jewish interpretations of these events as well as those at Sodom to assay
Iso'dad's meaning here. There is nothing in the context of these interpretations to justify the assumption that Iso'dad has invented a word to denote
same-sex desire and homoeroticism. All the evidence lends itself to the argument that Iso'dad is denoting the systematically cruel treatment of outsiders,
probably incorporating sexual violence and very likely including a cruel delight
in the victimization of others.

But Iso'dad's reading of the events at Gibeah highlights a fundamental
moral problem – a deep misogyny that also drives the Christian homophobic
interpretation of Sodom. Misogyny is crucial to understanding the threatened homophobic violence in both narratives. In attempting to rape the male
outsiders, apart from the sheer violence of such mass assault, the men of both
Sodom and Gibeah are invoking the symbolic feminizing of the penetrated
male. The penetrated male is like a woman and not a real man, at all. The
penetrated male is queer and an outsider. Homophobia's misogynistic basis
finds its most perverse expression in the Christian justification of Lot's offer
of his daughters. As Augustine and others would put it, it is better for women
to be raped than men. Furthermore, the grounding of Christian homophobia
in a discourse of the natural and unnatural, leads to an understanding of Lot's
offer as attempting to righteously convert the unnaturally homosexual Sodomites to the joys of natural heterosexual sex. This thoroughly perverse logic
is employed by Ambrose and Augustine, and is dramatized in the poem
Sodoma. To his credit, Augustine recognizes that there is something wrong
with this logic, but he is unable to understand where the problem lies. In so
doing he misses an opportunity to open a Christian ethical discourse on rape.

Misogyny and erotophobia are the moral flaws in Iso'dad's reading of Judges 19. For Iso'dad, it is still a good thing that a woman is raped (to death) instead of a man. His logic here is not the perversely twisted logic of homophobia but the blatantly (perversely) cruel logic of male patriarchal privilege. The woman had committed adultery and therefore deserved to die. While they committed a great sin deserving of death, the men of Gibeah had unwittingly enforced a rough application of the Law of Moses. Thus, according to Iso'dad, not only does the woman have the men of Gibeah to contend with, but also the god of Israel who is more outraged by the veneration of Micah's idols than by the horrible events in Gibeah. Unlike the god of Genesis 19 who intervenes to prevent such an outrage, this god stands with the Levite and the old man in orchestrating the death of the woman. The men of Gibeah become unwitting agents of divine patriarchy.

Perhaps, then, it is a blessing that Ambrose opted to read Judges 19–21 according to Josephus. In doing so, the woman is made a noble martyr to the cause of Ambrose's patriarchal privilege and, thus, his reading becomes one that attempts to speak for her. Her martyrdom means that her death is one that is vindicated and not one that is divinely endorsed. Given the consequences of the homophobic reading of Genesis 19 alone, I shudder to think of what might have been the consequences for women and for queer people, both, if Christian homophobia had had Sodom, Gomorrah and Gibeah at its disposal.

Chapter 6

THE SIN THAT ARROGANTLY PROCLAIMS ITSELF: INVENTING SODOMY IN MEDIEVAL CHRISTENDOM

1. *A Homophobic Project*

As Mark Jordan (1997) reminds us, the period of the medieval West is the time when the word/concept *sodomy* (L. *sodomia*) is invented as a clearly homophobic device. Furthermore this invention can be localized to a person and a text: Peter Damian and his *Book of Gomorrah*. This text was addressed to Pope Leo, who reigned from 1048 to 1054, so this invention can also be located very narrowly in time. As seen in Chapter 5, the invention of sodomy was rehearsed several times in the first Christian millennium, but only one of these attempts clearly foreshadowed Damian's move in its homophobic intent. I will be arguing that Damian should perhaps be better understood as the midwife at the birth of sodomy, a concept that had been gestating in the textual/cultural matrix of Latin Christianity. Before analysing Damian's work, I will explore some of that textual world in the form of medieval Latin penitential literature and biblical commentary. Following from Damian's achievement, however, exegesis will become stamped on language such that language is exegesis. Whereas Peter Damian is concerned solely with male-male sexuality, Peter Cantor (d. 1192) completes his project to incorporate female-female sexuality. This move will enable Thomas Aquinas to classify same-sex desire and sexuality as a specifically sodomitic species of the unnatural realm. Semantically, a disaster story, same-sex desire and homophobia are now fused in the lexicon. The Sodomite has become a person of dual nationality – on the one hand, a citizen of Sodom and on the other, a species of human associated with sexual transgression and same-sex desire. The story of Sodom functions as the Torah does for the Jew. It generates identity and community and just as Jewishness is not merely an ethnicity or genealogy but also a spirituality, so too Sodomy, the Sodomite avocation, denotes a spirituality – one of transgression, subversion and menace. The big difference is that Jewish identity is an internally generated and renewing autonomous lineage from the first standing at Sinai and therefore in some sense empowering. In contrast, the Sodomite identity is an imposed identity designed to disempower and destroy. There is no sustaining lineage from a covenant cut at Sodom. Instead the identity and the covenant are retrojected in time by those seeking to extirpate such a reality. The irony would be if, believing it to be true, subsequent communities embrace such a phobic fiction as their own for their own empowerment.

With the story of Gibeah no such metamorphosis occurs. Indeed, as in the first eight Christian centuries, the commentators seem to shun the story altogether, especially the incidents of Judges 19. The book of Judges appears not to be a desirable text for commentary and its ending even less so. For this reason I shall not include a specific section on Gibeah in this chapter, but incorporate material on Gibeah in the relevant sections. I remind the reader that because of their similarities, Gibeah serves here as a point of comparison to Sodom. What will be striking is that despite the similarity, Gibeah's story, with one exception, is generally ignored in the homophobic project.

2. *A Textual Matrix – Penitentials and Commentaries*

a. *Penitentials*

The penitentials are a body of literature that can best be called manuals or guides for confessors administering the sacrament of penance. The penitentials provide question and answer techniques for drawing out a confession, detailed discussions of particular sins and their mortal or venial nature. They also detail the penances to be imposed according to the type of sin and the estate of the confessor, that is whether they be laity, priest, monk, nun or bishop. The story of Sodom is frequently invoked in the penitential literature in the context of male-male or anal sex through the use of 'sodomite' as either an adjective to describe an act or as a noun, referring to a type of person who acts like a resident of Sodom. Thus, the seventh-century Penitential of Cummean refers to those who commit wickedness with men as the Sodomites did (*Cummean* 2.9) – *qui faciunt scelus virile ut Sodomite* (Bieler 1963: 114).[1] The Burgundian penitential, likewise, can refer to those who act as a Sodomite: *sicut sodomite fecerunt* (Payer 1984: 152). The Preface of Gildas contrasts natural fornication with fornication as a Sodomite: *fornicationem naturalem sive sodomitam* (Bieler 1963: 60). This usage is consistently employed so that, in the eleventh century, Burchard of Worms can, in his *Decretum* 19, refer to committing fornication as the residents of Sodom did (*fornicationem sicut Sodomitae fecerunt* [*PL* 140: 967D]). In the

---

1.   Both Bieler and McNeill and Gamer translate this phrase as 'those who commit sodomy' (Bieler 1963: 115; McNeill and Gamer 1965: 103).

early-thirteenth century Robert of Flamborough employs a similar phrase, *(q)ui fornicatus fuerit sicut sodomitae* (*Liber poenitentialis* 5.3, sec no 272). Egbert, in his *Canones de remediis peccatorum*, uses *sodomitae* as a shorthand instead of employing the whole phrase (*PL* 89: 446A, 448A). Thus, the act of 'fornicating as the Sodomites' becomes further subsumed under the name of Sodom. Sodomites are no longer residents of an ancient city but contemporaries of the confessor who fornicate as did the Sodomites. This sexual act awards citizenship of Sodom upon its practitioners. Such is certainly the case in the penitentials of Theodore where the reader finds a Capitula 'Concerning Sodomites' (*De Sodomitis*), which deals with those who fornicate as did the Sodomites (*PL* 99: 972C).

The adjectival use of sodomit/e/ic, much rarer than the noun (Payer 1984: 152), is occasionally accompanied by attempts to define its meaning. Peter of Poitiers confidently refers to the sodomitic vice, *sodomiticum vitium* (*Compilatio Praesens* 14.12), without any further need for clarification. Bede knows a sodomitic crime, *sodomiticum scelus* (*PL* 94: 570C) that he invokes in the context of sexual sins of the married to condemn sexual intercourse from behind (*PL* 94: 570C). This method of intercourse too closely resembles the sodomitic crime and is therefore to be shunned (Payer 1984: 29). Burchard of Worms is the most explicit and describes those men who have anal sex together as 'having sex with each other in the Sodomite manner' (*Decretum* 19; *PL* 140: 967D).[2] Columban also attempts a similar clarification. He sets the same penance (ten years) for monks found guilty of homicide or of committing the 'sodomitic sin', *aut sodomiticum fecerit peccatum* (*PL* 80: 225A).[3] He then sets a lower penance (seven years) for members of the laity guilty of fornication according to the 'sodomitic rite' (*PL* 80: 227C). He goes on to define this act as sinning by having 'female intercourse' with a man – *cum masculo, coitu femineo peccaverit* (*PL* 80: 227C).[4] Columban is here quoting the Levitical proscriptions from the Vulgate.[5] So not only is his usage one of the few occasions when the nature of sodomitic sin/fornication is given some clarification, it is also one of those few occasions where the story of Sodom is linked with the Levitical proscriptions on male-male anal sex.

2.   *Fecisti fornicationem sicut Sodomitae, ita ut in masculi terga et in posteriora virgam tuam immitteres, et sic secum coires more Sodomitico?*

3.   McNeill and Gamer translate this phrase as 'he commits...the sin of sodomy' (McNeill and Gamer 1965: 250).

4.   McNeill and Gamer translate this phrase as 'commits an act of homosexuality' (McNeill and Gamer 1965: 254).

5.   Lev. 18.22 – *cum masculo non commisceberis coitu femineo*; Lev. 20.13 – *qui dormierit cum masculo coitu femineo.*

Of course, the Levitical proscriptions are themselves not that clear. The Hebrew, literally translated, means something like 'with a male, a male not lying the lying down of a woman' (see Olyan 1997). Olyan (1997: 399) describes the proscriptions as being opaque because their meaning hinges on how the idiom translated as 'the lying down of a woman' is understood. He argues that the passages most likely condemn male-male anal sex only (Olyan 1997: 400). With the exception of Burchard and Columban, the references to Sodom in the penitentials are even more obtuse. As Mark Jordan says:

> Even in the penitentials, which are noted for their blunt speaking about sexual matters, references to Sodom or Sodomites are used both to conceal and to reveal. They reveal to those who already know what the geographico-biblical reference means. Otherwise they conceal (Jordan 1997: 42).

This strategy of concealment, ironically, is maintained by both the Bieler and McNeill and Gamer translations of the penitential literature. I have indicated above in footnotes how they have used the words 'sodomy' and 'homosexual' in translation. I have done this to show how such usage changes the meaning of the Latin text, whose authors had no concept of 'sodomy' (a word invented several centuries later) let alone 'homosexual', which was not invented until the late-nineteenth century. The use of these words actually serves to obfuscate further an already unclear text, as is clearly shown in McNeill and Gamer's translation of the penitiential canons from the sixth-century Welsh Synod of the Grove of Victory. They render canon 8 as follows, '(In substance), he who is guilty of sodomy in its various forms shall do penance for four, three, or two years according to the nature of the offense' (McNeill and Gamer 1965: 172). They also provide the Latin text in a footnote, *Qui facis scelus virile, ut sodomite, IV annis, Qui vero in femoribus, III annis, manu autem, sive alterius sive sua, II annis* (McNeill and Gamer 1965: 172, fn 20). It is clear that the Latin text is not listing three forms of sodomy or, more accurately, of acting as the Sodomites did. Several centuries later Peter Damian will make such an extension (see below) but in this context *sodomite* serves to separate out a particular act from two others, inter-femoral intercourse and (mutual) masturbation, the latter two being acts *unlike* that of the Sodomites.[6] The invocation of Sodom in the Latin demarcates as well as conceals, but in the translation it serves to conceal completely.

Ironically, the most explicit invocation of Sodom in a penitential text occurs in *Canones Hibernes* V (Bieler 1963: 172-75; see also McNeill and

6.   Similarly the passage in the Penitential of Cummean which refers to those who sin like the Sodomites is demarcating their sin from that of inter-femoral intercourse between men (*Cummean* 2.9-10 in Bieler 1963: 114-15; McNeill and Gamer 1965: 103).

Gamer 1965: 125-27). But here the issue is not male-male sex but hospitality, specifically towards those of high ecclesiastical office. The chapter opens citing Genesis 18–19:

> Let the wise man observe what benefits Abraham and Lot received for their kindness in receiving strangers; but let him likewise be aware what punishment Sodom brought upon itself by rejecting them and for its wicked deed (*Can. Hib.* V, 1).

But not only is this text noteworthy in that it declares Sodom's doom to be due to its inhospitality but it also continues almost as a midrash, weaving together material from various sources to underline the message of hospitality as an essential virtue. Included in this material are the gospel narratives concerning the preaching mission of the Twelve in Matthew 10 and Luke 9. The Matthean version explicitly refers to Sodom and Gomorrah in the context of inhospitality. The Canon quotes the Matthean Jesus saying, 'If anyone will not welcome you listen to your words shake off the dust from your feet (as you that…town)' (Mt. 10.14). Jesus then says that it will be easier for Sodom and Gomorrah than for that town in the day of judgement (Mt. 10.15). Clearly, for the authors of this Canon, not only the gospel references to Sodom and Gomorrah cited here, but also the original story of the cities in Genesis, are primarily concerned with the issue of hospitality. Immediately following Jesus' words, this penitential text declares:

> One who casts out a poor man slays him… Further, whoever is able to succour one who is about to perish and does not succour him, slays him; for the throat of a hungry stranger perishes when food is denied him (*Can. Hib.* V, 6).

In this context, the traditional association of the Sodomites and their sin with murder is quite logical. For travelling strangers, the refusal of food and drink by those they meet or with whom they take refuge has fatal consequences. As was seen in Jewish commentaries, this meanness of the Sodomites was understood as having murderous intent. This penitential illustrates dramatically the life and death importance of hospitality. Leaving aside the potentially lethal consequences of pack rape, or of the various tortures attributed to the Sodomites in Jewish tradition, plain Sodomite meanness is murder. That the western Christian tradition could take this lethal dimension of Sodom's sin of inhospitality and attribute it homophobically to same-sex love and desire is a particularly perverse twist. Given the fatal consequences for so many who could not be at home in this homophobic Christian regime, the perversity of this move is of such a quality that it would, no doubt, greatly delight the Sodomites of Midrash and Talmud.

b. *Commentaries*

In the penitentials, Sodom and its inhabitants were used as 'a way of designating a particular kind of sexual intercourse' (Jordan 1997: 41) even though this usage does not in itself always specify the type of intercourse involved. A similar use of the story will be seen in the medieval commentaries on Genesis. Sodom comes to represent a category of people who merit the general infamy of the biblical Sodom and its citizens and who consequently deserve to share in Sodom's fate. In these commentaries, it is clear that Sodom and Gomorrah are associated with a particular type of sexual activity but, as with penitential literature, the nature of this sexual activity is not clearly spelled out. However, while the specifics are vague, Sodom's infamy clearly pertains to male same-sex desire. My discussion of these Latin commentaries on Genesis will not cover their every detail, but will explore two significant issues. The first is the quality of the divine justice that destroys the children, especially the infants and newborn, with the parents. The second issue concerns the sin of Sodom, particularly in comparison with that of the generation of the Flood. The question is asked, why is water used for one and fire for the other? The answer relies on the fact that homoeroticism is non-reproductive or 'sterile', so as to give license to the most extreme omnicidal fantasy in which the earth itself is rendered forever lifeless. In none of these commentaries on Genesis does the similarity between the stories of Sodom and Gibeah arise as an issue. In order to give the reader some appreciation of how little the story of Gibeah figures in the medieval imagination, I shall conclude my discussion of the commentaries with an overview of the minimal treatment of Judges 19–21 to be found in medieval commentaries.

At first sight, it might be heartening to learn that medieval commentators were concerned about the children of Sodom and Gomorrah. Such concern was certainly not evident in the texts discussed in the earlier chapters, nor is it a major issue in texts from later periods, including our own. However, medieval answers to the question of whether it was just for the deity to destroy the children with their parents prove to be very disturbing, as their primary purpose is to justify the divine massacre. Indeed, in so doing, they provide a rationale for human agents of that divine entity when they feel inclined to do likewise. In his Inquiries and Answers on Genesis (*Interrogationes et Responsiones in Genesin*), Alcuin asks straightforwardly if the divine judgement can be just if the children are cremated with the parents. His answer betrays no doubt that the deity has acted justly. The children must die because if they were left to live they would continue in the way of their parents. Furthermore, the destruction of the children as well as their parents is a salutary warning to future generations not to imitate Sodom's example. Alcuin then says that the parents will be called to account in the final judgement for the death of their children and that the children themselves will be the accusers (*PL* 100: 541D). He completes his argument by stating that it is better for the children to perish than to grow up and be damned, and adds the chilling observation that it is good for a person not to be poor who is not able to be king (*PL* 100: 541D). This statement sounds like a misapplication of a popular adage but, as a rationale for genocide, it seems not to have been problematic for medieval exegetes because it is cited whenever the issue of the children comes up. Alcuin is quoted in full and without additional comment in the *Glossa Ordinaria* (*PL* 113: 132A). Alcuin's argument is also repeated virtually word for word by Angelomus in his own commentary on Genesis (*PL* 105: 186B). Comestor, in his *Historia Scholastica*, compares Sodom and Gomorrah to the generation of the Flood and extends Alcuin's argument to justify the death of the children in both disasters (*PL* 198: 1101B).

But what is it that could possibly merit such genocidal punishment, prompting commentators to say that it is better for the children not to be? The answer to this question inevitably elicits a comparison with the Flood. Once again Alcuin points the way. He asks why the generation of Noah was punished by water while the Sodomites were punished by fire. His answer is that the generation of Noah followed natural desires and sinned with women (*naturale libidinis cum feminis peccatum*), and therefore they were punished with a 'light' element. However, the Sodomites followed unnatural desires and sinned with men (*contra naturam libidinis peccatum cum viris*); hence they were wiped out with 'severe' elements (*PL* 100: 543A). He concludes that the earth was washed by water and could become green again, but the cities of the Plain were burned so as to dry up the land and render it forever sterile: *et illic terra aquis abluta revirescit; hic flammis cremata aeterna sterilitate arescit* (*PL* 100: 543A). Same-sex desire thus gives a warrant not only for genocide but omnicide.

Rabanus Maurus (*Commentariorum in Genesim* II) also links the fate of Sodom to same-sex or perverse desires (*perversa desideria*) and plays with imagery of the fires of lust and the fires of punishment in a manner that recalls the polemic of Gregory the Great. Like Gregory, too, Rabanus Maurus delights in the appropriateness of sulphur falling with the fire, because the stench of sulphur expels the stench of the (sins of the) flesh (*PL* 107: 558B). Similarly, in the *Glossa Ordinaria* Sodom's fate is compared to that of the Flood generation. The Sodomites' sin was much worse than that of the Flood generation who sinned naturally (*qua naturaliter peccabant*) whereas the Sodomites sinned against nature (*isti vero contra naturam*). They were destroyed in a flood of fire and sulphur, so that by their most severe condemnation and punishment they are an example to all of humanity (*PL* 113: 131D–132A). Rupert of Deutz also addresses the question of the significance of fire and brimstone as the tools of Sodom's doom. He says that fire and brimstone were appropriately employed because the Sodomites burned with the fire of that desire which is against nature: *ejus libidinis igne arserant, quae est contra naturam* (*PL* 167: 412C). The influence of Gregory the Great is again manifest because Rupert plays with the image of sulphur/brimstone. He points out the appropriateness of heaven raining brimstone with fire because it was in response to the awful stench of the (sins of the) flesh, sent up to heaven from Sodom. Sodom's fate is not only a warning but also an example of the eternal fire that awaits the damned at judgement. Both Angelomus Luxoviensis (*PL* 115: 187B) and Remigius Antissiodorensis (*PL* 131: 92C) likewise compare Sodom and Gomorrah to the Flood repeating, virtually word for word, Alcuin's original argument.

Compared to the wealth of material around Sodom and Gomorrah, material on Gibeah from this period is sparse. Of the six commentaries on Judges included in this section,[7] three give no more than about a half dozen lines to the events of chs. 19–21 as a whole. One focuses its discussion only on ch. 20 and only two give any extensive treatment of the events of Judges 19. Only one gives any consideration of the events of Judges 21. However, when compared to the commentaries on Genesis 19 this 'extensive treatment' seems quite circumspect. This circumspection is highlighted by the fact that all six of these commentators wrote on Genesis as well and have a lot more to say of the events around the destruction of Sodom than of those at Gibeah.

The compilers of the *Glossa ordinaria* seem to lose interest in the book of Judges as they proceed through the Samson story. There is less and less material found worthy of any comment as the chapters progress. After the Samson story they only comment on one verse from each chapter. At first the reader's interest might be aroused to find that v. 25 of Judges 19 has been singled out for comment, given that it recounts the concubine being pushed out to the mob. The commentary, however, does not condemn the Levite nor decry the concubine's fate. Instead, Augustine is quoted on the meaning of the word for 'concubine', pointing out that it is equivalent to the word for 'wife'. On ch. 20, v. 18 is cited, where the Israelites consult the deity at Bethel on their battle order against Benjamin. The commentary quotes abbreviatedly from Gregory the Great to the effect that it is good to submit oneself to the truth. In ch. 21, the opening verse is merely cited without any comment whatsoever (*PL* 113: 532C).

7.   Two others, by Peter Damian and Nicholas de Lyra, will be discussed later in this chapter in the sections on those writers.

As in the *Glossa ordinaria*, both Hugh and Andrew of St Victor also seem to lose interest in Judges as they approach the end. Both make only brief comments on 19.18 and 20.5. On 19.18, they both note that the tent at Shiloh was called the house of God. The second verse, 20.5, relates the Levite's explanation to the assembly of Israel concerning the reason he called them together. Both commentators say that the Levite omits mention of the immediate threat of the men of Gibeah out of shame at what they wanted to do to him: *Pudice de se tacet, quod facere voluerunt* (Hugh of St Victor, *In librum Judicum, PL* 175: 96B). Rabanus Maurus completely ignores the events of Judges 19 and focuses his attention on Judges 20, which he reads as a moral story against being carried away by revenge for evil. That Israel is defeated twice by Benjamin before they ultimately win meant that they had to purify themselves of vengeful thoughts. Maurus quotes Jn 8.7, 'let he who is without sin…', to underscore his argument (*PL* 108: 1200B).

There remain two more extensive treatments of Judges 19, though still quite brief when compared to the discussion of Genesis 19. Rupert of Deutz summarizes Judges 19, focusing on the events of the rape. He gives no reason for the Levite's wife (he uses the word *uxorem*) returning to her father's house in Bethlehem and ignores most of the events in Bethlehem. He describes how the men surround the old man's house and assail it, demanding the Levite be brought out to them. But Rupert omits the old man's intervention and his offer of both his daughter and the Levite's wife to the mob. Instead he states that, in the face of this demand, the Levite and his host were scarcely able to prevent the crime against nature being perpetrated on the Levite (*PL* 167: 1056A). They could only do so by providing the Levite's wife in exchange. She was abused the entire night, the mob being possessed by an extraordinary fury of desire: *facta commutatione nequissima uxorem ejus tota nocte abutendo, incredibili libidinis furore vexaverunt* (*PL* 167: 1056A). Rupert does not seem to be disturbed by the fate of the concubine. He neither condemns what happens to her, nor, more disturbingly, does he attempt to offer some justification of the Levite and the old man for their complicity in this crime. For Rupert, what is of concern in the outrage at Gibeah has to do with same-sex desire. However, he makes no attempt to compare this event with its most notorious counterpart in Sodom. It is as if the two stories are totally unrelated in Rupert's perspective. Furthermore, while he is prepared to use the events at Sodom to highlight the dangers of and punishment for same-sex desire (*PL* 167: 409A-C, 412B-C), he makes no such attempt here. Rupert seems to be impatient to get through ch. 19 because he is more interested in the events of Judges 20. He also ignores completely the events of Judges 21, which should not be a cause for surprise, considering his lack of concern at the concubine's fate and considering that this chapter deals primarily with mass rape.

Peter Comestor's *Historia Scholastica* is most noteworthy because he gives an inclusive account of the events of Judges 19–21, and also because he acknowledges Josephus' version of the events at Gibeah. The *Historia* is a retelling of the biblical narratives, supplemented by glosses from a number of commentaries. For the events of Judges 19–21, Comestor refers frequently to Josephus, but on those occasions where Josephus contradicts the biblical text, Comestor makes no attempt to harmonize the two. He largely follows the Vulgate account of the outrage at Gibeah, referring to the concubine as the Levite's wife (*uxorem*) who returns to her father because she was angry with her husband. Comestor recounts how the Levite and his party were given hospitality by the old man from Ephraim and that the house was surrounded by a crowd of men demanding that the Levite be brought out for them to abuse (*abutamur* as per the Vulgate). Comestor then tells the reader that, according to Josephus, the mob did not come for the Levite but to rape his wife (*PL* 198: 1291C). However, he makes no attempt to explain this discrepancy, but leaves it to the reader to decide whether or not to accept Josephus' version. Comestor simply resumes the biblical account of the old man offering his daughter and the concubine to the mob, in lieu of the Levite, without further comment. Similarly he recounts, without comment, the fate of the concubine being raped all night by the mob until her death. Like Rupert, he makes no attempt to justify or condemn the Levite and the old man for the concubine's fate. In his account of the events of ch. 20 he focuses on the horrified reaction of the assembly of Israel and the ensuing civil war. Significantly, he omits the Levite's account of events as if a third version of the outrage might be too much for the reader to assimilate. Comestor's account of the events of Judges 21 is largely a summary of the biblical text, and closes with the well-known words from 21.25, 'In those days there was no king in Israel and everyone did what was right in their eyes' (*PL* 198: 1292C).

c. *Summary*

Surveying these medieval commentaries and penitentials, the reader is struck by the association of Sodom and Gomorrah with same-sex desire and in particular with one sexual act between men. This sexual act is rarely specified but, on the few occasions when it is, the act is clearly male-male anal sex. This is identified as the sodomitic crime, or sinning as the Sodomites did, and is also known as the crime against nature. Although such usages are not very specific, they do serve to distinguish the act from other forms of male-male sex such as inter-femoral sex and mutual masturbation, which, while sinful, are not sinning as did the Sodomites. However, such distinctions are most apparent in the penitential literature. Over the centuries the distinctions begin to blur, such that Sodom is associated with (male) same-sex desire *per se*. What contributes to this shift is the blurring of the meaning of the term 'Sodomite' itself. The word comes to denote a species of humanity, distinguished by a sex act or a form of sexual desire, namely for a member of one's own sex. In the commentaries this propensity for the homoerotic is so horrendous that it can justify the mass murder of children in an act of genocide because it is better for the children not to be alive than to grow up and become members of such a tribe. Same-sex desire is against nature, utterly disordered. The gravity of this sin is demonstrated by the massacre of the children and the sterilization of the land. The commentators argue that not only is the massacre of children justified to completely extirpate homoeroticism and to save those children from growing up to embrace it, but even the sterilization of the earth itself is warranted in Sodom and in any place where sodomitic sins take hold. The sterilization of places where such sterile desire has thrived ensures that no life can arise there that might embrace that sin. It is as if traces of that sin lurk as spores of infection in the environment, despite such 'disinfection' and wasting of the land. Such drastic action is required because the tribe of Sodomites did not perish with the cities of the Plain, but is found in every town and monastery of Christendom and beyond.

While Sodom and her sisters in the Plain are transformed into a foundational homophobic myth of same-sex desire for Western Christendom, no such process takes place for Sodom's stepsister, Gibeah. Despite the similarity of the two stories, no one even remarks on that similarity. Gibeah is doomed to a life of drudgery in the commentaries, unlike Sodom, which becomes stamped on language itself. A reader exploring those few commentaries would be hard pressed indeed to ascertain that a woman was actually raped and murdered there. In the case of Gibeah, commentary has served to cover up a crime. What follows is a description of four, solo, homophobic performances of medieval Christian themes associated with Sodom and Gomorrah. All four of these virtuoso performances produce morbidly fascinating and repellent variations of the Sodom myth of medieval Christian homophobia, which further shape that myth not only for the medieval period but beyond, into our own time.

3. *Peter Damian and the Invention of Sodomy*

Peter Damian's eleventh-century work against clerical homosexuality, *The Book of Gomorrah*, represents a crucial turning point in the history of Sodom and in the history of homophobia. In this work the word 'sodomy', *sodomia*, is first coined with all its homophobic associations. Consequently, Mark Jordan argues that to Peter Damian belongs the dubious honour of inventing sodomy as a word and a concept. *Gomorrah* contains many references to Sodom and Gomorrah in which the cities are portrayed as places that gave themselves over to same-sex desire. Because of their fate, they graphically illustrate the deity's abhorrence for same-sex desire and homoerotic relationships. Damian's work is a fierce polemic that draws on many biblical threads to make its case, and he is not averse to creating his own biblical texts to support his case. Nowhere in *Gomorrah*, does Damian give a single overview of the events of Genesis 19, but he makes reference to aspects of the story throughout the work. Nor does he make reference to the events of Judges 19–21, although he knew of them. The oversight suggests that he did not regard the story of Gibeah as primarily concerning the evil of homoeroticism.

In *Gomorrah* is embedded a very rudimentary Sodom story comprising the elements of sin, outrage and punishment/destruction. All the male characters are present (the deity, the angels, Abraham, Lot, the Sodomites) but none of the female characters (Sarah, Lot's wife, Lot's daughters). Abraham is briefly mentioned in *Gomorrah*, chapter 24, where, because he settled at Mamre and kept distant from Sodom, he serves as an example of those who steer clear of Sodomites and keep their passions under control (*Gomorrah* 86). The Sodomites represent the 'lustful plagues of the flesh' and the people who yield to such drives, especially by surrendering to same-sex desire. In contrast to both Abraham and the Sodomites, Damian employs Lot as a figure for those whose passions are not so well-yoked or who are unable to live in a Sodomite-free environment.

As for the sin/s of Sodom and Gomorrah, Damian is in no doubt that they pertain to the free expression of same-sex desire. In the discussion of the penitentials, I noted that they employed Sodom to distinguish a particular sex act from other sex acts that were acts of *not* sinning as the Sodomites. With Damian, however, it is clear from the title of his work that he wants to expand Sodom semantically to stand for same-sex desire and not just a particular act. In his opening Preface, addressed to Pope Leo, he lays down the gauntlet saying that a 'certain abominable and terribly shameful vice (*quoddam autem nefandum et ignominiosum valde vitium*) has grown up in our region' (*Gomorrah* 27; *PL* 144: 161A). It is the vice 'against nature' (*vitium contra naturam*), which 'creeps in like a cancer' and 'rages like a bloodthirsty beast in…the sheepfold of Christ' and 'even touches the order of consecrated men' (*Gomorrah* 27). Then in his first chapter he sets out to clarify what this vice against nature is and gives it four orders or types

> ...some sin with themselves alone; some commit mutual masturbation; some commit femoral fornication; and, finally, others commit the complete act against nature. (*Alii sequidem secum, alii aliorum manibus, alii inter femora, alii denique consummato actu contra naturam delinquunt*) (*Gomorrah* 29; *PL* 144: 161C).

If the reader has any doubt that these practices are all offshoots of the one vine of Sodom (cf. Deut. 32.32), Damian declares,

> ...whether one pollutes himself or another in any manner whatsoever, even if discretion is observed, nevertheless he is undoubtedly to be convicted of having committed the crime of Sodom. Nor do we read that the inhabitants of Sodom corrupted others only by the consummated act. We should rather believe that under the impulse of unbridled lust they acted shamefully alone and with others in different ways (*Gomorrah* 78).

In the penitentials, Sodom is used to identify a particular expression of same-sex desire, anal sex, as against other expressions such as mutual masturbation and inter-femoral sex. Damian's move is quite breathtaking because he has semantically equated Sodom with all expressions of same-sex desire, including the implicit homoeroticism of the solo act of masturbation. In so doing, he has equated all expressions of same-sex desire with the singular 'vice against nature' and made them all expressions of the sin of Sodom. According to Damian, this vice against nature was already being punished with severity by the deity even 'before he had placed the bridle of legal precept on the other vices' and the proof of this claim is the destruction of Sodom and Gomorrah (*Gomorrah* 32). Therefore, having made these moves, it should come as no surprise that Damian makes his most important semantic move namely the invention of sodomy as an abstract concept representing the homoerotic. He says,

> ...if blasphemy is the worst, I do not know in what way sodomy is better. Blasphemy makes a man to err, sodomy to perish (...*quia si pessima est blasphemia, nescio, in quo sit melior sodomia. Illa enim fecit hominem errare; ista perire*). The former divides the soul from God, the latter joins it to the devil... If we are careful to search into which of these crimes weighs more heavily on the scales of divine scrutiny, sacred scripture fully instructs us in what we seek...the Sodomites perished in heavenly fire and sulphur, devoured in the holocaust (*Gomorrah* 89; *PL* 144: 188D-189A).

This subsumption of Damian's four forms of unnatural vice or same-sex desire under Sodom not only creates the abstract entity of sodomy. It also transforms the S/sodomite most effectively, from a resident of Sodom to a member of a species marked by same-sex desire. If sodomy is the state and expression of same-sex desire, then the sodomite is the person given over to sodomy or same-sex desire. The fires of Peter Damian's Sodom implicitly give birth to the homosexual and the bisexual.

However, continuing with the birth image, I would argue that Damian's role is that of midwife rather than mother. There is a textual/cultural matrix from which Damian has drawn or made explicit the Sodomite identity that had been gestating there. This midwifing role is also evidenced in a second narrative element where Damian makes explicit another image, long implicit in the commentaries, the equation of Lot's angelic guests with the deity. This equation first appeared implicitly in Philo, and remains implicit as long as Christians understood Abraham's visitation at Mamre by the deity/angels as a revelation of the Trinity.

Damian makes this narrative move early in *Gomorrah* as part of his agenda of vilification, to portray 'sodomite' clergy in the worst possible light. He uses the image of blindness, saying that such clergy who continue in their sacramental roles are blinded by their iniquity. This moral/spiritual blindness is not accidental, but results from 'the rule of divine justice' whereby those who so 'defile themselves…are struck by a judgement of deserved punishment and incur the shades of blindness' (*Gomorrah* 38). Damian then cites Gen. 19.9-11, where the angels intervene to rescue Lot from the mob besieging his house. Damian follows with his narrative leap, employing Gen. 19.18-19 and building on that biblical citation:

> Moreover, it is clearly not incongruous to see the persons of the Father and the Son signified by those two angels who, we read, came to blessed Lot. This is apparent from what Lot himself says to them, 'O no my Lord! Surely your servant has found favor with you…' For it is certain that Lot spoke to the two in the singular as if to one since he worshipped one substance in two persons (*Gomorrah* 38).

Damian now collapses all the categories of story and argument, deity and angels, Sodomites and sodomite clergy as he ties together polemic, theology and narrative. He declares, 'So Sodomites try to break in violently on the angels when unclean men attempt to approach God through the offices of sacred orders' (*Gomorrah* 38). He then employs the image of the blinded Sodomites ferociously seeking entry to Lot's house to develop his attack on sodomite clergy. They cannot find the entranceway to approach the deity. They try to enter where they ought not and, attempting 'to break into the office of the sacred altar…they…strike their foreheads on the rocks of Sacred Scripture' (*Gomorrah* 38-39). The imagery of attempted forced entry evokes very strongly, for me, rape as well as invasion. This rape is attempted every time a sodomite priest performs or tries to perform the sacred offices. I would suggest that Damian draws on Catholic theology of the Mass to infer that sodomite clergy re-present that ancient siege of Lot's house. They do so by virtue of their sodomite status in the same way that Christ's death and resurrection are made present in the Mass. This 'sodomizing' of the sacred in Damian's polemic reminds one of anti-Semitic libels concerning the consecrated host, in which Jews were alleged to steal such hosts for a blasphemous re-crucifixion of Christ. Sodomites, like Jews, are, thus, a race or community apart from Christendom and, like the Jews, are a constant threat to Christendom. Unlike the Jews, Sodomites are hidden within the body of Christendom and must be rooted out. So along with the birthing of the homosexual/bisexual species, perhaps Damian can also be seen as midwife to the birthing of the closet.

It is clear that Damian is determined to expose the Sodomite 'menace' within the Church. That they are a menace is due to the Sodomite propensity to masquerade as good sons of the Church. Despite such appearances, Damian is convinced that their real agenda is 'to overturn the walls of the heavenly homeland' so as to busily repair 'the renewed bulwarks of Sodom' (*Gomorrah* 63). While outwardly Christian, the Sodomite soul has separated 'from God to join...with devils' (*Gomorrah* 63). Sodomy, and by implication, the Sodomite collectivity is feminized by Damian as the 'most pestilential queen...who pants to satisfy her desire for pleasure, but...fears lest she become exposed and come out in public and become known to men' (*Gomorrah* 64). And nowhere does this closet become more apparent than in the secrecy of confession. In confession, the confraternity of the closet is made manifest because here they 'confess to one another to keep the knowledge of their guilt from becoming known to others' (*Gomorrah* 43). Furthermore, this Sodomite conspiracy has been able to insert 'deceptive and sacrilegious items...in the sacred canons', the penitentials, themselves (*Gomorrah* 50). The invention of the closet suits Damian's rhetorical agenda because he is determined to expose it, to lay bare before the reader the spectacle of the closet, the spectacle of the inherent secrecy of the Sodomite, which guarantees success. It is only by exposing the Sodomite that Damian can defeat him (although occasionally feminized, Damian is under no doubt that his Sodomite enemy is male). The Sodomite menace works clandestinely, behind the scenes, hiding behind masks of clerical legitimacy. But Damian is not afraid to break down the closet door, to out the Sodomite from his lair, to address him in his sanctuary:

> Now I meet you face to face, carnal man, whoever you are. Do you ever refuse to confess to spiritual men what you have committed... See, O good Sodomite man, in your own scripture which you singularly love, which you eagerly love, which you fasten to yourself as a shield of defence, see before your own eyes that it makes no difference whether one sins with a female

servant of God or with a male.... Unmanned man, speak! Respond, effeminate man! What do you seek in a male which you cannot find in yourself?
(*Gomorrah* 45, 51-2, 68).

Damian's frenzied outing of Sodomites in the ranks evokes Eve Kosofsky
Sedgwick's observations of the all-male military environment and the factors
that generate and maintain the official homophobia found there. Damian's
clerical confraternity is like the military in that it is a regime where

> compulsory...male friendship, mentorship, admiring identification, bureau-
> cratic subordination, and heterosexual rivalry...force men into the arbitrarily
> mapped, self contradictory, and anathema-riddled quicksands of the middle
> distance of male homosocial desire. In these institutions...the *pre*scription
> of the most intimate male bonding and the *pro*scription...of 'homosexuality'
> are both stronger than in civilian society – are, in fact, close to absolute
> (Sedgwick 1994: 186)

What results is homosexual panic and heterosexual paranoia. *Gomorrah* is a
paranoid text, which speaks the language of pestilence, contagion and conspiracy. There is also a certain amount of projection. Damian virtually
accuses the Sodomites of tampering with the penitentials, 'the sacred canons'.
However, he is not himself averse to interfering with sacred scripture. This
interference is, ironically, part of an appeal to the Sodomites to give up the
arrogance by which they do not believe themselves to be condemned. This
arrogance, this 'pride', Damian attributes to the diseased nature of sodomy,
the 'plague of Gomorrah' now living 'in the dwelling of your body' (*Gomorrah*
69). This plague is like the pestilence with which David cursed the house of
Joab in 2 Kings (Vulgate reckoning) 3.29. Damian cites v. 29, 'let there not fail
from the house of Joab one that hath an issue of seed, or that is a leper' (D-R),
but renders it as, 'let there not fail from the house of Joab one doing a deed of
Gomorrah' (*Gomorrah* 70). Needless to say there is no such reference to 'one
doing a deed of Gomorrah' anywhere in the Hebrew Bible or the Christian
New Testament. Damian acknowledges that the biblical text reads 'one suffering from a discharge of semen, or a leper, or one unmanly (from the
Vulgate), one falling by the sword, or one in need of bread' but he calls this a
'second translation' (*Gomorrah* 70). However, as if to cover himself, he gives a
reading of this verse linking semen, unmanliness and leprosy to suggest an
implicit condemnation of same-sex desire and thus to demonstrate that his
created text is inferred by the biblical text.

   It is important to note that Damian employs quite a variety of scriptural
citations in developing his argument. The story of Joab is one example of how
creative he can be in his reading of biblical texts to buttress his polemic.
Furthermore, he does not simply rely on the traditional condemnations of

same-sex desire found in Leviticus and the Pauline corpus or on the many references to Sodom and Gomorrah in the biblical texts. For example, the character of Eli in 1 Samuel is made to serve as a warning to sodomite clergy that they will eventually be punished by the deity (*Gomorrah* 87). Damian even employs the image of Samson's strength, restored after he falls into the hands of the Philistines, as a sign of divine acknowledgement of a sinner's repentance (*Gomorrah* 82). However, there is one biblical narrative that Damian ignores completely, and that is the outrage at Gibeah. Given his creative endeavours with the curse of Joab, I can only be left puzzled by his oversight.

It is not as if Damian was unaware of the story. In the anthology of letters and sermons that make up his commentary on the Old Testament is found a short discussion of the events, *In Librum Judicum* XIII (*In epistola ad canonicus Fanenses*). The focus of the discussion is Judges 20 and the Israelite reverses in the war with Benjamin. Damian is aware of the outrage at Gibeah or, as he calls it the outrage of Benjamin, *scelus Benjamin* (*PL* 145: 1090C). This outrage inflamed the Israelites with righteous zeal such that they recklessly attacked Benjamin and were severely defeated on two occasions. It is only when they make peace with the deity and accept the leadership of Judah that they triumph. Like Rabanus Maurus,[8] Damian reads the events as a cautionary tale about being carried away with righteous zeal and cites the gospel verse 'let those without sin cast the first stone' (Jn 8.7) to prove his point. (It is a pity that he didn't follow his own advice and hold back rather than writing his *Book of Gomorrah*.)

4. *Peter Cantor and the Sodomitic Vice*

Much briefer than Damian's *Gomorrah*, Peter Cantor's *De vitio sodomitico* is a condemnation of same-sex desire in the form of a quasi-midrash on Genesis 18–19. The work opens invoking the outcry of Sodom's sin and closes with Lot's wife looking back on Sodom, weaving together into this structure a variety of scriptural references to Sodom and Gomorrah and to same-sex desire. Unlike Damian, who invents the word 'sodomy' and applies it to categories of male same-sex erotic activity, Peter Cantor refers always to the sodomitic vice, *vitio sodomitico*, which he applies to same-sex desire. He extends this term to cover female same-sex desire as well as male.[9]

8. Or does he merely repeat Maurus?
9. For my discussion, I am using John Boswell's translation (1980: 375-78) along with the Latin text in *Patrologiae cursus completus Series Latina*, vol. 205.

Cantor opens by citing Ezek. 16.49 to the effect that Sodom's sin was pride, abundance of bread and excess of wine. However, whereas Ezekiel is concerned to highlight the selfish hoarding of resources and the resultant abuse of the poor, Cantor uses the verse to invoke the medieval concept of *luxuria*, which Jordan points out is best understood as disordered desire. The surrender to such disordered desire results in self-indulgence and self-gratification. In medieval thought this concept becomes especially focused on sexual sin because *luxuria* 'is housed in the genitals as in a part of the body…given over to demonic control' (1997: 39). For Cantor, same-sex desire represents the epitome of *luxuria*. By giving in to pride, gluttony and drunkenness, the Sodomites thus fan the flames of same-sex desire and become possessed by it. Through their surrender to such pleasures, they give themselves over to the 'novelty of a sin so great and unheard of', which 'evokes astonishment and wonder'. Being 'perpetrated openly', it causes an outcry that marvels the deity who is 'amazed at such a crime' and is prompted to investigate it (Boswell 1980: 375). There are only two sins whose gravity calls out to heaven, murder and the sodomitic vice (*PL* 205: 334A). It is important to realize that so far Cantor has not identified the nature of this sodomitic vice, though it is clear that he is drawing on the presumed homoerotic associations with Sodom in the mind of his audience. However, in explaining why this sin is comparable to murder, Cantor makes plain that it is same-sex desire. Such desire resembles murder because it repudiates divinely sanctioned reproductive sexuality.

Cantor develops his argument by citing the Genesis 1 account of human creation in which he understands the deity to have decreed as a commandment that humans reproduce and multiply. Murderers and 'sodomites' (*sodomitae*) set themselves up as adversaries of this divine schema. By their deeds they say, 'You have created men that they might be multiplied, but we shall strive to undermine and wreck your labour' (Boswell 1980: 375). Despite the reference to murderers here, they are secondary in Cantor's mind to sodomites. It would appear that the sodomitic vice is worse than murder:

> Furthermore, when the Lord assigns the punishments to be inflicted for various sins, he seems to abandon his native patience and kindness with this one, not waiting for the Sodomites to come to justice but, rather, punishing them temporally with fire sent from heaven, as he will ultimately exact justice through the fires of hell (Boswell 1980: 375).

Cantor then reverts to his argument from Genesis 1 and argues that 'male and female he created them' (1.27) should be understood to mean, 'There will not be intercourse of men with men or women with women, but only of men with women and vice versa' (Boswell 1980: 375-75). To further his argument he cites Church regulations on hermaphrodites by which they must choose which 'organ' they will use and foreswear use of the other. Subsequent use of that other organ is like 'the role inversion' of sodomitic vice (Boswell 1980: 376).

To further develop his argument of a divine disavowal of same-sex desire, Cantor then cites a variety of biblical texts. Some of these are expected because they either refer to same-sex desire (Rom. 1.26-27; Lev. 18.22, 20.13) or to the Genesis 19 account of Sodom and Gomorrah (Isa. 1.9; Deut. 32.32; Jude 7). He expands the phrase 'going after strange flesh' in Jude 7 by glossing it with 'males doing evil with males, women with women' (Boswell 1980: 376). But Cantor will also apply the biblical curse on any who would rebuild Jericho in Josh. 6.26 to any latter day sodomite, 'he who raises up the sin of Sodom' (Boswell 1980: 377).

Cantor gives a novel twist to the fate of Lot's wife. Her fate underscores divine abhorrence of same-sex desire because she is 'changed into earth and a pillar of salt, as if the Lord were saying, "I wish that no memory of this crime should remain, no reminder, no trace of its enormity" ' (Boswell 1980: 377). Yet Lot's wife only looks back on the destruction of the cities. The 'crime' to which Lot's wife is a witness is the divine destruction, and according to Cantor's logic 'the LORD' is covering up the incriminating evidence of his act. Narratively, it is Lot and his daughters who are the witnesses to Sodom's outrages. It is they who should perish so that there is truly no one left to maintain any memory of Sodom's crimes.

Concluding his argument, Cantor betrays the contingencies of biblical translation. His Bible is the Latin Vulgate and the verses he cites carry a homoerotic overtone absent from the Hebrew or Greek Bibles. Thus, the men of Sodom 'were struck not only dumb but blind'. These are the type of whom Jeremiah laments that they 'abused the young men indecently, and boys have perished on wood' (Boswell 1980: 377, citing Vulg. Lam. 5.13),[10] as those condemned by Joel for having 'placed a boy (in a brothel)' (Boswell 1980: 378, citing Vulg. Joel 3.3).[11]

There are two points of significance in Cantor's short text. The first is that he expands his understanding of the crime of Sodom to include female homoeroticism. Unlike Peter Damian, who is primarily concerned about

10. The NRSV renders this verse, 'Young men are compelled to grind, and boys stagger under loads of wood'. The JPS version is, 'Young men must carry millstones, and youths stagger under loads of wood' while in the LXX the verse reads 'The chosen men lifted up the voice in weeping, and the youths fainted under the wood'.

11. This last verse is obscure and is variously rendered as 'traded boys for prostitutes' (NRSV), 'they bartered a boy for a whore' (JPS, Joel 4.3), 'the boy they have put in the stews' (D-R), 'they...have given a boy for an harlot' (KJV).

homoeroticism amongst the male clergy, Peter Cantor is addressing a broader societal concern. The second concerns Judges 19–21 and the outrage at Gibeah. Cantor weaves many scriptural quotations into his argument; indeed much of his text is comprised of carefully selected and arranged quotations with a minimum of commentary on his part. Yet, like Peter Damian before him, he strangely neglects to use the outrage at Gibeah as part of his argument.

5. *Thomas Aquinas*

Thomas Aquinas has been regarded as the greatest theologian and philosopher of Western medieval Christendom and his influence has been paramount in Roman Catholic thinking, not least through his monumental *Summa Theologiae*. In the *Summa Theologiae*, Thomas Aquinas employs Sodom and the events of Genesis 19 by way of illustration and to confirm his conclusions in the discussion of three issues. First, Lot figures in a discussion of whether a person's drunkenness excuses them of subsequent sin. Aquinas concludes that, as Lot was made drunk by his daughters rather than deliberately, he is not culpable for what followed (*Summa* 2a2æ. 150, 4). Second, the Sodomites illustrate negatively whether righteousness can be rewarded materially and temporally or only in the next life. As they suffered temporal punishment for their sins, it can be argued that temporal rewards can be received for righteousness (*Summa* 12æ. 114, 10). However, the most significant role of the story is Aquinas's third issue, 'unnatural vice' and its relationship to the sin of Lust (*Summa* 2a2æ. 154, 11 and 12).

In the two articles that make up this discussion, Aquinas clearly understands that same-sex desire and homoeroticism are the defining sins of Sodom. At issue in article 11 is whether 'unnatural vice', *vitium contra naturam*, is a form of lust or lechery (*luxuriae*) or should instead be understood as a form of bestiality or brutality. Aquinas notes that lust has normally been considered to be associated with potentially reproductive sexual activity, in which case 'unnatural vice', being ungenerative, could not be a form of lust. However, he notes a gloss on 2 Cor. 12.21, listing the sexual sins of uncleanness, fornication and lasciviousness, which equates uncleanness with 'unnatural lust' (*luxuria contra naturam*). He argues from this point that sins of lust show an 'especial ugliness making sex activity indecent', being 'in conflict with the natural pattern of sexuality for the benefit of the species'. Such acts are forms of 'unnatural vice' (*vitium contra naturam*) and therefore can be considered sins of lust. Aquinas then identifies four categories of such 'unnatural vice'. Three categories are masturbation, intercourse with animals, and non-vaginal intercourse between a woman and man. This latter category qualifies as unnatural as it is intercourse not using the proper organs. The fourth category of unnatural sexuality is sodomitic vice (*sodomiticum vitium*),[12] which Aquinas defines as sexual relations 'with a person of the same sex, male with male and female with female' (*Summa* 2a2æ. 154, 11). The *Summa Theologiae* is one of the rare texts that explicitly links female same-sex desire with 'sodomitic vice' and to further underscore this position Aquinas cites Rom. 1.26. So, for Aquinas, like Peter Cantor, Sodom is the epitome of the homoerotic between women as well as men. Nevertheless, while the sodomitic or homoerotic is an 'unnatural' form of sexual desire, it is only one of several such 'unnatural' forms of the erotic.

In article 12 Aquinas turns to the question of whether 'unnatural vice' is the worst of all kinds of lust. Aquinas argues affirmatively, citing Augustine's *Confessions* to this effect.

> On the other hand there is Augustine holding that of all kinds of unchastity that against nature is worst...the plan of nature comes from God, and therefore a violation of this plan, as by unnatural sins, is an affront to God, the ordainer of nature. Augustine says, *Those foul offences against nature should be detested and punished everywhere and at all times, such as were those of the people of Sodom, which, should all nations commit then would all stand guilty of the same crime by God's law, which has not made men that they should so abuse one another. For then even the very intercourse which should be between God and us is violated when that same nature, of which he is the author, is polluted by the perversity of lust* (*Summa* 2a2æ. 154, 12, citing *Confessions* 3.8).

Jordan points out that Aquinas is here misreading Augustine to develop his own argument. First, Aquinas shifts Augustine's stress on the perversity of all lust to the misuse of created bodies and further 'changes the allusion to the Sodomites from the ferocity of their punishment to the (presumed) species of their crime' (Jordan 1997: 148). Augustine is not employing a sexual taxonomy but addressing offences against nature in contrast to offences against human custom. Jordan rightly points out that Augustine does not, in *Confessions*, specify the nature of these unnatural crimes for which Sodom was punished. The fate of Sodom here illustrates Augustine's point concerning the consistency and immutability of Divine justice. Augustine's purpose, in this passage at least, is not to condemn same-sex desire specifically. However, Aquinas understands Augustine's reference to Sodom as distinguishing

---

12. Both translations of the *Summa*, Gilby (1964-76, vol. 43) and the Dominican translation (1947–48, vol. 2), employ 'sodomy' to translate each occasion of *sodomiticum vitium*.

unnatural sins from sins that do not violate nature. He defines fornication and adultery and rape as natural. Unlike these sexual sins, the sins against nature are 'sins against God' and 'graver than sacrilege' (*Summa* 2a2æ 154, 12). In accordance with Aquinas' thinking is the Christian tradition of exonerating Lot for offering his daughters in place of the angels. As was seen in Chapter 5, Augustine gave some credence to the notion that it was better for women to be raped than men.

Aquinas concludes his argument by applying the fourfold taxonomy outlined in article 11 to rank the unnatural sins of lust in order of gravity. The least serious is masturbation. The worst is sexual intercourse with animals, as it blurs the boundaries of the species. Just above it is the sodomitic vice (*sodomiticum vitium*) because it 'does not observe the due sex' (*Summa* 2a2æ 154, 12). Taken for granted throughout Aquinas' arguments on sins against nature is the equation of Sodom and Gomorrah with same-sex love and desire. Homoeroticism, the desire of male for male and female for female, is the sodomitic vice, and Aquinas quotes the passage from the *Confessions*, because it speaks of both Sodom and sins against nature in a way that associates the one with the other.

6. *Nicholas De Lyra*

In the *Postilla Super Totam Bibliam* (*PSTB*) of Nicholas de Lyra (1265–1349) a reader finds, at last, a thorough commentary on the complete Vulgate bible. Lyra gives an extensive commentary on Genesis 18–19 in which he discusses and debates a variety of issues. Unlike the other medieval commentaries seen above, Lyra also does not hesitate to give a rather detailed commentary on Judges 19–21 and, in particular, on the events of Judges 19. In his discussion of the events at Gibeah, he refers to the story of Sodom on a number of occasions. Furthermore, unlike the commentaries discussed earlier in this chapter, Lyra shows himself to be familiar with many details of Jewish exegesis, some of which he incorporates uncritically into his commentary but most of which he will critique.[13] My discussion of Lyra's commentary will focus first on his treatment of Sodom and Gomorrah and then on the closing chapters of Judges.[14]

I begin with Lyra's commentary on the outcry to heaven against Sodom and Gomorrah (Gen. 18.20-21). He points out that three sins cry out to the

13. He is reputed to have been a convert from Judaism.

14. The edition of the Postilla I am using is the 1971 facsimile of the 1492 printed edition and I must here acknowledge the assistance of Dr Keith Atkinson in transliteration and translation.

deity: the killing of the innocent, the defrauding of the labouring poor and the sin against nature (*peccatum contra naturam*) (*PSTB* Gen. 18.20, note l). For an example of the first, he cites the murder of Abel, whose blood cries out from the earth (Gen. 4.10), and for the last he states 'just as it says here' (*PSTB* Gen. 18.20, note l). In other words, Lyra affirms that the story of Sodom has to do with divine punishment of the sin against nature. It becomes clear, as his commentary progresses, that the sin against nature is same-sex desire and homoeroticism. However, Lyra seems to allow another perspective. The Vulgate renders Gen. 18.20 as 'The (out)cry of Sodom and Gomorrah is multiplied and their sin is become exceedingly grievous'. In commenting on this latter phrase, Lyra surprises the reader by referring to Jewish traditions of the rebellious daughters in Sodom. He states that the Jews understand Sodom's evil to have escalated in the killing of a girl who was caught giving food to a beggar (*PSTB* Gen. 18.20, note n). He then quotes Ezek. 16.49, that in their 'pride, excess of food and prosperous ease', the Sodomites 'did not aid the poor and needy' (NRSV). Whether Lyra is citing Ezekiel as a source for the Jewish tradition or to verify it, the overall effect would seem to undercut his association of same-sex desire with the outcry against Sodom. Lyra certainly does not oppose this tradition and a few lines down uses it to explicate the roles of the angels at both Mamre and Sodom (*PSTB* Gen. 18.20, note p). However, I suggest that Lyra uses it, with Ezekiel, to illustrate how giving into same-sex desire leads a society to abrogate responsibilities to the poor and the weak and the maintenance of justice. Same-sex desire results in the arrogant pursuit of self-gratification over everything else.

Lyra outlines four sections to his commentary on Genesis 19: the events that cause the destruction of Sodom, the flight of Lot and his family, the destruction of Sodom and, finally, the 'incest' of Lot and his daughters. I will focus primarily on the first and final sections, together with his observations on the fate of Lot's wife. Lyra's first section concerns vv. 1-8, and it is clear that, for him, the 'vice against nature', *vicium contra naturam*, same-sex desire, is responsible for Sodom's destruction. This section is the most extensive of his commentary on ch. 19 because Lyra is very greatly exercised by the question of whether Lot was right to offer his daughters to protect his guests. Here his familiarity with Jewish commentary re-emerges.

On 19.1, Lyra rehearses the Jewish interpretation that, of the two angels who arrive at Sodom, one is sent to overthrow the city and the other to ensure the escape of Lot and his family (*PSTB* Gen. 19.1, note a). There is one feature of Jewish exegesis, however, that Lyra will not accept: that Lot is sitting at the city gates because he has been appointed chief justice of the city. He acknowledges that Jewish exegetes understand this as the reason behind the Sodomite rebuke of Lot in v. 9 (that Lot has set himself up as judge over them). But Lyra prefers the explanation that Lot learnt hospitality in the house of Abraham and thus would come to the city gates every evening to look for travellers and take them to his house (*PSTB* Gen. 19.1, note c). Lot does not know that the two men are angels, for they obviously arrive in the form of travellers (*PSTB* Gen. 19.1, note d). Lot, he notes, is said by the text to bow to the angels because such deference was intended to persuade them to accept his hospitality. But the angels refused Lot's invitation in order to test his piety and thus to make him an example of hospitality to others (*PSTB* Gen. 19.2, note g). Comparing this incident with Luke's account of the encounter between two disciples and an incognito risen Christ on the road to Emmaus (Lk. 24.13-35), Lyra draws a further moral. Just as the disciples constrained the incognito Jesus to stay and dine with them, so Lot also presses his hospitality on the angels. He does so because hospitality requires that guests not be invited superficially and lightly but with great insistence (*PSTB* Gen. 19.3, note h).

In his discussion of the siege of Lot's house, however, Lyra ignores Jewish understandings of the events, including condemnation of Lot's offer of his daughters to the mob. This omission is quite striking because Lyra has a lot to say on the issue of whether Lot sinned when he offered his daughters. The first point Lyra addresses is the question of how literally to read the statement in v. 4 that *all* the people (or more accurately, all the males, from youngest to eldest) gathered at once outside Lot's house. He does not accept the interpretation that 'all' means every male, but is hyperbolic, and thus opens up the thorny question, seen in other medieval commentaries, of the justice of the deity's destruction of the children of Sodom along with their parents. But Lyra does not address the question of divine justice at all.

Lyra has no doubt about the mob's intentions and summarizes them tersely, *concubitu nephario* (*PSTB* Gen. 19.5, note l). He also states that Lot goes out to face the mob because he believes his guests to be men (*PSTB* Gen. 19.6, note m), then embarks on his second major discussion, whether Lot sinned by offering his daughters to the mob. Relying on Augustine, and possibly attempting to resolve some of the ethical problems within Augustine's reasoning, Lyra begins with the point that Lot acts to avoid a greater evil (*maius malum*) namely the sin against nature (*vicium contra naturam*) and violence against his guests (*PSTB* Gen. 19.8, note n). Clearly the sin against nature is a greater evil than the defloration of virgins (*PSTB* Gen. 19.8, note n). Thus Moses allowed the (male) Israelites to divorce their wives even though this is subsequently declared illicit by the Saviour (*PSTB* Gen. 19.8, note n): divorce prevented a greater evil, wife-killing. Lot, then, acted correctly in offering his daughters in order to avoid the sin against nature and violence against his guests (*PSTB* Gen. 19.8, note n). However, Lyra then reprises Augustine's critique of this argument. Specifically citing *Against Lying*, Lyra summarizes Augustine's arguments and concludes that

> Lot could not offer his daughters in such a way without consenting to something that was a sin in its very nature, not only a venial one, such as an obliging lie, but indeed a mortal one. And yet he was exonerated to some extent, even if not completely, partly by reason of the disturbed mental state he was in, partly to ward off the most foul vice (*vicio pessimo*) in his co-citizens and the violence against his guests (*PSTB* Gen. 19.8, note n).

So Lot is partially exonerated due to the derangement he experienced by his confrontation with the spectre of the sin against nature.

Unsurprisingly, Lyra betrays no real understanding of the enormity of rape and the issue for him is the potential loss of the daughters' virginity rather than the violence they would suffer. While he is aware of the threat of violence to the guests on the part of the mob, I do not believe that it is this violence that is so execrable and abominable (*nephario*) as the unnatural quality (*contra naturam*) of sexual relations (*concubitu*) among people of the same sex. We know from his commentary on Gen. 18.20 that it is this same-sex desire, running rampant in Sodom, that cries out to heaven for divine intervention. In his comments on the destruction of Sodom, Lyra underscores this position by repeating the argument of his predecessors, such as Alcuin and Rabanus Maurus and Gregory the Great before them, concerning the fitting nature of Sodom's fiery doom. The fire and brimstone that fall on Sodom are appropriate to the sin of the Sodomites, the sin against nature. The stench of brimstone and the burning fire signify the stench of the sins arising from the fires of same-sex desire (*PSTB* Gen. 19.24, note p).

Lyra also records the Jewish interpretation of the fate of Lot's wife encountered earlier in Iso'dad, pointing out that 'the Hebrews' say that she is turned to salt because she sinned by salt on the preceding night (*PSTB* Gen. 19.26, note p), pretending to the angels that they have no salt and thus begrudging hospitality, in Sodomic style. Lyra's is one of the few Christian texts that betray awareness of this Jewish story, a story that highlights the meanness and inhospitality of Sodom. In his discussion of Lot and his daughters Lyra again shows his knowledge of Jewish exegesis. Here, however, he will dispute various aspects of it. At issue for Lyra is the moral culpability of the various protagonists who, interestingly for Lyra, include the deity. He indicates the existence of a Jewish tradition that the daughters can get their father drunk because the deity miraculously provided wine in the cave for that purpose, and disputes such a notion saying that the deity would not facilitate an act of incest (*PSTB* Gen. 19.32, note b). He solves the problem by suggesting that as they had been given ample warning by the angels of the impending destruction of the cities, they had spent the previous night putting together supplies to take with them including bread and wine (*PSTB* Gen. 19.32, note b) and even added something to the wine to intoxicate Lot and awaken his desire (*PSTB* Gen. 19.32, note b).

So does this mean that Lot's daughters are to be condemned? Surprisingly, Lyra seems averse to such condemnation of them and grudgingly allows that they acted with good intentions. He states that Lot flees Segor (Zoar) because he fears that the city will still be overthrown. Indeed, Lyra states that, when Lot and his daughters go up to the hills, Segor is destroyed (*PSTB* Gen. 19.30, note y). Is it surprising, then, that they believe that they have survived the destruction of the world by fire they heard their father speak about (*PSTB* Gen. 19.31, note a)? Lyra concludes that their motives were noble, namely the preservation of the human race (*PSTB* Gen. 19.31, note a), but he condemns their action as abominable and unlawful (*PSTB* Gen. 19.31, note a), and also the older daughter for being so shameless as to name her son Moab, exposing the foulness of his conception by his father (*PSTB* Gen. 19.37, note f). Lyra is clearly embarrassed by the action of the daughters because he does not refer to the Jewish tradition that the Messiah comes from Sodom through this action, perhaps because the messianic implications of their act would be almost impossible to deny.

But what of Lot himself? He is the third protagonist whose culpability is discussed. While Lyra partially excuses Lot, he echoes Jewish scepticism concerning Lot's innocence, specifically that it was impossible to have sex with a woman, especially a virgin, and not know she was his daughter. However, Lyra exonerates Lot by suggesting that under the wine's influence he forgot his wife was dead and thought she was the woman having sex with him (*PSTB* Gen. 19.33, note c). Nevertheless, there is a problem in that the situation is repeated the following night with the younger daughter (*PSTB* Gen. 19.33, note c). Lyra concludes that it is for this reason that the text says that Lot was not aware (*non sensit*), when each daughter lay down with him or got up, but *not* that he did not know (*cognovit*) whether or not she was his daughter (*PSTB* Gen. 19.33, note c).

On Judges 19, Lyra's is one of the most extensive Christian commentaries. While he refers to the Hebrew text and draws on Josephus, he rarely refers to rabbinic commentary in his discussion. He does compare the events in Gibeah with those of Sodom, especially revisiting his discussion of the morality of offering a daughter and a concubine up for abuse by a mob. For the purposes of this book, discussion focuses on Lyra's understanding of the events in Judges 19 and their similarity to those of Genesis 19.

At the outset, Lyra informs his readers that the events of this story are the effects of excessive desire – *nimia libidine* – and that in Gibeah there were some men, ruffians, who were excessively wicked and wanton (*PSTB* Judg. 19.1, note a). The events are a clear example of the perils of such unrestrained desire. It is also important to remember that Lyra's Latin Bible simply states that the concubine 'left him (the Levite) and returned to her father's house in Bethlehem' (Judg. 19.2, D-R), omitting the adultery leading to the concubine's departure, though Lyra acknowledges this detail in the Hebrew version. He draws from this fact two possible scenarios to account for the concubine leaving. Either the Levite could have thrown her out on account of her behaviour, or she left him to commit the adultery and afterwards, not daring to return to him, she went to her father's house instead (*PSTB* Judg. 19.2, note c). So while he does not say it outright, Lyra seems to suggest that the chain of events, in this story about the evil of unchecked sexual desire, are set in motion by the sinful desire of the concubine herself. But Lyra says no more concerning her role in the marital breakdown.

However, Lyra is more interested in what happens to the Levite's party at Gibeah than in what happens beforehand. Why does no one offer hospitality to the Levite's party as they wait in the town square? According to Lyra, the townspeople have been intimidated by the ruffians and are fearful that their homes will be attacked if they take in travellers (*PSTB* Judg. 19.15, note l). These men were not only themselves averse to practising hospitality but felt free to prevent others practising it (*PSTB* Judg. 19.15, note l). The words that Lyra chooses to describe the men, evil (*mali*), arrogant or haughty (*insolentes*) and vagrant or vagabond (*vagi*), paint a picture of a ruthless predatory pack of men accountable to no one but themselves and usurping or defying proper authority. He develops this portrait further in his comment on v. 22. The Latin text of Judges inserts, after 'sons of Belial', 'that is without a yoke'. Lyra comments that it has been added to explain the Hebrew, indicating that such men are without the rule and way of God (*PSTB* Judg. 19.22, note o). Thus, Lyra builds up a picture of Gibeah as a town at the mercy of a band of ruthless gangsters who know no law but their own arrogance and lust. Travellers or outsiders are especially prey to their rapaciousness. This portrait could suggest that Lyra is developing a theme of hospitality and inhospitality here. However, I argue that he is establishing the equation of sexual excess with a broader lawlessness and social chaos that results in abuse of the weak. But I suspect that Lyra's attempts to attribute this excess and lawlessness to same-sex desire are hampered by two problems. First, it is the concubine who falls victim to the mob and not the Levite. Second, Lyra uses two contradictory versions of the story, the biblical account and Josephus.

Lyra invokes the spectre of Sodom to explicate the siege of the old man's house in Gibeah. The 'sons of Belial' demand that the Levite be brought out so that they can know him. Lyra is explicit in saying that they meant to have sodomitic sex – *concubitu sodomitico* – with him, with which most interpreters are in agreement. However, he then points out that, according to Josephus, the men really wanted the concubine. Therefore it could be argued that they threatened the Levite with sodomitic sex in order to coerce both him and the old man into handing her over to them (*PSTB* Judg. 19.22, note q). If she was not given to them they intended to kill the Levite. This interpretation is subsequently borne out by their focusing their sexual attentions on the concubine when she is given to them (*PSTB* Judg. 19.22, note q). Lyra further notes that the Levite's account of events in Judges 20.5 back up this interpretation.

Attention then turns to the old man's intervention and the offer of his daughter. Here, Lyra echoes his commentary on the similar events in Sodom, noting that some have argued that the old man did not sin because he was offering his daughter to avoid a greater evil, the sin against nature (*peccatum contra naturam*) (*PSTB* Judg. 19.24, note s). But Lyra strongly disagrees, reminding the reader of his extensive discussion concerning Lot. He repeats his position that no one can consent to a sin to prevent others from sinning (*PSTB* Judg. 19.24, note s). This statement represents Lyra's last word on the subject because on the old man's offer of the concubine he comments only that the Latin text here refers to the woman as a concubine for the first time rather than as a wife. He states that the two words mean the same thing and cites 2 Sam. 16 (Vulg. 2 Kgs 16): the concubines of David must have been his wives, otherwise Absolom could not commit adultery with them (*PSTB* Judg. 19.24, note t).

Lyra has nothing to say on the handing over of the concubine to the mob, but only on her fate. In doing so he attempts to evoke Sodom's ghost again by stating that the mob subjected her to such sexual abuse that they even used her for unnatural sex – *talis concubitus erat abusus vel qui utebantur ea concubitu innaturali* (*PSTB* Judg. 19.25, note v). The biblical text is not so specific and this evocation of anal sex suggests to me that Lyra is attempting to link the sin of Gibeah with that of Sodom, a suspicion reinforced by his treatment of the Levite's account of events in Gibeah. Lyra gives two alternative ways of understanding the Levite's statement that the men wanted to kill him. The first is, as Josephus recounts, that the Levite was threatened with death unless he gave over his concubine (*PSTB* Judg. 20.5, note i). The second option is a further attempt to raise the ghost of Sodom. Lyra completes the Levite's statement that they wanted to kill him by adding, through 'assaulting me and by abominable sex' – *(vel) alfligendo* (sic) *me carnali concubitu et nephario* (*PSTB* Judg. 20.5, note j). Importantly, Lyra uses the phrase *concubitu...nephario*, the same description he gave of the Sodomites' intentions.

However, the problem remains that a woman is raped by the mob, not a man. She might have been subjected to unnatural sex, but is it sodomitic sex? Lyra, himself, has reserved that term to describe the intentions of the mob vis-à-vis the Levite. Sodomitic sex is also *concubitu nephario*, a term Lyra employs to describe the Sodomite intentions towards Lot's guests, perhaps to avoid tautology. It is a phrase he also uses to describe the possible sexual intentions of the mob in Gibeah toward the Levite, but he does not use i in relation to the concubine's fate. The fact that the penitential literature reserves the invocation of Sodom to refer to sex between men must also be considered. While often unclear about the specific act, these texts refer to it clearly as an act between men. Furthermore, Peter Damian has left no doubt that any male to male sex is sodomitic. Finally, while Aquinas and Peter Cantor associate women with Sodom, they only do so in the context of same-sex desire: sodomitic sex is sex between men or between women. Of course, for Aquinas, sodomitic sex is but one category of unnatural sex. As was seen above, Aquinas regards non-vaginal sex between a man and a woman as a species of unnatural sex, but it is a separate species from sodomitic or homo-sexual sex. If Lyra is attempting, then, to conscript the story of Gibeah for a homophobic agenda by making it a *petit* Sodom, the textual/semantic tradi-tion has failed him. Sodom has become associated exclusively with same-sex desire and in Gibeah the mob accepts a woman in place of a man. No genuine Sodomite could be content with such an offer. While Lyra is suspicious of it, Josephus has provided a plausible alternative, that the sexual threat to the Levite was merely a ploy to force him to hand over the real object of the mob's desire, the concubine. Josephus is backed up by no less an authority than Ambrose, who cites his account as if it were Scripture, while the subse-quent commentary tradition has turned the final chapters of Judges into a cautionary tale about being carried away by righteous zeal. It will not be until the invention of the concept of the bisexual, in the late-twentieth century, that the story of Gibeah will be employed as another Sodom to provide a paradigm for the evil of same-sex desire.

7. *Conclusion*

In the medieval Latin West the story of Sodom is consolidated as a founda-tional Christian homophobic myth. In the early Christian period, Sodom was more associated with particular proscribed behaviours. By the late-medieval period, Sodom is associated with a state of desire, a state of nature, or, more appropriately, a state of anti-nature. The Sodomite is a creature whose same-sex desire expresses a rebellion against both God and the divinely mandated natural order. Same-sex desire is a state of rebellion, for which the only response can be genocidal mass murder. Indeed, same-sex desire is something that warrants the omnicidal sterilizing of the earth.

Sodom stands as a sort of anti-Sinai and from it stems a Sodomite conspiracy. According to Peter Damian, Sodomites masquerade as good Christians, even as good clergy, but all their efforts are devoted to rebuilding the walls of Sodom. Sodomites are in league with devils and pervert and corrupt everything holy. They even re-write Scripture and the canons. They make of the Mass a blasphemous re-enactment of the attempted rape of the divine on that fateful night in Sodom. For Peter Cantor, too, the Sodomite has rejected divine mandate and seeks to restore that ancient city. Sodomites are like Jews in being a race apart. But, unlike Jews, they lurk within the body of Christendom, sheltering in the closet, seeking to pervert it. The deity's action at Sodom proves just how evil Sodomites are, for this is one occasion when the deity loses all control and indulges in genocidal rage. There can be no questioning of the divine justice involved in such genocide. It is better that the innocent burn than for anyone not to understand how abhorrent same-sex desire is to the deity and how abhorrent, therefore, it should also be to humans.

What is missing in all these homophobic polemics is any invocation of Sodom's shadow, Gibeah. Damian and Cantor are very inventive in their application of scripture, but also ignore that story. Only Lyra attempts to connect Gibeah and Sodom and to read both as describing similar events. However, he is defeated, partly because of the tradition behind him that the threat to the Levite was merely a ploy to force the hand-over of the concubine, and partly because it is a woman who is raped and murdered here. Lyra wants an essentialized unambiguous portrayal of same-sex desire, something denied him in Gibeah by the broken body of the concubine.

Chapter 7

CONCLUSION: DETOXIFYING SODOM AND GOMORRAH

While my goal has been to create a resource in the struggle against homophobia, I have not set out to write a history of homophobia or of the acceptance or otherwise of homoeroticism in either Christianity or Judaism. I
have attempted to destabilize one of the mythological foundations of
religiously based homophobia. To that end I have demonstrated that the
invention of the myth of Sodom and Gomorrah as a site of divine genocide
in response to homoeroticism has been primarily a Christian enterprise. I
have done so, in part, through retrieving the rich world of Jewish readings
of the story with their focus on hospitality and the abuse of the poor and
outsider. Bringing this textual world into conversation with the early Christian readings puts the latter in a new light. Much that is odd about these
early Christian readings, from a homophobic perspective, makes better
sense if they are understood as sharing the Jewish understanding of the
story, not the later homophobic understanding. Early Christian references
to Sodom and its sins should not be automatically understood as homophobically inspired unless clearly indicated in the text. I maintain that it is
up to those who want to argue a homophobic intent from such references
to prove such claims and not to rely on the strength of later homophobic
traditions. Furthermore, I argue that it is not enough to use only Christian
materials to prove a homophobic intent and so discount Jewish (and other)
traditions. Christianity began as a Jewish sect and the story of Sodom is
part of the Torah, the fundamental scripture of Judaism. If Christians such
as Origen and Jerome were both familiar with, and utilized, Jewish interpretation in their own readings, then it is foolhardy to read such Christian
texts today without being informed by that world of Jewish interpretation.

Crucial to my whole enterprise, too, has been the juxtaposing of Sodom
with Gibeah. Indeed, without Gibeah, I may not have found a number of
fairly crucial texts such as Iso'dad's commentary, in which he invents a
form of 'sodomy'. Similarly, Nicholas of Lyra's reading of Sodom cannot be
considered complete without his failed attempt to turn Gibeah into a *petit*

Sodom. Furthermore, a homophobic reading of Sodom's story has to take into account the observation of both Nahmanides and Yitzchaq Arama that there was no divine intervention in Gibeah because, unlike the men of Sodom, the men of Gibeah were only interested in sex. Both of these commentators were pre-modern rabbis, authorities within Jewish tradition, and were not attempting to promote the legitimacy of same-sex desire and homoeroticism. While they were as homophobic as their Christian contemporaries, they did not share the Christian homophobic understanding of Genesis 19.

In tracing Gibeah's story, the relative paucity of its reception raises important questions for anyone wanting to maintain the homophobic interpretation of Sodom. Given the striking similarity of the two stories why is it that Gibeah has not caught the homophobic imagination? Indeed, why is it that two classic texts of Christian homophobia, Damian's *Book of Gomorrah* and Cantor's *De Vitio Sodomitico* make no reference to Gibeah whatsoever? Is it because a woman is raped and murdered there? Is the very similarity of the two stories something to be covered up if the homophobic interpretation of Sodom is to be maintained? Certainly there is a similar paucity of reception in the world of Judaism, but nowhere near the same extent as in Christianity. Furthermore, Nahmanides and Arama are quite prepared to discuss and compare the events of the two stories. Christians do not seem to be willing to do so to the same degree. Indeed, no Christian commentator addresses the similarity of the stories as forthrightly as these two rabbis do. Is it because a homophobic interpretation of Gibeah is much harder to sustain, so that such an interpretation of Sodom requires its near-suppression? Is not this suppression an act of complicity in the woman's rape and murder? Does not the very success of the Christian homophobic interpretation of Sodom entail the failure of Christians to develop any meaningful moral discourse on rape?

I raise these questions not to posit a superiority of one religion over another, although as a gay man I must confess that I find the traditional Jewish reading of Sodom and Gomorrah refreshing if not liberating. After reading so many homophobic Christian texts on Sodomites and sodomy, I confess I not only prefer the rabbis' Sodom but regard it as the more true reading, if any reading can be true. Of course, it is not without its own dilemmas, but at least these dilemmas are common to any story in which the rage of the outcast and oppressed is allowed full expression in the heavenly fires of vengeance and vindication. The destruction of the World Trade Center is a stark reminder of such rage to the affluent West and an instantiation of those dilemmas. Yet in contrast to the rabbinic Sodom, I must confess to being appalled by the rabbinic Gibeah. While Sodom might not be a site of rabbinic homophobia, Gibeah certainly is a site of rabbinic misogyny. Similarly, if Christians cannot successfully turn Gibeah into a homophobic example, they also do not hide their own misogyny in the rare occasions when they read the story. The most positive reading of all is that of Ambrose. However, he turns the concubine into a martyr for patriarchal privilege. Of course, in actual fact she is a victim of patriarchal privilege and Ambrose's heroic reading of the concubine provides a cruel model for women to follow. Nevertheless, his reading effectively quarantined Gibeah from the homophobic reading imposed on its sister city of Sodom.

These observations serve to maintain a fiction of closure, but the stories of both Sodom and Gibeah are not closed. The fires of Sodom still fuel the engine of Christian homophobia, a homophobia that, as I said in my introductory chapter, is now turning its attention to Gibeah. The Christian Sodom has even entered the Jewish world pushing aside the older tradition (Jakobovits 1971). It is also found in Islam, where its seeds, possibly planted in the Prophet's day, have found the right conditions to sprout and grow. Does a trace of the Christian Sodom even lie behind the rejection of the homoerotic in the youngest Abrahamic religion, Bahai? Questions like these mean that there can be no closure. I have elsewhere argued that the interpretation of Sodom's story by such Reformation figures as Luther discloses a blueprint for a new and rigid erotic order sustained by an underlying homosexual panic and abjection of the homoerotic (Carden 2003). In the Reformation, the Christian homophobic interpretation of Sodom nurtured in medieval cloisters metastasizes into the regime of the godly and compulsory heterosexual society based on the tyranny of marriage. The compulsory nature of this heterosexuality derives from an apocalyptic anxiety that everyone is at heart a Sodomite, every heterosexual is at heart a homosexual. Hence the strident homophobia of the Christian Right and Defence of Marriage initiatives.

The detoxification of the story of Sodom has a number of implications for Christianity. Jewish tradition reads Sodom as a society where principles of oppression and exclusion were the rule. These principles operated in every sphere of Sodomite society including the sexual sphere. I have, thus, identified Sodom as epitomizing the phallocentric and patriarchal heterosexual economy of penetration that was the dominant sexual system of the ancient Mediterranean world. Christianity, by turning the story into a homophobic ideo-story, ironically served to reproduce, reinforce and refine the system against which the biblical story protests. It is further ironic that the pioneer of the homophobic reading is the pre-Christian philosopher, Philo of Alexandria. His own reading collapses because he cannot reconcile the various positions of virgin, eunuch and the hierarchy of penetration that is patriarchal marriage. I would suggest that in early Christianity with its valorization of eunuchs and, in particular, with its central image of Virgin Mother and Divine Eunuch Son, there are discourses of protest against that hierarchy of penetration epitomized by both patriarchal marriage and the sexual violence of Sodom. These discourses have found expression over history in such movements as the Shakers, the various Russian sectarian movements, but also within Catholicism, in the whole impulse towards celibacy and same-sex community. Mark Jordan observes that 'queer and Catholic is what the Christian church has been for much of its history' (2000: 257). The central images and main impulses of Catholic Christianities, I would suggest, are far from heterosexual. The Divine Eunuch Son opposes heteronormative masculinity while Virgin Motherhood's utopian dimensions may only be fully realized in lesbian co-parenting (on Mary as a Sapphic model see Vanita 1996: 14-36). Perhaps, Catholic can only ever be queer to be Catholic? As Sedgwick observes,

> Catholicism...is famous for giving countless gay and proto-gay children the shock of the possibility of adults who don't marry, of men in dresses, of passionate theatre, of introspective investment, of lives filled with what could, ideally without diminution, be called the work of the fetish (1994: 140).

Thus, nurtured as it was in the Catholic bosom, the homophobic reading of Sodom represents a fundamental contradiction within Catholicism. The healing of this contradiction will only take place through Catholicism's overcoming the erotophobia and homophobia that generated that reading and by recognizing the original utopian impulse now corrupted by that erotophobia and homophobia. That impulse, I would suggest, is the attempt to explore liberating alternatives to a patriarchal heterosexual system. Paradoxically, by denying the utopian vision, the erotophobic and homophobic energies resulted in the restoration of a new and improved patriarchal heterosexual order in the Reformation. However, it would be wrong to ignore the reality that much of the Reformation energy marshalled in the construction of that order was itself a utopian impulse to break down the erotophobic hierarchy of celibacy, with all the injustices and hypocrisy it entailed. I would suggest, too, that Protestant traditions recognize their own early utopian impulse against an erotophobic order. In other words, then, Catholic discourse for celibacy and same-sex community and Protestant discourse for marriage have embedded in them utopian impulses against sexual power structures of oppression and exclusion. Sodom's history in the tapestry of Christianity shows that by replacing power structures of oppression and exclusion with more power structures of oppression and exclusion one is simply building a new Sodom on the ruins of the old.

BIBLIOGRAPHY

Aland, K., M. Black, C.M. Martini, B.M. Metzger and A. Wilkgren (eds.)
1983   *The Greek New Testament* (Stuttgart: United Bible Societies).
Alcuin
        'Interrogationes et Responsiones in Genesin', in *PL* 100: 515-69.
Alshech, Moshe ben Chayim
1988   *Torat Moshe: Commentary of Rabbi Moshe ben Chayim Alshech (Hakadosh)
        on the Torah* (trans. and condensed by Eliyahu Munk; Jerusalem: Rubin Mass).
Alter, Robert
1994   'Sodom as Nexus: The Web of Design in Biblical Narrative', in Goldberg
        1994: 29-42.
Ambrose of Milan
1954   *Letters* (trans. M.M. Beyenka; New York: Fathers of the Church).
1962   'De Abraham', in *Opera* I (New York and London: Johnson Reprint Corpora-
        tion; [Prague: Tempsky, 1897]): 501-638.
1972   'Flight from the World', in *Seven Exegetical Works* (trans. M.P. McHugh;
        Washington, DC: Catholic University of America Press): 279-323.
Andersen, F.I.
1983   '2 (Slavonic Apocalypse of) Enoch', in Charlesworth 1983: I, 92-100.
Andrew of St Victor (Andreae de Sancto Victore)
1986–1896 *Opera: 1. Expositio super Heptateuchum* (ed. Charles Lohr and Rainer Berndt;
        Corpus Christianorum Continuatio Mediaevalis, 53; Turnholti: Brepols).
Angelomus (of) Luxoviensis
        'Commentarius in Genesin', in *PL* 115: 107-244.
Aphrahat
1969   'Demonstrations', in John Gwynn (ed. and trans.), *A Select Library of Nicene
        and Post-Nicene Fathers of the Christian Church, Second Series.* XIII. *Gregory
        the Great: Part II, Ephraim Syrus, Aphrahat* (Reprint of 1890–1900 edition;
        Grand Rapids: Eerdmans): 345-412.
Arama, Yitzchaq
1986   *Aqaydat Yitzchaq: Commentary of Rabbi Yitzchaq Arama on the Torah*
        (trans. and condensed by Eliyahu Munk; Jerusalem: Rubin Mass).
Athanasius
1971   'Against the Arians', in *A Select Library of Nicene and Post-Nicene Fathers of
        the Christian Church.* IV. *St Athanasius: Selected Works and Letters* (trans.
        Cardinal Newman; rev. A. Robertson; Grand Rapids: Eerdmans): 306-447.
1971   'De Synodis', in *A Select Library of Nicene and Post-Nicene Fathers of the
        Christian Church.* IV. *St Athanasius: Selected Works and Letters* (trans.
        Cardinal Newman; rev. A. Robertson; Grand Rapids: Eerdmans): 451-80.
1971   'Encyclical Letter', in *A Select Library of Nicene and Post-Nicene Fathers of*

the Christian Church. IV. *St Athanasius: Selected Works and Letters* (trans.
M. Atkinson; rev. A. Robertson; Grand Rapids: Eerdmans): 92-96.

1971   'Life of Antony (vita Antoni)', in *A Select Library of Nicene and Post-Nicene
Fathers of the Christian Church*. IV. *St Athanasius: Selected Works and
Letters* (trans. H. Ellershaw; rev. A. Robertson; Grand Rapids: Eerdmans):
195-221.

Augustine

'Quaestionum in heptateuchum, libri VII', in *PL* 34: 547-825.
'Locutionum in heptateuchum, libri VII', in *PL* 34: 485-546.

1835–1839   *Opera omnia: post Lovaniensium theologorum recensionem: opera et studio
monachorum ordinis Sancti Benedicti e Congregatione S. Mauri* (Paris:
Gaume).

1952   *The City of God: Books VIII–XVI* (trans. G.G. Walsh and G. Monahan; Washington, DC: Catholic University of America Press).

1953   'Against Lying', in *Treatises on Various Subjects* (trans. M.S. Muldowney;
Washington, DC: Catholic University of America Press): 125-81.

1953   *Confessions* (trans. V.J. Bourke; Washington, DC: Catholic University of
America Press).

1953   'The Christian Life', in *Treatises on Various Subjects* (trans. M.S. Muldowney;
Washington, DC: Catholic University Of America Press): 9-45.

1954   *The City of God: Books XVII–XXII* (trans. G.G. Walsh and D.J. Honan; Washington, DC: Catholic University of America Press).

1957   *Against Julian* (trans. M.A. Schumacher; New York: Fathers of the Church).

1958   *Quaestionum in heptateuchum, libri VII; Locutionum in heptateuchum, libri
VII de octo quaestionibus ex veteri testamento* (Turnholti: Typographi Brepols
Editores Pontificii).

1991   *On Genesis: Two Books on Genesis against the Manichees* and *On the Literal
Interpretation of Genesis, an Unfinished Book* (trans. Roland J. Teske; Washington, DC: Catholic University of America Press).

1992   *Confessions* (commentary by James J. O'Donnell; Oxford: Clarendon Press;
New York: Oxford University Press).

Baer, Richard A.

1970   *Philo's Use of the Categories Male and Female* (Leiden: E.J. Brill).

Bahya ben Asher ben Hlava

1980   *Encyclopedia of Torah Thoughts (Rabbeinu Bachya/Kad ha-kemah)* (trans.
and annotated by Charles B. Chavel; New York: Shilo Publishing House [cited
as Bachya 1980]).

Bailey, Derrick Sherwin

1955   *Homosexuality and the Western Christian Tradition* (London: Longmans,
Green & Co.).

Bal, Mieke

1988   *Death and Dissymmetry: The Politics of Coherence in the Book of Judges*
(Chicago and London: University of Chicago Press).

1989a   'Between Altar and Wondering Rock: Towards a Feminist Philology', in Bal
(ed.) 1989: 211-31.

1989b   'Introduction', in Bal (ed.) 1989: 11-24.

1993   'A Body of Writing: Judges 19', in Brenner 1993: 208-230.

Bal, Mieke (ed.)

1989   *Anti-Covenant: Counter-Reading Women's Lives in the Hebrew Bible*
(JSOTSup, 81; Sheffield: Almond Press).

Bar Hebraeus
1932   *The Chronography of Gregory Abu'l Faray the Son of Aaron, the Hebrew*
           Physician Commonly Known as Bar Hebraeus, Being the First Part of his
           Political History of the World (trans. from the Syriac by Ernest A. Wallis
           Budge; London: Oxford University Press).
Basil of Caesarea
1955   *Letters: Volume II (186-138)* (trans. R.J. Deferrari; New York: Fathers of the
           Church).
1962   *Ascetical Works* (trans. Sister M. Monica Wagner; Washington: Catholic
           University of America Press).
1963   *Exegetic Homilies* (trans. Agnes Clare Way; Washington: Catholic University
           of America Press).
Beal, Timothy K.
1992   'Ideology and Intertextuality: Surplus of Meaning and Controlling the Means
           of Production', in Fewell (ed.) 1992: 27-39.
Bede
           'Questiones in Genesim', in *PL* 93: 233-364.
           'Questiones in Librum Judicum', in *PL* 93: 423-30.
           'De remediis peccatorum', in *PL* 94: 567-76.
ben Isaiah, Abraham, and Benjamin Sharfman (eds. and trans.)
1949   *The Pentateuch and Rashi's Commentary (Hamishah humshe Torah: 'im*
           perush Rashi): A Linear Translation into English – Genesis (Brooklyn: S.S. &
           R. Publishing [cited as Rashi 1949]).
Bernhardt-House, Phillip
2000   'Serving Two Masters: Bisexual Theological Foundations' (Unpublished MA
           thesis, Gonzaga University, USA).
Berzbach, Ulrich
1999   'The Varieties of Literal Devices in a Medieval Midrash: Seder Eliyyahu
           Rabba, Chapter 18', in Judit Targarona Borrás and Angel Sáenz-Badillos
           (eds.), *Jewish Studies at the Turn of the Twentieth Century: Proceedings of the*
           6th EAJS Congress, Toledo, July 1998. I. *Biblical, Rabbinical, and Medieval*
           Studies (Leiden, Boston and Cologne: E.J. Brill): 384-91.
Bible and Culture Collective
1995   *The Postmodern Bible* (New Haven: Yale University Press).
Bieler, Ludwig (ed.)
1963   *The Irish Penitentials* (Appendix by D.A. Binchy; Dublin: Dublin Institute for
           Advanced Studies).
bin Gorion, Emmanuel (ed.)
1976   *Mimekor Yisrael: Classical Jewish Folk Tales,* I (Collected by Micha Joseph
           Bin Gorion; trans. I.M. Lask; introduction by Dab Ben-Amos; Bloomington
           and London: Indiana University Press).
Birnbaum, Philip
1979   *Encyclopedia of Jewish Concepts* (New York: Sanhedrin Press).
Bischoff, Bernhard, and Michael Lapidge (eds.)
1994   *Biblical Commentaries from the Canterbury School of Theodore and Hadrian*
           (Cambridge: Cambridge University Press).
Blok, Anton
1981   'Rams and Billy-Goats: A Key to the Mediterranean Code of Honour', in *Man*
           (NS) 16 (1981): 427-40.

Boling, Robert G.
    1975   *Judges: Introduction, Commentary and Translation* (Garden City, NY: Dou-
              bleday).
Boswell, John
    1980   *Christianity, Social Tolerance and Homosexuality: Gay People in Western
              Europe from the Beginning of the Christian Era to the Fourteenth Century*
              (Chicago and London: University of Chicago Press).
Braude, William G. (trans.)
    1968   *Pesikta Rabbati: Discourses for Feasts, Fasts and Special Sabbaths* (New
              Haven and London: Yale University Press).
Braude, William G., and Israel J. Kapstein (trans.)
    1981   *Tanna debe Eliyyahu: The Lore of the School of Elijah* (Philadelphia: Jewish
              Publication Society of America).
Brenner, Athalya (ed.)
    1993   *A Feminist Companion to Judges* (Sheffield: JSOT Press).
Brenton, Sir Lancelot C.L. (trans.)
    1986   *The Septuagint with Apocrypha: Greek and English* (Peabody, MA: Hen-
              drickson).
British and Foreign Bible Society
    undated   *Torah, Nebiim, w'Kethubim: The Hebrew Bible* (St Ives: Clays).
Brown, Francis, S.R. Driver and Charles A. Briggs
    1977   *A Hebrew and English Lexicon of the Old Testament* (Oxford: Clarendon
              Press [1907]).
Brownmiller, Susan
    1976   *Against our Will: Men, Women and Rape* (Harmondsworth: Penguin Books).
Brundage, James A.
    1987   *Law, Sex, and Christian Society in Medieval Europe* (Chicago: University of
              Chicago Press).
Burchard of Worms (Burchardus Vormatiensis)
              'Decretorum liber', in *PL* 140: 537-1091.
Caesarius of Arles
    1964   *Sermons: Volume II (81-136)* (trans. M.M. Mueller; Washington: Catholic
              University of America Press).
Carden, Michael
    1999   'Homophobia and Rape in Sodom and Gibeah: A Response to Ken Stone',
              JSOT 82: 83-96.
    2003   'It's Lonely at the Top: Patriarchal Models, Homophobic Vilification and the
              Heterosexual Household in Luther's Commentaries', in Roland Boer and
              Edgar Conrad (eds.), *Redirected Travel: Alternative Journeys and Places in
              Biblical Studies* (JSOTSup, 382; London and New York: T. & T. Clark
              International): 185-200.
Carroll, Robert P.
    1992   'The Discombobulations of Time and the Diversities of Text: Notes on the
              Rezeptiongeschichte of the Bible', in Robert P. Carroll (ed.), *Text as Pretext:
              Essays in Honour of Robert Davidson* (Sheffield: JSOT Press): 61-85.
    1993   'Intertextuality and the Book of Jeremiah: Animadversions on Text and
              Theory', in Clines and Exum (eds.) 1993: 55-78.
Cathcart, Kevin, and Robert Gordon (trans.)
    1989   *The Targum of the Minor Prophets* (with a Critical Introduction, Apparatus
              and Notes; Edinburgh: T. & T. Clark).

Catholic Bible Association
    1970   *The New American Bible* (Paterson, NJ: St Anthony Guild Press).
Challoner, Richard
    1989   *The Holy Bible (Douay Reims Version): Translated from the Latin Vulgate* (Rockford, IL: Tan Books and Publishers).
Charles, R.H. (trans.)
    1908   *The Testaments of the Twelve Patriarchs* (London: A. & C. Black).
Charlesworth, J.H. (ed.)
    1983–1985   *The Old Testament Pseudepigrapha* (2 vols.; Garden City, NY: Doubleday).
Clement of Alexandria
    1954   *Christ the Educator* (trans. S.P. Wood; New York: Fathers of the Church).
Clines, David J.A.
    1993a   'A World Established on Water (Psalm 24): Reader-Response, Deconstruction and Bespoke Interpretation', in Clines and Exum (eds.) 1993: 79-90.
    1993b   'Possibilities and Priorities of Biblical Interpretation in an International Perspective', *Biblical Interpretation* 1.1 (1993): 67-87.
Clines, David J.A., and Cheryl Exum
    1993   'The New Literary Criticism', in Clines and Exum (eds.) 1993: 11-25.
Clines, David J.A., and Cheryl Exum (eds.)
    1993   *The New Literary Criticism and the Hebrew Bible* (Sheffield: JSOT Press).
Cohen, A. (ed.)
    1965   *The Minor Tractates of the Talmud: Massektoth Ketannoth* (trans. into English, with Notes, Glossary and Indices; foreword by Israel Brodie; London: Soncino Press).
Cohen, Jeremy
    1989   *'Be Fertile and Increase, Fill the Earth and Master It': The Ancient and Medieval Career of a Biblical Text* (Ithaca: Cornell University Press).
Cohn, Norman
    1996   *Noah's Flood: The Genesis Story in Western Thought* (New Haven: Yale University Press).
Columban(us)
           'De poenitentiarum mensura taxanda liber', in *PL* 80: 223-30.
    1957   *Opera* (ed. G.S.M. Walker; Dublin: Dublin Institute for Advanced Studies).
Cyprian
    1958   'Exhortation to Martyrdom, To Fortunatus', in Roy J. Deferrari (ed. and trans.), *Treatises* (New York: Fathers of the Church): 311-44.
Cyril of Alexandria
           'Glaphyra', in *PG* 69: 9-678.
de Jonge, M. (ed.)
    1978   *The Testaments of the Twelve Patriarchs: A Critical Edition of the Greek Text* (ed. in cooperation with H.W. Hollander, H.J. de Jonge and Th. Korteweg; Leiden: E.J. Brill).
Delaney, Carol
    1987   'Seeds of Honour, Fields of Shame', in David Gilmore (ed.), *Honor and Shame and the Unity of the Mediterranean* (Washington, DC: American Anthropological Association): 35-48.
Diodorus Tarsensis
           'Fragmenta ex Catenis: In Genesin', in *PG* 33: 1561-1580.
           'Fragmenta ex Catenis: In Librum Judicum', in *PG* 33: 1587-1588.

Dover, K.J.
    1978   *Greek Homosexuality* (London: Gerald Duckworth).
Egbert
    'Canones de remediis peccatorum', in *PL* 89: 443-54.
Ephrem the Syrian/Ephraem Syrus
    1969   'Selections from the Hymns and Homilies', in *A Select library of Nicene and post-Nicene Fathers of the Christian Church, Second series. XIII. Gregory the Great, Part II: Ephraim Syrus, Aphrahat* (trans. John Gwynn; reprint of 1890–1900 edition; Grand Rapids: Eerdmans): 163-341.
    1989   *Hymns* (trans. and Introduction by Kathleen E. McVey; Preface by John Meyendorff; New York: Paulist Press).
    1994   *Selected Prose Works: Commentary of Genesis, Commentary on Exodus, Homily on Our Lord, Letter to Publius* (ed. Kathleen McVey; trans. Edward G. Mathews, Jr, and Joseph P. Amar; Washington, DC: Catholic University of America Press).
Epstein, I. (ed.)
    1961   *The Babylonian Talmud* (London: The Soncino Press).
Eron, Lewis John
    1990   'Early Jewish & Christian Attitudes toward Male Homosexuality as Expressed in the *Testament of Naphtali*', in *Homophobia and the Judaeo-Christian Tradition* (ed. Michael L. Stemmeler and J. Michael Clark; Dallas: Monument Press, 1990): 25-49.
Fewell, Danna Nolan
    1992   'Introduction: Writing, Reading and Relating', in Fewell 1992: 11-20.
Fewell, Danna Nolan (ed.)
    1992   *Reading Between Texts: Intertextuality and the Hebrew Bible* (Louisville, KY: Westminster/John Knox Press).
Fishelis, Avrohom, and Shmuel Fishelis (trans.)
    1991   *Judges: A New English Translation; Translation of Text, Rashi and Commentary* (New York: Judaica Press [cited as Rashi 1991 for Rashi's Commentary and JCD for the other Commentary Digest]).
Fone, Byrne R.S.
    2000   *Homophobia: A History* (New York: Metropolitan Books).
Freedman, H., and Maurice Simon (eds.)
    1939   *Midrash Rabbah* (trans. into English with notes, glossary and indices with a foreword by Rabbi Dr. I. Epstein); *Genesis* (trans. H. Freedman); *Leviticus* (trans. J. Israelstam and J. Slotki); (London: Soncino).
Friedlander, Gerald (trans.)
    1981   *Pirke de Rabbi Eliezer (The Chapters of Rabbi Eliezer the Great): According to the Text of the Manuscript Belonging to Abraham Epstein of Vienna* (annotated with Introduction and Indices by Gerald Friedlander; New York: Sepher-Hermon Press; [London: Kegan Paul, Trench, Trubner, 1916]).
Frontain, Raymond-Jean (ed.)
    1997   *Reclaiming the Sacred: The Bible in Gay and Lesbian Culture* (New York and London; Harrington Park Press).
Gaster, Moses (trans.)
    1927   *The Asatir: The Samaritan Book of the Secrets of Moses; Together with the Pitron or Samaritan Commentary and the Samaritan Story of the Death of Moses* (with Introduction and Notes by Moses Gaster; London: Royal Asiatic Society).

Gennadius, Patriarchae CP
    'Fragmenta in Genesin', in *PG* 85: 1623-1664.
Ginzberg, Louis
1937–1966   *The Legends of the Jews* (7 vols.; trans. Henrietta Szold; Philadelphia: Jewish
    Publications Society of America).
Goldberg, Jonathan
1992   *Sodometries: Renaissance texts, Modern Sexualities* (Stanford, CA: Stanford
    University Press).
1994   'Introduction', in Goldberg (ed.) 1994: 1-22.
Goldberg, Jonathan (ed.)
1994   *Reclaiming Sodom* (New York and London: Routledge).
Goodich, Michael
1979   *The Unmentionable Vice: Homosexuality in the Later Medieval Period* (Santa
    Barbara and Oxford: ABC-Clio).
Goss, Robert, and Mona West (eds.)
2000   *Take Back The Word: A Queer Reading of the Hebrew Bible* (Cleveland, OH:
    Pilgrim Press).
Goyer, Peter F., and Henry C. Eddleman
1984   'Same-Sex Rape of Nonincarcerated Males', *American Journal of Psychiatry*
    141.4 (April 1984): 576-79.
Graves, Robert, and Raphael Patai
1964   *Hebrew Myths: The Book of Genesis* (London: Cassell).
Greenberg, David F.
1988   *The Construction of Homosexuality* (Chicago and London: University of
    Chicago Press).
Greenstein, Edward L.
1984   'Medieval Bible Commentaries', in Holtz 1984: 213-59.
Gregory of Nyssa
1967   *Ascetical Works* (trans. V. Woods Callahan; Washington, DC: Catholic Uni-
    versity of America Press).
Gregory the Great
    'De Expositione Veteris ac Novi Testamenti', in *PL* 79: 683-1424.
1950   *Pastoral Care* (trans. and annotated by Henry Davis; Ancient Christian
    Writers, 11; Westminster: Newman Press).
1952   *Morales sur Job: Livres 1 et 2* (Introduction and notes by Robert Gillet; trans.
    Andre de Gaudemaris; Sources Chretiennes, 32; Paris: Editions du Cerf).
1959   *Dialogues* (trans. O.J. Zimmermann; New York: Fathers of the Church).
1974–1975   *Morales sur Job, Livres XI-XVI: texte latin* (Introduction, trans. and notes by
    Aristide Bocognana; Sources Chretiennes, 212 and 221; Paris: Editions du
    Cerf).
1982   *Registrum Epistularum* (ed. Dag Norberg; Corpus Christianorum Series
    Latina, 140-140A; Turnhout, Belgium: Brepols).
Gregory of Nazianzus
1987   'Concerning His own Affairs', in *Three Poems* (trans. Denis Molaise Meehan;
    Supplemenary Notes by Thomas P. Halton; Washington, DC: Catholic
    University of America Press): 25-45.
Grossfeld, Bernard (trans.)
1988   *The Targum Onqelos to Genesis* (with a Critical Introduction, Apparatus and
    Notes; Edinburgh: T. & T. Clark).

Groth, Nicholas, Ann Wolbert Burgess and Lynda Lytle Holmstrom
    1977   'Rape: Power, Anger and Sexuality', *American Journal of Psychiatry* 134.11
             (November 1977): 1239-1243.
Groth, Nicholas, and Ann Wolbert Burgess
    1980   'Male Rape: Offenders and Victims', *American Journal of Psychiatry* 137.7
             (July 1980): 806-811.
Halitgarius Cameracensis
             'Liber poenitentialis', in *PL* 105: 651-93.
Hallam, Paul
    1993   *The Book of Sodom* (London and New York: Verso).
Handelman, Susan A.
    1982   *The Slayers of Moses: The Emergence of Rabbinic Interpretation in Modern
             Literary Theory* (Albany: State University of New York Press).
Harrington, D.
    1985   'Pseudo-Philo', in Charlesworth 1985: II, 297-303.
Harrington, Daniel J., and Anthony J. Saldarini (Introduction, Translation and Notes)
    1992   *Targum Jonathan of the Former Prophets* (Edinburgh: T. & T. Clark).
Hawk, L. Daniel
    1992   'Strange House Guests: Rahab, Lot and the Dynamics of Deliverance', in
             Fewell 1992: 89-97.
Herbert, A.
    1962   *Genesis 12–50: Introduction and Commentary* (London: SCM Press).
Herring, Basil F.
    1982   *Joseph ibn Kaspi's Gevia' Kesef: A Study in Medieval Jewish Philosophic Bible
             Commentary* (New York: Ktav).
Higgins, Lynn A., and Brenda R. Silver
    1991   'Introduction: Rereading Rape', in *eadem* (eds.), *Rape and Representation*
             (New York: Columbia University Press): 1-11.
Hill, Robert
    1990   See John Chrysostom 1990
Hollander, H.W., and M. de Jonge
    1985   *The Testaments of the Twelve Patriarchs: A Commentary* (Leiden: E.J. Brill).
Holtz, Barry W.
    1984   'Midrash', in Holtz (ed.) 1984: 177-211.
Holtz, Barry W. (ed.)
    1984   *Back to the Sources: Reading the Classic Jewish Texts* (New York: Summit
             Books).
Horner, Tom
    1978   *Jonathan Loved David: Homosexuality in Biblical Times* (Philadelphia: West-
             minster Press).
Horowitz, Isaiah
    1992   *Shney Luchot Habrit on the Written Torah*. I. *Bereshit* (trans. and annotated
             by Eliyahu Munk; Jerusalem: Eliyahu Munk).
Hugh of St Victor (Hugo de Sancto Victore)
             'Adnotationes elucidatoriae in Pentatuechon', in *PL* 175: 29-86.
             'Adnotationes elucidatoriae in librum Judicum', in *PL* 175: 87-96.
Ibn Ezra, Abraham
    1988   *Commentary on the Pentateuch: Genesis (Bereshit)* (trans. and annotated by
             H.N. Strickman and Arthur M. Silver; New York: Mesorah Publishing).

Ide, Arthur Frederick
    1985   *The City of Sodom and Homosexuality in Western Religious Thought to 630
          CE* (Dallas: Monument Press).
International Bible Society
    1978   *The Holy Bible: New International Version* (East Brunswick, NJ: International
          Bible Society).
Irenaeus
    1883   'Against Heresies', in *The Writings of Irenaeus*, II (trans. A. Roberts and W.H.
          Rambaut; Edinburgh: T. & T. Clark): 1-155.
Isho Bar Nun
    1962   *Selected questions of Ish⁻o Bar N⁻un on the Pentateuch* (ed. and trans. Ernest
          G. Clarke; Leiden: E.J. Brill).
          Isidore (Isidorus Hispalensis).
          'Questiones in Genesin', in *PL* 83: 207-287.
          'Questiones in Librum Judicum', in *PL* 83: 379-90.
Iso'dad of Merv
  1950–1955 *Commentaire d'Iso'dad de Merv sur l'Ancien Testament. I. Genese* (ed. and
          trans. J.M. Voste and C. Van den Eynde; Corpus Scriptorum Christianorum
          Orientalium, 126 and 156; Louvain: Dubecq).
  1962–1963 *Commentaire d'Iso'dad de Merv sur l'Ancien Testament. III. Livres des ses-
          sions* (ed. and trans. Ceslas van den Eynde; Corpus Scriptorum Chris-
          tianorum Orientalium, 229 and 230; Louvain: Secretariat du CorpusSCO).
Jacobson, Howard
    1996   *A Commentary on Pseudo-Philo's Liber Antiquitatum Biblicarum: With Latin
          Text and English Translation* (Leiden and New York: E.J. Brill).
Jakobovits, Immanuel
    1971   'Homosexuality', in *Encyclopedia Judaica*, VIII (Jerusalem: Keter Publishing
          House): 961-62.
Janssen, Thijs
    1992   'Transvestites and Transsexuals in Turkey' (trans. Peter op't Veldt), in Schmitt
          and Sofer (eds.) 1992: 83-91.
Jerome
    1933   *Select Letters* (English trans. F.A. Wright; London: Heinemann).
  1959–1970 *Opera exegetica* (Turnhout, Belgium: Brepols).
    1963   *The Letters* (trans. Charles Christopher Mierow; Introduction and Notes by
          Thomas Comerford Lawler; Westminister: Newmann Press).
    1966   *Homilies* (trans. M.L. Ewald; Washington, DC: Catholic University of America
          Press).
    1995   *Saint Jerome's Hebrew Questions on Genesis* (Introduction, Translation and
          Commentary by C.T.R. Hayward; Oxford: Clarendon Press; New York: Oxford
          University Press).
Jewish Publication Society
    1985   *Tanakh: The Holy Scriptures: The New JPS Translation according to the Tra-
          ditional Hebrew Text* (Philadelphia: Jewish Publication Society).
John Cassian
    1973a   'The Conferences Part I (i-x)', in *A Select Library of Nicene and Post-Nicene
          Fathers of the Christian Church. XI. Sulpitius Severus, Vincent of Lerins, John
          Cassian* (trans. Edgar C.S. Gibson; Grand Rapids: Eerdmans): 295-409.
    1973b   'The Conferences Part II (xi-xvii)', in *A Select Library of Nicene and Post-*

Nicene Fathers of the Christian Church. XI. *Sulpitius Severus, Vincent of Lerins, John Cassian* (trans. Edgar C.S. Gibson; Grand Rapids: Eerdmans): 411-74.

1973c   'The Twelve Books of the Institutes of the Coenobia', in *A Select Library of Nicene and Post-Nicene Fathers of the Christian Church. XI. Sulpitius Severus, Vincent of Lerins, John Cassian* (trans. Edgar C.S. Gibson; Grand Rapids: Eerdmans): 201-290.

John Chrysostom

1889   *On the Priesthood; Ascetic Treatises; Select Homilies and Letters; Homilies on the Statues* (trans. W.R.W. Stephens; ed. Philip Schaff; A Select Library of the Nicene and Post-Nicene Fathers of the Christian Church, First series, 9; New York: Christian Literature).

1969   *Homilies on the Epistles of Paul to the Corinthians* (trans. Talbot W. Chambers; ed. Philip Schaff; A Select Library of the Nicene and Post-Nicene Fathers of the Christian Church, First series, 12; Grand Rapids: Eerdmans).

1969   *Homilies on the Acts of the Apostles and the Epistle to the Romans* (trans. J.R. Morris and W.H. Simcox; rev. with notes by George B. Stevens; ed. Philip Schaff; A Select Library of the Nicene and Post-Nicene Fathers of the Christian Church, First series, 11; Grand Rapids: Eerdmans).

1975   *Homilies on the Gospel of Saint Matthew* (trans. George Prevost, rev. with notes by M. Riddle; ed. Philip Schaff; A Select Library of the Nicene and Post-Nicene Fathers of the Christian Church, First series, 10; Grand Rapids: Eerdmans).

1979   *Discourses against Judaizing Christians* (trans. Paul W. Harkins; Washington: Catholic University of America Press).

1983   *Commentaire sur Isaie* (Introduction, Critical Text and Notes by Jean Dumortier, trans. Arthur Liefooghe; Paris: Editions du Cerf).

1984   *On the Incomprehensible Nature of God* (trans. Paul W. Harkins; Washington, DC: Catholic University of America Press).

1989   *A Comparison between a King and a Monk; Against the Opponents of the Monastic Life: Two Treatises* (trans. with Introduction by David G. Hunter; Lewiston, NY: Edwin Mellen Press).

1990   *Homilies on Genesis 18–45* (trans. R.C. Hill; Washington, DC: Catholic University of America Press).

John of Damascus

1958   *Writings* (trans. F.H. Chase; New York: Fathers of the Church).

Johnston, Craig, and Robert Johnston

1988   'The Making of Homosexual Men', in *Staining the Wattle: People's History of Australia since 1788*, IV (ed. Verity Burgmann, Jenny Lee and Vic Fitzroy: McPhee Gribble and Penguin Books): 87-99.

Joint Committee on the New Translation of the Bible

1970   *The New English Bible* (Oxford: Oxford and Cambridge University Press).

Jones, Alexander (ed.)

1974   *The Jerusalem Bible: Popular Edition* (London: Darton, Longman & Todd).

Jongeling, B., C.J. Labuschagne and A.S. van der Woude (trans. and annotations)

1976   *Aramaic Texts from Qumran*, I (Leiden: E.J. Brill).

Jordan, Mark

1997   *The Invention of Sodomy in Christian Theology* (Chicago and London: University of Chicago Press).

2000   *The Silence of Sodom: Homosexuality in Modern Catholicism* (Chicago: University of Chicago Press).

Josephus
1926–1965   *Josephus in Nine Volumes* (Loeb Classical Library; trans. H. St J. Thackeray, Ralph Marcus, Allen Wikgren and L.H. Goldman; London and Cambridge, MA: William Heinemann & Harvard University Press).

Justin Martyr
1948   *Writings* (trans. T.B. Falls; Washington, DC: Catholic University of America Press).

Kamuf, Peggy
1993   'Author of a Crime', in Brenner (ed.), 1993: 187-207.

Kaufman, Arthur, Peter Divasto, Rebecca Jackson, Dayton Voorhees and Joan Christy
1980   'Male Rape Victims: Noninstitutionalised Assault', *American Journal of Psychiatry* 137.2 (February 1980): 221-23.

Kee, H.C.
1983   'Testaments of the Twelve Patriarchs', in Charlesworth 1983: I, 776-81.

Kimhi, David
1983   *Perush Radak 'al Sefer Shoftim = The Commentary of Rabbi David Kimhi on the Book of Judges* (ed. Michael Celniker; Toronto, ON and Buffalo, NY: Rabbi Dr M. Celniker Book Committee).

Kugel, James L.
1997   *The Bible As It Was* (Cambridge, MA: Belknap Press of Harvard University Press).

Lampe, G.W.H.
1961–1968   *A Patristic Greek Lexicon* (Oxford: Clarendon Press).

Lancaster, Roger N.
1988   'Subject Honor and Object Shame: The Construction of Male Homosexuality and Stigma in Nicaragua', *Ethnology* 27.2 (April 1988): 111-25.

Langermann, Y. Tzvi (trans.)
1996   *Yemenite Midrash: Philosophical Commentaries on the Torah* (with Introduction; San Francisco: HarperSanFrancisco).

Lasine, S.
1984   'Guest and Host in Judges 19: Lot's Hospitality in an Inverted World', *JSOT* 29 (1984): 37-59.

Lazar, M. (ed.)
1989   *Libro de las Generaciones (Ms. 17633, B.N. Madrid); and the Book of Yashar (English anonymous translation)* (Culver City, CA: Labyrinthos).

Leander of Seville
1969   'The Training of Nuns and Contempt for the World', in *Iberian Fathers* (trans. C.W. Barlow; Washington, DC: Catholic University of America Press), I: 183-228.

Levine, Abraham (ed.)
1951   *The Early Syrian Fathers on Genesis: From a Syriac MS on the Pentateuch in the Mingana Collection* (first 18 chapters of the MS with Introduction, Translation and Notes; study in comparative exegesis by A. Levine; London: Taylor's Foreign Press).

Lewis, Jack P.
1968   *A Study of the Interpretation of Noah and the Flood in Jewish and Christian Literature* (Leiden: E.J. Brill).

Liddell, Henry George, and Robert Scott
    1940   *A Greek-English Lexicon* (revised and augmented throughout by Henry Stuart Jones, with the assistance of Roderick McKenzie; Oxford: Clarendon Press).
Linscheid, John
    1996   *Surviving Fire: A Queer Look at Sodom* (www.seas.upenn.edu/~linsch/ Sodomtxt.html, last accessed 23/1/98).
Loader, J.A.
    1990   *A Tale of Two Cities: Sodom and Gomorrah in the Old Testament, Early Jewish and Early Christian Traditions* (Kampen, Netherlands: J.H. Kok).
Louth, Andrew (ed. and Introductions)
    1987   *Early Christian Writings: The Apostolic Fathers* (trans. Maxwell Staniforth; Harmondsworth: Penguin).
Lovelace, Richard F.
    1979   *Homosexuality and the Church: Crisis, Conflict, Compassion* (London: Lamp Press).
Maher, Michael (trans.)
    1987   *Targum Pseudo-Jonathan: Genesis* (with Introduction and Notes; Edinburgh: T. & T. Clark).
Maimonides, Moses
    1956   *The Guide for the Perplexed* (trans. from the original Arabic text by M. Friedlander; New York: Dover Publications).
Martin, James D.
    1975   *The Book of Judges: A Commentary* (Cambridge: Cambridge University Press).
Matthews, Victor H.
    1987   'Entrance Ways and Threshing Floors: Legally Significant Sites in the Ancient Near East', *Fides et Historia* 19: 25-40.
    1992   'Hospitality and Hostility in Genesis 19 and Judges 19', *Biblical Theology Bulletin* 22.1: 3-11.
MacDonald, John (ed. and trans.)
    1963   *Memar Marqah: The Teaching of Marqah* (Berlin: Alfred Töpelmann).
Madden, Ed
    1997   '*The Well of Loneliness*, or The Gospel According to Radclyffe Hall', in Frontain 1997: 163-86.
McKim, Donald K. (ed.)
    1998   *Historical Handbook of Major Biblical Interpreters* (Leicester, UK; Downers Grove, IL: InterVarsity Press).
McMullen, Richie J.
    1990   *Male Rape: Breaking Silence on the Last Taboo* (London: Gay Men's Press).
McNamara, Martin (trans.)
    1992   *Targum Neofiti 1: Genesis* (with Apparatus and Notes; Edinburgh: T. & T. Clark).
McNeil, John
    1977   *The Church and the Homosexual* (London: Darton, Longman & Todd).
McNeill, John T., and Helena M. Gamer (trans.)
    1965   *Medieval Handbooks of Penance: A Translation of the Principal libri poenitentiales and Selections from Related Documents* (New York: Octagon Books).
Migne, J.P. (ed.)
 1844–1905   *Patrologiae cursus completus Series Latina: in qua prodeunt patres, doctores,*

scriptoresque ecclesiae Latinae a Tertulliano ad Innocentium III (221 vols.; Paris: Garnier Fratres).

1959–96   *Patrologiae cursus completus Series Graeca* (Turnhout, Belgium: Brepols [repr. of edn published 1857–1868]).

Milikowsky, Chaim Joseph

1981   'Seder Olam: A Rabbinic Chronography, I (Introduction); II (Text and Translation)' (Unpublished PhD dissertation, Yale University).

Moffat, James

1953   *A New Translation of the Bible Containing the Old and New Testaments* (London: Hodder & Stoughton).

Moore, George F.

1895   *A Critical and Exegetical Commentary on Judges* (Edinburgh: T. & T. Clark).

Morris, Paul

1992   'A Walk in the Garden: Images of Eden', in Morris and Sawyer 1992: 21-38.

Morris, Paul, and Deborah Sawyer (eds.)

1992   *A Walk in the Garden: Biblical, Iconographic and Literary Images of Eden* (JSOTSup, 136; Sheffield: JSOT Press).

Muhammad Ali, Maulana

1951   *The Holy Qur'an* (Arabic text, Translation and Commentary by Maulana Muhammad Ali; Lahore: Ahmadiyyah Anjuman Isha' at Islam).

Murphy, Frederick J.

1993   *Pseudo-Philo: Rewriting the Bible* (New York and Oxford: Oxford University Press).

Nahmanides

1971   *Commentary on the Torah: Genesis* (trans. C.B. Chavel; New York: Shilo).

National Council of Churches in the USA

1990   *The Holy Bible: New Revised Standard Version* (Nashville: Thomas Nelson).

Neusner, Jacob

1971   *Aphrahat and Judaism: The Christian-Jewish Argument in Fourth-Century Iran* (Leiden: E.J. Brill).

1977   *The Tosefta* (New York: Ktav).

1985   *Genesis Rabbah: The Judaic Commentary to the Book of Genesis – A New American Translation* (3 vols.; Atlanta: Scholar's Press).

1986   *The Fathers According to Rabbi Nathan: An Analytical Translation and Explanation* (Atlanta, GA: Scholars Press).

1987   *Pesiqta de Rab Kahana: An Analytical Translation* (Atlanta, GA: Scholars Press).

1989   *Ruth Rabbah: An Analytical Translation* (Atlanta, GA: Scholars Press).

1991   *Confronting Creation: How Judaism Reads Genesis – An Anthology of Genesis Rabbah* (Columbia, SC: University of South Carolina Press).

1993   *The Mother of the Messiah in Judaism: The Book of Ruth* (Valley Forge, PA: Trinity Press International).

Nicholas of Lyra

1971   *Postilla Super Totam Bibliam* (reissued facsimile of Strasbourg 1492; Frankfurt/ Main: Minerva GmbH).

Niditch, S.

1982   'The Sodomite Theme in Judges 19-20: Family, Community and Social Disintegration', *Catholic Biblical Quarterly* 44: 365-78.

Nilus (abbas)

'Epistolarum Libri 1-4', in *PG* 79: 58-582.

Noah, Mordecai M. (trans.)
1972–73   *The Book of Yashar* (New York: Hermon Press).
Novatian
1974   *The Trinity. The Spectacles. Jewish Foods. In praise of Purity. Letters* (trans. R.J. DeSimone; Washington, DC: Catholic University of America Press and Consortium Press).
O'Donovan, Connell
1996   *Reclaiming Sodom* (www.geocities.com/WestHollywood/1942/sodom, last accessed 5/5/98).
Olyan, Saul
1997   '"And with a Male You Shall Not Lie the Lying Down of Woman": On the Meaning and Significance of Leviticus 18:22 and 20:13', in Gary David Comstock and Susan E. Henking (eds.), *Que(e)rying Religion: A Critical Anthology* (New York: Continuum): 398-414.
Omosupe, Ekua
1991   'Black/Lesbian/Bulldagger', *Differences* 3.2: 101-111.
Origen
1982   *Homilies on Genesis and Exodus* (trans. R.E. Heine; Washington, DC: Catholic University of America Press).
1990   *Homilies on Leviticus: 1–16* (ed. and trans. Gary Wayne Barkley; Washington, DC: Catholic University of America Press).
1993   *Homélies Sur Les Juges: Texte de la Version Latine de Rufin* (Introductions, Translation, Notes and Index by Pierre Messeé, Louis Neyrand, Marcel Borret; Paris: Les Editions Du Cerf).
1998   *Homilies on Jeremiah: Homily on 1 Kings 28* (trans. John Clark Smith; Washington, DC: Catholic University of America Press).
Orosius, Paulus
1964   *The Seven Books of History against the Pagans* (trans. R.J. Deferrari; Washington, DC: Catholic University of America Press).
Parker, Simon B.
1991   'The Hebrew Bible and Homosexuality', *Quarterly Review* 11.3: 4-19.
Parkes, Geoff
2001   *Suicide Is Never Painless* (http://www.remyforum.net/geoff/gsuicide1.htm, last accessed 28/2/02).
Paulinus of Nola
1967   *Letters of St. Paulinus of Nola* (trans. and annotated by P.G. Walsh; Westminster, MD: The Newman Press).
Payer, Pierre J.
1984   *Sex and the Penitentials: The Development of a Sexual Code, 550–1150* (Toronto: University of Toronto Press).
Penchansky, David
1992   'Staying the Night: Intertextuality in Judges and Genesis', in Fewell (ed.) 1992: 77-88.
Peter Cantor (Petrus Cantor)
'Verbum abbreviatum: de vitio sodomitico', in *PL* 205: 333-36.
Peter Comestor
'Historia Scholastica', in *PL* 198: 1043-1721.
Peter Damian (Petrus Damianus)
'Liber Gomorrhianus', in *PL* 145: 159-90.

'Collectanea in Vetus Testamentum: In Librum Judicum', in *PL* 145: 1079-1092.

1982   *Book of Gomorrah: An Eleventh-Century Treatise against Clerical Homosexual Practices* (trans. with Introduction and Notes by Pierre J. Payer; Waterloo, ON: Wilfrid Laurier University Press).

Peter of Poitier (Petrus Pictor)

1980   *Summa de confessione: compilatio praesens* (ed. Jean Longere; Corpus Christianorum Continuatio Mediaevalis, 51; Turnholti: Brepols).

Philo

1929–1962   *Philo* (Loeb Classical Library; 10 vols. and 2 supp. vols.; trans. F.H. Colson; London: Heinemann; Cambridge, MA: Harvard University Press).

1987   *The Works of Philo: Complete and Unabridged* (trans. C.D. Yonge; Peabody, MA: Hendrickson).

Procopius of Gaza

'Commentarii in Genesin', in *PG* 87: 19-510.

'Commentarii in Judices', in *PG* 87: 1042-1080.

Prudentius

1965   *The Poems of Prudentius*, II (trans. M.C. Eagan; Washington, DC: Catholic University of America Press).

Rabanus Maurus

'Commentariorum in Genesim libri quatuor', *PL* 107: 439-670.

'Commentarium in librum Judicum', *PL* 108: 1111-1200.

'De Vitiis et Virtutibus', *PL* 112: 1335-1398.

Rashbam (Rabbi Samuel ben Meir)

1989   *Perush ha-Torah Bereshit = Rabbi Samuel ben Meir's Commentary on Genesis: An Annotated Translation* (trans. Martin I. Lockshin; Lewiston, Lampeter and Queenston: Edwin Mellen Press).

Rashi

1949   See Abraham ben Isaiah and Benjamin Sharfman (ed. and trans.).

1991   See Avrohom Fishelis, and Shmuel Fishelis (trans.).

1997   *Perush Rashi 'al ha-Torah = Rashi: The Torah: With Rashi's commentary* (translated, annotated, and elucidated by Yisrael Isser Zvi Herczeg, in collaboration with Yaakov Petroff and Yosef Kamenetzky; Brooklyn, NY: Mesorah Publications).

Reeves, Peggy Sanday

1989   'Rape and the Silencing of the Feminine', in Sylvana Tomaselli and Ray Porter (eds.), *Rape: An Historical and Cultural Enquiry* (Oxford and New York: Basil Blackwell): 84-101.

Remigius (Monachus S. Germani) Antissiodorensis

'Commentarius in Genesin', in *PL* 131: 52-134.

Robert of Flamborough

1971   *Liber poenitentialis* (Critical edition with Introduction and Notes; ed. J.J. Francis Firth; Toronto: Pontifical Institute of Mediaeval Studies).

Roberts, Alexander, and James Donaldson (eds.)

undated   *Constitutions of the Holy Apostles (Ante-Nicene Christian Library: Translations of The Writings of the Fathers Down to A.D. 325, XVII)* (Edinburgh: T. & T. Clark).

Rosenbaum, M., and A.M. Silbermann (trans.)

1929   *Pentateuch with Targum Onkelos, Haphtaroth and Prayers for Sabbath and Rashi's Commentary*. I. *Genesis* (London: Shapiro, Valentine & Co.).

Ruether, Rosemary Radford
    1983   *Sexism and God-Talk: Toward a Feminist Theology* (Boston: Beacon Press).
Runia, D.T.
    1988   'God and Man in Philo of Alexandria', in *Journal of Theological Studies* 39 (April 1988): 39-75.
Rupertus Abbas Tuitiensis
             'Commentarorium de operibus S. Trinitatis libri XLII – In Genesim', in *PL* 167: 199-565.
             'Commentarorium de operibus S. Trinitatis libri XLII – In Judicum', in *PL* 167: 1023-1060.
Ryle, Herbert E.
    1921   *The Book of Genesis: In the Revised Version with Introduction and Notes* (Cambridge: Cambridge University Press).
Saldarini, Anthony J. (trans. and Commentary)
    1975   *The Fathers According to Rabbi Nathan (Abot de Rabbi Nathan) Version B* (Leiden: E.J. Brill [cited as Saldarini for his Commentary]).
Salvian the Presbyter
    1962   *Writings* (trans. J.F. O'Sullivan; Washington, DC: Catholic University of America Press).
Saperstein, Marc (trans. and Introduction)
    1989   *Jewish Preaching 1200–1800: An Anthology* (New Haven and London: Yale University Press).
Sawyer, John F.A.
    1996   *The Fifth Gospel: Isaiah in the History of Christianity* (Cambridge: Cambridge University Press).
Schmitt, Arno
    1992   'Different Approaches to Male-Male Sexuality/Eroticism from Morocco to Usbekistan', in Schmitt and Sofer (eds.) 1992: 1-24.
Schmitt, Arno, and Jehoeda Sofer (eds.)
    1992   *Sexuality and Eroticism among Males in Moslem Societies* (New York: Haworth Press).
Schneemelcher, W. (ed.)
    1974   *New Testament Apocrypha.* II. *Writings Relating to the Apostles, Apocalypses and Related Subjects* (London: SCM Press).
Sedgwick, Eve Kosofsky
    1985   *Between Men: English Literature and Male Homosocial Desire* (New York: Columbia University Press).
    1993   *Tendencies* (Durham: Duke University Press).
    1994   *The Epistemology of the Closet* (London: Penguin Books).
Sforno, Obadiah ben Jacob
    1997   *Be'ur 'al ha-Torah le-Rabi 'Ovadyah Sforno = Commentary on the Torah.* I. *Beresheis/Genesis, Sh'mos/Exodus* (trans. and Notes by Raphael Pelcovitz; Brooklyn, NY: Mesorah Publications).
Sherwood, Yvonne
    2000   *A Biblical Text and its Afterlives: The Survival of Jonah in Western Culture* (Cambridge: Cambridge University Press).
Skinner, John
    1930   *A Critical and Exegetical Commentary on Genesis* (Edinburgh: T. & T. Clark).
Sly, Dorothy
    1990   *Philo's Perception of Women* (Atlanta: Scholars Press).

Smith, R. Payne (ed.)
1999   *Thesaurus Syriacus* (Hildesheim: Georg Olms).
Sofer, Jehoeda
1992   'Testimonies from the Holy Land: Israeli and Palestinian Men Talk about
          their Sexual Encounters', in Schmitt and Sofer (eds.) 1992: 105-119.
Soggin, J. Alberto
1987   *Judges: A Commentary* (trans. John Bowden; London: SCM Press).
Sontag, Susan
1966   'The Imagination of Disaster', in *Against Interpretation and Other Essays*
          (New York: Dell Publishing): 209-225.
Sperling, Harry, and Maurice Simon (trans.)
1984   *The Zohar* (Introduction by J. Abelson; London and New York: Soncino
          Press).
Stone, Ken
1995   'Gender and Homosexuality in Judges 19: Subject-Honor, Object-Shame?',
          JSOT 67: 87-107.
2001   'Queer Commentary and Biblical Interpretation: An Introduction', in Stone
          (ed.) 2001: 11-34.
Stone, Ken (ed.)
2001   *Queer Commentary and the Hebrew Bible* (Cleveland, OH: Pilgrim Press;
          Sheffield: Sheffield Academic Press).
Tapp, Anne Michele
1989   'An Ideology of Expendability: Virgin Daughter Sacrifice', in Bal (ed.) 1989:
          157-74.
Tertullian (attributed)
          'Sodoma', *PL* 2: 1159-1162.
1870   'A Strain of Sodom', in *The Writings of Quintus Sept. Flor. Tertullian* (trans.
          S. Thelwall; Edinburgh: T. & T. Clark): III, 284-92.
Tertullian
1878   *The Five Books against Marcion* (trans. Peter Holmes; Ante-Nicene Christian
          Library, 7; Edinburgh: T. & T. Clark).
1880   *The Writings* (trans. S. Thewall and P. Holmes; Ante-Nicene Christian
          Library, 11, 15, 18; Edinburgh: T. & T. Clark).
1920   *Tertullian against Praxeas* (trans. A. Souter; London: Society for Promoting
          Christian Knowledge; New York: Macmillan).
1950   *Apologetical Works and Minucius Felix Octavius* (trans. Rudolph Arbesmann,
          Sister Emily Joseph and Edwin A. Quain; Washington: Catholic University of
          America Press).
1954   *Opera: Pars 2, Opera Montanistica* (Corpus Christianorum Series Latina, 15;
          Turnhout, Belgium: Brepols).
Theodore Bar Konai
1981–1982 *Livre des Scolies (Liber Scholiorum): Recension de Seert* (trans. Robert Hespel
          and Rene Draguet; Lovanii: Peeters).
1983   *Livre des Scolies (Liber scholiorum): Recension d'Urmiah* (ed. Robert Hespel;
          Lovanii: Peeters).
Theodore of Canterbury
          'Capitula Theodori', in *PL* 99: 935-87.
Theodoretus Cyrensis
          'Questiones in Genesim', in *PG* 80: 77-226.

'Questiones in Judices', in *PG* 80: 485-518.

Theodorus Prodomus
'Epigrammata in Vetus et Novum Testamentum', in *PG* 133: 1101-1221.

Thomas Aquinas
1947–1948   *Summa theologica* (literally translated by Fathers of the English Dominican Province, with synoptical charts; London: Burns & Oates).

1964–1976   *Summa theologiae: Latin Text and English Translation, Introductions, Notes, Appendices and Glossaries* (ed. Thomas Gilby; London: Blackfriars [in conjunction with Eyre & Spottiswoode]).

Thunberg, L.
1966   'Early Christian Interpretations of the Three Angels in Gen. 18', *Studia Patristica* VII.1 (1966): 560-70.

Trible, Phyllis
1984   *Texts of Terror: Literary-Feminist Readings of Biblical Narratives* (Philadelphia: Fortress Press).

Vanderkam, James C. (trans.)
1989   *The Book of Jubilees* (Lovanii, Belgium: E. Peeters).

Vanita, Ruth
1996   *Sappho and the Virgin Mary: Same-Sex Love and the English Literary Imagination* (New York: Columbia University Press).

Vermes, Geza (ed.)
1995   *The Dead Sea Scrolls in English* (London: Penguin Books).

Von Rad, Gerhard
1961   *Genesis: A Commentary* (trans. John H. Marks; Philadelphia: Westminster Press).

Walafrid Strabo (attributed)
'Glossa ordinaria', in *PL* 113.

Warne, Graham J.
1988   'The Soul in Philo and Paul' (PhD dissertation, submitted Studies in Religion Department, University of Queensland).

Warner, Marina
1995   'In and Out of the Fold: Wisdom, Danger and Glamour in the Tale of the Queen of Sheba', in Chistina Buchmann and Celina Spiegal (eds.), *Out of the Garden: Women Writers on the Bible* (London and New York: HarperCollins): 150-65.

Webb, Barry G.
1987   *The Book of Judges: An Integrated Reading* (JSOTSup, 46; Sheffield: JSOT Press).

1994   'Homosexuality in Scripture', in *idem* (ed.), *Theological and Pastoral Responses to Homosexuality* (Adelaide: Openbook Publishers): 65-103.

Weber, Robert (ed.)
1994   *Biblia Sacra: Iuxta Vulgatam Versionem* (Stuttgart: Deutsche Bibelgesellschaft).

Westermann, Claus
1987   *Genesis: A Practical Commentary* (trans. David E. Green; Grand Rapids: Eerdmans).

Whiston, William (trans.)
c. 1876   *The Works of Flavius Josephus* (London: George Routledge and Sons).

1987   *The Works of Josephus: Complete and Unabridged* (Peabody, MA: Hendrickson).

Wikan, Unni
    1977   'Man Becomes Woman: Transsexualism in Oman as a Key to Gender Roles',
            Man (NS) 12 (1977): 304-319.

Wilson, Nancy
    1995   *Our Tribe: Queer Folks, God, Jesus and the Bible* (San Francisco: Harper
            Collins).

Wintermute, O.S.
    1983   'Jubilees', in Charlesworth 1983: II, 35-51.

Wright, William Aldis (ed.)
    1909   *The Authorised Version of the English Bible 1611* (Cambridge: Cambridge
            University Press).

Yacowar, Maurice
    1995   'The Bug in the Rug: Notes on the Disaster Genre', in Barry Keith Grant (ed.),
            Film Genre Reader (Austin: University of Texas Press), II: 260-79.

Zlotowitz, M. (trans. and Commentary)
    1986   *Bereishis: Genesis/A New Translation with a Commentary Anthologized from
            Talmudic, Midrashic and Rabbinic Sources* (Overviews by N. Scherman;
            Brooklyn, NY: Mesorah Publications [cited as GCD]).
    1996   *The Book of Ruth: Megillas Ruth/A New Translation with a Commentary
            Anthologized from Talmudic, Midrashic and Rabbinic Sources* (Overview by
            N. Scherman; Brooklyn, NY: Mesorah Publications [cited as Ruth Comm.
            Digest]).

Zornberg, Avivah Gottlieb
    1996   *The Beginning of Desire: Reflections on Genesis* (New York: Doubleday).

INDEX

INDEX OF REFERENCES

HEBREW BIBLE/OLD TESTAMENT

OTHER TEXTS.